THE

HISTORY OF STANDON:

PARISH, MANOUR, AND CHURCH,

WITH TWO HUNDRED YEARS OF REGISTERS.

BY

EDWARD SALT, B.A.,

RECTOR OF STANDON.

"NULLUM ESSE LIBRUM TAM MALUM UT NON EX ALIQUA
PARTE PRODESSET."—*Pliny.*

BIRMINGHAM: CORNISH BROTHERS, NEW ST.

LONDON: SIMPKIN, MARSHALL, & CO.

1888.

J. AND C. MORT, PRINTERS, 39, GREENGATE STREET, STAFFORD.

I DEDICATE THIS TO MY WIFE,

ANNA CAROLINE,

AND MY ELDEST SON,

ALEXANDER EDWARD WROTTESLEY SALT,

WITH WHOM I HAVE SPENT MANY PLEASANT HALF-HOURS

IN DISCUSSING

THE ANCIENT HISTORY OF STANDON.

PREFACE.

In writing a short account of the Parish of Standon, I had intended at first merely giving the Registers for a certain number of years, and the names mentioned in the Court Rolls; but the work itself opened out other subjects, and thus I have taken up a short history of the early customs and ancient nomenclature from those days, when, in all probability, the parish and manour began to be defined. I have thus tried to connect, from such an early date, a kind of succinct narrative down to later times.

Imperfect as my work must be, I have little doubt that, in the hands of an abler writer, such a parish and manour as Standon would offer great advantages; not because it is historically famous, nor because it is grown into importance on account of commerce and increase of population, but because it is one of those parishes which has had a kind of simple history from the early time of Domesday: a history which shows up the gradual changes from primitive times down to more recent dates, and which have not affected considerably the boundaries of the manour nor caused any diminution of interest which such an ancient manour as Standon must arouse.

And though it cannot claim, as some manours do, the same possessing family, or direct descendants of a family, commencing from Domesday, it can claim the site of the original manour house; the same church, altered though it may be; and the present existing mill on a near site to the more ancient one; all of which are mentioned in the Domesday account.

Another reason remains for writing this book, viz., that a great amount of the papers which I had recourse to were collected by my late uncle, Mr. William Salt, F.R.S., no doubt, it may be conjectured, purposely for making Standon one of the chief places, out of many others, he had intended writing a history of. Also many of the books and MSS. now at the William Salt Library, Stafford, and which partially help to swell the " History of Staffordshire," edited by the William Salt Archæological Society, were lodged for some time in the very house in which I now reside. Those books are now at Stafford, under Mr. Mazzinghi's care, whose courteousness and aid I must especially acknowledge.

In conclusion, I may say, if there is any profit from this work, I intend it to be used towards the Home for Orphan and Destitute Boys, established in the Parish of Standon.

STANDON RECTORY,
June, 1888.

CONTENTS.

THE

HISTORY OF STANDON:

PARISH, MANOUR AND CHURCH.

CHAPTER I.

"THE ORIGIN OF OUR ANCIENT VILLAGES, PARISHES, AND MANOURS."

EFORE beginning to discuss the successive line of possessors in the manour of Standon, and the names of persons connected more or less with the manour, I purpose to give some account of the origin of villages and manours, and the numerous laws that are connected with the foundation of separate estates. In all probability it is to the Romans first we owe the building up of many of our villages, and then afterwards to the Saxons.

The Romans were in the habit of building, along their great roads, cities and inns for the accommodation of travellers,[1] but we do not find them often raising places of dwelling away or apart from their roads.

The Saxons, on the other hand, were more of the class of scattered settlers, choosing their places of abode on account of water, wood, or open ground, according as these sites were of advantage.

The Romans made their way by engineering; the Saxons by adopting, here and there, land which seemed suitable for cultivation.

---

[1] Camden, "Brittannia," Vol. I., LXXX.

A

In many places in Staffordshire we have not only the
Roman name of a place, but also remains have been
discovered pointing to a Roman camp or dwelling.

There is little doubt Berry Bank, near Stone, was a
Roman fort;[2] again, at Wotton,[3] near Eccleshall, there was
most likely a paved Roman way. So, too, we have Walford
in our parish, the ford of the wall (Vallum), evidently the
first syllable (Wal) being Roman, and the second (ford)
Saxon, but beyond this we have no proof of any Roman road
or remains in the parish.   And so it is not till the Domesday
account of Standon, which I reserve for the next chapter,
that we obtain substantiative and written proof of its
existence, although it may be fairly conjectured it existed in
early Saxon times ; and, supposing that to be the case, we can
the more readily trace the gradual changes which occurred
during different periods up to the time of the Norman
Conquest.

The five centuries of Saxon period were (though difficult
to define) periods of development and progress, and the
survey given by Domesday would, no doubt, show a great
advancement from the period and time of Bede.[4]

We may suppose, then, in Saxon times places were chosen
for abode according to their position or resources, and each
man would have his croft and farm, and with buildings and
enclosures, and in northern countries such would go by the

[2] "His. Coll. of Staff.," Vol. VI., Part I., p. 9. "It would appear
from this deed that there had been originally a Roman military post
near Darlaston or Stone, on the site now known as Berry Bank."

[3] Camd. "Britt." Vol. I., p. 638. Also we find in the Emperor
Antoninus' Itinerary through Britain, that in his second route he
mentions "Pennocrucio," Penkridge, lying between Uxacon (near
Sheriff Hales) and Etoceto (Wall, near Lichfield).   Whether this
Pennocrucio was Penkridge, or Stretton, close to Penkridge, has been
an open question, but the name would rather suggest the village of
Penkridge, which is actually on the Penk, than Stretton, which is
mile or so from the River Penk.

[4] See Stubbs's "Constitutional History," Vol. I., p. 165.

name of " Odal," or " Edhel," and the mother village would be Athelby, or Athelham ; and from the same root we get Adel, or Athel—one of noble descent; also Adaling—a nobleman. And in connection with the same root, there is little doubt the word " Alod " [5]—an hereditary estate—is derived. In England we get the name Ethel applied to the Royal Family. From the Saxon time we may presume that the military service existed, and it grew into a more perfect form and administration after the Norman Conquest. But however indistinct this Saxon time is, there seems to be a bias in favour of the military[6] service, and the people had to go out in arms, whether they were landowners or dependents.

The land was also the best means of taxation for military service.

When land became more defined as to its measurement, it had, according to its extent, to maintain a man at arms, and every owner of the land was called upon for service in war.

Land, however, in these Saxon days, had already come under the distinguishing names Folkland and Bokland, and for an interesting account of these conditions of holding, a note is given by Hallam at the end of the 2nd Vol. of his " Middle Ages."[7]

Folkland would be the land which was the revenue of the country, and no part of it could be alienated without the consent of the National Council ; and although individuals might hold portions of it paying rent, it could not be given in inheritance. The taxes on Folkland were more numerous than on Bokland.

When either Folk or Bokland was let for a life it received the name of Lænland, i.e., leased or lent for a life. The Folkland became at the last " *Terra Regis* " (the land of the king). Bokland was, on the other hand, heirable property.

---

[5] See Stubbs' " Constitutional History," Vol. I., p. 52.

[6] Hallam's " Middle Ages," Vol. II., p. 294.

[7] Hallam's " Middle Ages," Vol. II., Note ix.

On the exact meaning of Folkland and Bokland there has been some difference.[8]

The simplest definition seems to be that Folkland was State and public property.

Bokland was originally land held by some gift from the owner, such as a spear, a drinking horn, a staff, &c., till the time came of giving a charter, when, although these gifts were not entirely done away with, a written charter was drawn up. Even in later times there is the existence of the same custom: the Dukes of Wellington and Marlborough holding their estates, Strathfieldsaye and Blenheim, by annual presentation to the crown, of flags.

After the institution of Bokland, the land held in full ownership, and which was known by the name of Ethel, was sunk into that of Bokland.

Bokland was exempt from most payments, except what was termed the "Trinoda Necessitas," or the "Rata Expeditio," or "Hostis," which consisted in service in three ways, (a) Military Service, (b) Repair of Bridges, (c) Maintenance of Fortifications. However, in some cases, religious houses were exempt.

On the other hand Folkland had to contribute to these services; and taxes were levied as well in support of any king coming through the territory, affording relay of horses, even giving assistance to their servants and attendants.

As a community increased, and formed itself into a village or town, the different districts would have their separate names given to them, and thus in the village of Standon we find different names for townships, such as Bowers, Walford, Weston, and The Rudge.

The different names that were applied to distinguish the formation of a town or village are of interest.

---

[8] See Spelman, who thought Bookland implied a written title, while Folkland was based on the witness of the people.

Phillips thought Bookland feudal; and Folkland alodial (independent).

The Latin language gives us " vicus" and " viculus;" the first meaning a street with houses on each side, the second more a lane than a street.

Township is derived from " tun scipe," tun being the hedge that surrounded either that portion of the village, or even the farm itself. Burgh is the fortified house in the village, probably the residence of the great man.

We also get the word yard, in our own language, from the Norse " garde." And the common term " hamlet," having originally the same meaning as gard, is derived from the German " heim." In the present day the smaller townships have been lost in the more general name of the whole parish, but no parish has a township within it which has a portion also of that township within another parish. Townships have been made into parishes, but a township (I believe) has never existed as lying between two parishes, *i.e.*, one portion belonging to one parish, and the other to another.

The township seems to prove the existence of the land-owner, and the division of land into farms, and other resources from the land. The township grew into the parish, but we do not find manorial rights vested in the whole parish, but in that of the township.

In Edward the Confessor's day, Siward held the land in Stantone and Rigge (Standon and The Rudge), and Godwin, in Westone (Weston), three different townships.

But the ecclesiastical parish of Standon contained these three townships, with also Bowers and Walford.

In the time of Bede we read that the churches were increased, and he urges on Egbert to attend to this.[9]

---

[9] " Necessarium satis est ut plures tibi sacri operis adjutores adsciscas, presbyteros videlicet ordinando, atque instituendo doctores qui in singulis viculis praedicando Dei verbo et consecrandis mysteriis coelestibus ac maxime peragendis sacri baptismatis officiis ubi opportunitas ingruerit insistant."—Epis. ad Egbert, v. 3.

It is very necessary that you bring into use helpers for the divine work, by ordaining priests forsooth, and by instituting the learned, who, in each village, by preaching the word of God nd by consecrating

Very often, at first, a cross at which the missionaries would perform the sacred ordinances of baptism and holy communion, with a burial-place near it, would be in existence before the church was built. (See chapter on Standon Church.)

I quote Dr. Stubbs, Bishop of Chester, as probably the highest authority on the payment to the clergy of the Saxon day.[10] He says:—"The maintenance of the clergy thus settled was provided chiefly by the offering of the people; for the obligation of tithe, in its modern sense, was not yet recognised. It is true that the duty of bestowing on God's service a tenth part of the goods was a portion of the common law of Christianity, and as such was impressed by the priest on his parishioners. But it was not possible or desirable to enforce it by spiritual penalties, nor was the actual expenditure determined, except by custom or by the will of the bishop, who usually divided it between the church, the clergy, and the poor. It was thus precarious and uncertain, and the bestowal of a little estate on the church of the township was probably the most usual way of eking out what the voluntary gifts supplied." And although the land property of the church, during later ages, in some cases was largely extended, the same extent of land as now supports some parish churches may have existed. The manour would thus soon grow into a state not unsimilar to that of the Norman time. And it is not likely that the manour was formed as a new desmesne under the Norman Conqueror, though given and passed by his hand. The name of manour is of French, or rather Latin, origin: from *manere*,[11] to remain. And the

the heavenly mysteries, and especially carrying out the offices of sacred baptism, may be urgent as opportunity may afford.

[10] Stubbs, "Constitutional History," Vol. I., p. 227.

[11] A manour—"manerium," "A manendo"—because the usual residence of the owner, seems to have been a district held by lords or great personages, who kept in their own hands so much land for the use of their families, which were called demesne lands.—Blackstone, Vol. II., p. 90.

right of jurisdiction of the thanes was the same as that in the after-Norman age of manorial owners. In the manour, we should find in the Saxon times the thane and the ceorl, the highest of which would be the king's thanes, whose lives would be valued at 1,200 shillings. After that the thanes whose lives would be valued at half that sum, and the ceorls whose lives would be valued at 200 shillings. "If a ceorl came to possess land to the extent of five hides (about 600 acres), and built, or had a mansion of his own, with a church, he was raised to the rank of a thane."[12]

The grade of society was in proportion to the amount any one could pay to commute a sentence of punishment; this was called "weregild;" and in the case of a king's thane was valued at 1,200 shillings.[13] The alderman in Saxon times was the highest in rank after the royal family. The office of alderman was sunk into that of a magistrate after the Norman conquest, and to each county there was an alderman. The sheriff was the under officer to the alderman. The alderman had jurisdiction over the shire (Saxon word meaning division), which shire was composed of different districts, generally named hundreds. County, as the name for a district, would evidently have its derivation from *comes*, a lord; or *comitatus*, a lord's or prince's court. In time we find that the earlderman, or alderman (earl) becomes the comes (count); the sheriff becomes the vicecomes, and the thane in all probability the baron.

The baron was a Norman creation, and the baron exercised authority over his tenants, and if he was sufficiently great would, no doubt, have councillors, stewards, and other officers.

In the Saxon times we get the geref (a sheriff) of the township, and the bydel (beadle), which no doubt become eventually the Norman steward and the bailiff.

[12] Hallam, " Middle Ages," Vol. II., p. 276.
[13] Blackstone, Vol. IV., p. 188.

We do not find that the questions of disputes between the owner of land and his serfs were settled in private courts till the later period of the Saxon times, though the grants of sac[14] and soc implied the power of the jurisdiction and the territory, sac being taken as meaning the jurisdiction, and soc the territory.

As soon as this jurisdiction arose we may well understand the constant litigations connected with the owner's rights; which jurisdiction it might have been supposed would almost have taken away the power of the king as supreme; but, to prevent this, the king had power in all breach of the peace, and it must be remembered that he had officers who acted for him, and he had power of jurisdiction through the landowners.

But we must also remember that military service was in a most essential way connected with land, and this in a great measure kept up the king's authority. It is clear, as I have mentioned, that every hide of land supported its soldier, and that every landowner and dependent had to serve, and thus grew up the feudal system, beginning from the king, and drawing in everyone of importance, down to the smallest landowner.

Although the system of feudalism can be traced from the day of the Franks down to later times of the middle ages, there is little doubt the feudal system was in a certain sense in existence[15] in Saxon days, though we may not see its full development till the Norman conquest. I purpose taking a general view of the feudal system rather than attempt to define the time when the feudal system took its first growth in England.

---

[14] On the words sac and soc there seems to have been a good deal of difference of opinion. The opinion of Ellis seems the simplest —that sac was the jurisdiction, and soc the territory.

[15] See Hallam, "Middle Ages," Vol. II., p. 294.

Dr. Robertson,[16] in his "History of Scotland," says :—"The genius of the feudal government, uniform in all its operation, produced the same effects in small as in great societies, and the territory of a baron was, in miniature, the model of a kingdom."

"The word feudal is taken from feudum, fief or fee, from the German word for cattle; Gothic, faihre; Anglo-Saxon, feoh.[17] The secondary meaning being goods or chattels." Dr. Robertson also says :—"A feudal kingdom was properly the encampment of a great army. Military ideas predominated; military subordination was established; and the possession of the land was the pay which the soldiers received for their personal service."

Two systems existed in the feudal state which helped to keep alive, as it were, the existence of feudalism. One, which was called the "Beneficium," the other the practice of commendation. The first was originated from the king giving gifts of land to kinsmen and dependents, and exacting from them a promise or pledge of fidelity,—in fact, vassalage.

Sometimes landowners put their land under the protection of churches, giving service for so doing.

By the practice of commendation, the weaker put himself under his lord, and became a vassal,[18] a dependent, though he did not give up his share in the estate.

---

[16] Dr. Robertson, "History of Scotland," Vol. I., p. 71.

[17] Dr. Stubbs, "Constitutional History," Vol. I., p. 251.

[18] The act of becoming vassal was performed by placing the vassal's hands between that of his lord, and taking the oath of fealty. —Stubbs, "Consti. History," Vol. I., p. 253. Lingard gives, in Vol. I., "History of England," p. 192, the exact words used. The vassal, putting his hands between those of his chief, said this oath :—"By the Lord, I promise to be faithful and true, to love all that thou lovest, and shun all that thou shunnest, conformably to the laws of God and man, and never in will or weald (power), in word, or work, to do that which thou loathest, provided thou hold me as I mean to serve, and fulfil the conditions to which we agreed when I subjected myself to thee and chose thy will."

By these means the lord and vassal were bound together, the lord being called upon to defend, and the vassal to be faithful.

How hardly and cruelly this system must have worked upon the lowest, it is not my purpose to mention; but the lowest state of servitude existed under this system, as we see so graphically described in after times in Sir W. Scott's "Ivanhoe."—(See Chapt. II., p. 24, note 6.)

The Saxon courts consisted of the "Witenagemot," the assembly of wise men—the highest court. This court assembled three times in the year, occasionally oftener. The number of its constitution has been a subject of debate; however, the king, his sons, bishops, abbots, thanes, abbesses, the queen occasionally, were members of it; and, attending it as outside hearers would be, no doubt, the great men's vassals. This court might be called the Parliament of the Saxon kingdoms.

Next to this would be the Shire mote[19] (the Shire court). The king could call a Shire mote whenever he travelled through the territories of his realm, and to this court would be summoned the great men of the shire.

Beneath this would rank the Hundred mote, summoned once a month by the ealdermen, or great men, and was attended by the clergy, and the reeve,[20] and chief men from the township. In this court civil causes were tried, and offenders brought to trial; but as reading and writing were not common accomplishments, this court was made use of for private business, such as arrangement of contracts; also exchanges and purchases were enrolled.

Next to this would be the Hall mote, so called because being held in the hall of the lord. According to the power of jurisdiction given to the thane or lord, would be the extent and importance of this court.

[19] Mote, Gemot: A court; an assembly.

[20] Reeve: Officer of the manour, or officer of the shire.

From this hall mote is derived the baron court of the manour, which is the civil jurisdiction ; and court leet,[21] which had jurisdiction over criminals.

I give, as an illustration of a sitting of the shire gemot in the time of Canute, a literal translation from a Saxon document as given by Hallam.[22] This is a good example of showing the mode of the business of the shire gemot :—" It is made known by this writing that in the shire gemot (county court) held at Agelnothe-stane (Aylston, in Herefordshire) in the reign of Canute, there sat Athelstan the Bishop, and Ranig the Alderman, and Edwin his son, and Leofwin Wulfig's son ; and Thurgil the White and Fofig came there on the king's business ; and there were Bryning the sheriff, and Athelweard of Frome, and Leofwin of Frome, and Goodric of Stoke, and all the thanes of Herefordshire. Then came to the mote Edwin son of Enneawne, and sued his mother for some lands called Weolinton and Cyrdeslea. Then the bishop asked who could answer for his mother.

" Then answered Thurkil the White and said that he would if he knew the facts, which he did not. Then were seen in the mote three thanes that belonged to Fehgly (Fawley), Leofwin of Frome, Aegelwig the Red, and Thinsig Stægthman. and they went to her and inquired what she had to say about the lands which her son claimed. She said she had no land which belonged to him, and fell into a noble passion against her son, and, calling for Leofleda, her kinswoman, the wife of Thurkil, thus spake to her before them : ' This is Leofleda, my kinswoman, to whom I give my lands, money, clothes, and whatsoever I possess, after my life.' And this said, she then spake to the thanes : ' Behave like thanes, and declare my message to all the good men in the mote, and tell them

21 Leet, probably from Gothic leita, to inquire. " You would present her at the ' leet ' because she brought stone jugs and no sealed quarts." (Shakespeare, " Taming of the Shrew.")

22 Hallam, " Middle Ages," Vol. II., p. 283. Hallam has taken his translation from Hickes.

to whom I have given my lands and all my possessions, and nothing to my son,' and bade them be witnesses to this; and thus they did—rode to the mote, and told all the good men what she had enjoined them.   Then Thurkil the White addressed the mote and requested all the thanes to let his wife have the lands which her kinswoman had given her; and thus they did, and Thurkil rode to the church of St. Ethelbert, with the leave and witnesses of all the people, and had this inserted in a book in the church."

The household of the king, or great man, would be composed of four great officers. In the Salian law we get the following names:—Major, Infertor, Mariscalcus, and Pincerna, which respectively in our English language[28] correspond as follows:—Major Præfectus, or Præpositus, to the groom of the chamber; Infertor, to the house steward; Marisculus, to the master of the horse; and Pincerna, the cup-bearer. In the Saxon household these names would correspond to the following names, which also seem to distinguish their office. The Major Præfectus, Maitre d'Hotel, would be termed the gerefa, or steward of the household.

The infertor or steward (dapifer) would answer to the disc thegn, that is, nominally speaking, the thane of the dish (the German disch = dish), the servant (thane) who brings in the banquet array.

---

[28] In Ducange, "Glossaries of Latin Words," we get the following descriptions:—Major qui domui seu famulis præest—major who is over the house and household. Infertor (steward), qui dapes infert—who brings in the banquet, in Greek παρα θετης. In a year 1038, quidam bene valens vir Conradus, Infertor ciborum Imperatoris, cum aliis interfectus est—a certain very strong steward of the food (of the table) of the Emperor's was slain with others. Charta Hugonis, Epis. Gratianop Ann. Pincerna, qui vinum convivis miscet—he who mixes the wine for the guests—from Greek πινειν κιρνα. Bouteiller, Butler, Apud Hariulfum, Lib. 4, Cap. 22, Hugo Pincerna Regis. Mariscalcus Horsthegn : Equarius Medicus : the veterinary or farrier in the Pactus Leg. Sal. Edit. Eccardt, tit., § 6.   We find that Mariscalcus had the whole care of the horses given to him; Strator was only over the grooming of the horses and accoutreing them, and bringing them into the domain.

Pincerna would be the cup-bearer (the butler), and the Mariscalous would be the "horsthegn." I would take horsthegn to mean the man who had the care of the stables—the stud-groom, as we should call him now.

Statores, the men who had to bed down, groom, and harness the horses.

These offices in the Norman time gradually developed into greater importance. The major becomes not the maitre d'hotel, but the master of the household, and the horsthegn the master of the horse.

We find also in the Norman household the Justiciar[94]—the royal treasurer—who seems to have swallowed up many of the offices of the steward, if not some of the perquisites, and becomes of the first importance in the royal household.

The master of the horse—the horsthegn in Saxon—becomes eventually the constable. (The lord of the stable, comes stabuli.) And eventually this office becomes of great importance, for later on we have the constables of the Tower of London, of Dover, and Carnarvon.

There is another definition given in Lord Herbert of Cherbury's life, that " Constable, anciently in France, was the first officer in the army, and so called from placing the king where he should stand in battle." It is rather with this definition we should see the source of the meaning of constable as custodian of the Tower and Dover Castle, than in connection with horses or stables, both the Tower and Dover appointments being given without exception, I believe, to military men.

In the reign of Edward the Confessor, we first hear of Chancellor, and he was the first in the list of Anglican kings to have a seal, of which the Chancellor was the keeper. From the Norman Conquest the office has followed in direct succession, and was generally held not by a layman but an ecclesiastic.

[94] The Justiciar acted in the king's absence, and thus the importance of his office.

The word Chancellor, we find, is derived from "a cancellis," that is lattice work, behind which all secretarial work was transacted. The chancellor gradually assumed many of the duties of the justiciar.

The Chamberlain was another grand official of the Norman time; but by his work seems more to have been in connection with auditing the accounts than receiving money.[25]

Leaving the (Curia Regis) Court of the King and the Court of Exchequer for the chapter which I purpose to give on the researches made by the W. Salt Archæological Society in connection with Standon, I pass on in conclusion to an account given in the Duke of Argyll's book, " Scotland as it was and as it is," of the household of a monastery, as given in the early times. At the same time there is no reason to suppose Standon came under any monastic house; but the account as given shows how the Church was, in the most primitive time, the pioneer of all agricultural industry, an industry which is conducted in not an unsimilar way in our modern days. The Duke writes: " In the narrative of the life led by St. Columba on the Island of Iona, 1,300 years ago, left us by the Abbot Adamnan, we see a quiet picture of all the operations of a farm hardly differing at all from those which constitute the ordinary operations of a modern farm, except that they were more complete, and embraced a more varied provision for the comforts of life. There was a smithy for needed iron work; there was a kiln for the drying of corn; there was a mill in which the monks ground their own corn into meal; there were cows and a cowhouse or byre; there were milk pails, carried, from the pastures to the monastery, on horseback; there was a barn for the storage of grain; there was a baker for baking the meal or the flour into bread—moreover, it is significant that

---

[25] See Dr. Stubbs, " Constitutional History," Vol. I., p. 352.

this skilled official was a Saxon ; there were wheeled carts or carriages for the conveyance of heavy articles.[26]

In sketching out some of the principal and leading characteristics of the Saxon days I come now in the succeeding chapters to the more definite description of names and places connected with Standon. I cannot conclude this chapter without mentioning that Standon,[27] as a name, is eminently Saxon, Stan being the same as Stanes—stone, a rock, and "don" is a hill. Standon in Saxon would be the Stone Hill, or Rocky Hill or Height. The geological structure of parts of Standon bears this out very clearly ;[28] so also Bowers is the same as Bury, Perry Brough (Borough), also Saxon for a town, or a place of retreat. From Brough we get the names of places, such as Broughton and Burton. Close by again we have Chorlton, which is evidently the same as Ceorl, the town or place of abode of the Ceorl. And so if we have no authoritative proof of the existence of Standon as a place in Roman times, we have a proof of its existence in Edward the Confessor's day, and with that proof I commence the next chapter.

[26] Duke of Argyll's "Scotland as it was and as it is," Vol. I., p. 102.

[27] Saxon Chronicle. By Rev. J. Ingram, B.D. 1823.

[28] The churchyard of Standon is in many places very rocky. The cellars of the Rectory House are cut entirely out of rock. A deep cutting is known on the Walford road, and three cottages bear the name of Rock Cottages from being built actually out of the very rock.

CHAPTER II.

AN ACCOUNT OF THE DOMESDAY RETURN OF WILLIAM THE
CONQUEROR, WITH THE MENTION MADE IN THAT RETURN
OF STANDON.

[This account of Domesday I contributed to the *Staffordshire
Advertiser* in 1886, but did not specify Standon.]

N the more ancient days, before the actual Domesday return of William the Conqueror, we find the
expense of defending the State in England lay
equally upon all the land. Land that extended to five hides
had to equip a man for service ; and, as the hides of land in
England were estimated at 243,600 hides, the armed men
furnished would be 48,720. It is conjectured that the first
actual Domesday return made was in the reign of
Alfred, and that it was preserved at Winchester.[1] I believe
we are right in supposing that record does no longer exist,
but the Domesday Book of William the Conqueror is still
kept in its original form in the keeping of the Exchequer.
Domesday or Doomsday, is the day of universal judgment,
from the Saxon word "dom;" and we have the same kind

---

[1] Ingulfus, p. 8.

of meaning in the word "domesman,"[2] an umpire, a judge. It is almost impossible to give the actual value of the Domesday Book of William the Conqueror. All historians who write of those times speak of its value. Mr. Green, in his "History of the English People," says:—"A jury empanelled in each hundred declared on oath the extent and nature of each estate; the names, number and condition of its inhabitants; its value before and after the Conquest; and the sums due from it to the Crown." Mr. Freeman says:— "The value of the Domesday Survey, as an historical monument, cannot be overrated. It is a map and a picture of England at a moment of which a map and a picture is unusually precious. Domesday tells us by whom every scrap of land was held in the later days of William, and also by whom it had been held in the days of Edward the Confessor.[3] It is a terrier of a gigantic manor setting out the lands held in demesne by the lord and the lands held by the tenants under the lord. Domesday teaches us, better than any other witness of those times can teach us, that the England of the nineteenth century and the England of the eleventh century are one and the same thing. We seem to be brought nearer to those times when the commissioners stop to notice a new church, a new and goodly house 'Domus optima,' or a fertile vineyard, 'Et vinea bona.' We feel at home as we read of the mill, 'Mola,' which for lack of water in the hot season could be worked in the winter only. Even the entries which caused special wrath at the time, the searching inquiries which left no ox, or cow, or swine unrecorded, help to bring the general picture of the land more vividly before us." But the two names connected most prominently with elucidating this

[2] "And Jesus stood before the domesman, and the justise axide him and seide, Art thou kyng of Jewis?"—Wicliffe, St. Matt. xxvii.; A.D. 1380.

[3] In reading the entry of a tenant holding, as a rule the perfect tense gives the tenant who held in Edward's time, as, "Siward (the Saxon) tenuit," held, &c., i.e., in Edward's time, "Briend tenet," holds, &c., i.e., in William's time.

B

work of Domesday are those of the late Sir H. Ellis, F.R.S., and the late Rev. Mr. Eyton. From the former all the different class qualifications of persons at that time are specially gleaned.

The first documentary evidence about Standon is given us in this Domesday Return of William the Conqueror, about 1085. In it we get the names, first of all, of holders of the land before the Conquest—men who lived in the time of Edward the Confessor (he reigned from A.D. 1041 to 1065). One is Siward, who held land in Stantone (Standon) and the Rigge (The Rudge), and Godwin, who held in Westone (Weston).

Siward, on the authority of Hon. C. Wrottesley, of All Souls, Oxon, I believe to be a Danish name.

Godwin is a Saxon name—win meaning in Saxon war, or strength, or the esteem of the people. So it may be either interpreted as good in war, or good in the esteem of the people.

We have also the first mention at this early day of Christian worship, for we read here at Standon there was a priest; later on we get the definite mention of a church at Standon, but this first mention of a priest is sufficient to let us take for granted the existence of a stone church at that date, if not before; but I reserve further mention of this till the chapter on the Church of Standon.

We also get the mention of the mill and its value. The tenant-in-chief in William the Conqueror's time at Standon was Robertus de Stafford; and the tenant under him, the tenant in fee or possession, was Briend de Standon.

From this time we obtain an almost successive line of inhabitants at Standon by name and ancestry. But we owe to the William Salt Archæological and Historical Collections of Staffordshire a great debt for giving us, or rather, I should say, deciphering, the names of so many persons connected with different manours and parishes of Staffordshire in so early a period of our country.

THE DOMESDAY RETURN ABOUT STANDON IS THEN AS FOLLOWS:—

Ipse "R." tenet II. hid in Stantone (Standon) et in Rigge (Rudge) Briend de eo.
Siward tenuit et lib ho fuit.
Tra. e. VI. car.
In dnio e. una.
Et XI. villi et III. bord et III. Servi cu V. car.
Ibi pbr et molin de V. sol.
Ibi II. ac pti XIIII. ac grave valet XL solid,
Ipse R. tenet in Westone una v. tre et Briend de eo.
Godwin tennit et liber fuit. Tra. e. II. car.
In dnio e. una car et VI. servi et IV. villi et II. bord cu I. car.
Silva dimid leuu lg et II. q3 lat valet XX. sol.

Domesday Name.	Saxon Possessor. Temp of Rex Edwardius Confessor.	Domesday Tenant in Capite.	Tenant in Fee or possession.	Sub-Tenants. Presbyter.	Hides	Virg.	Carucates.
							Domesday measure.
In Stantone et In Rigge	Siward	Robertus de Stafford.	Briend.	Presbyter.	2	0	0
In Westone	Godwin	Robertus de Stafford.	Briend.		0	1	0

Terra quot. Carucis.
In Stantone 6
In Rigge 2
In Westone 2

Acre Prati. 2

Silva (Wood) of Domesday.
14 Acre Grave.
dim. ten lg. et ii q3 lat.
(half-a-mile in longitude and two furlongs in latitude)

Acres of Wood.	Value in Domesday.
14	£2 : s0 : d0
120	1 : s0 : d0

Domesday features and particulars.
Ibi molinus de V. solidis—ibi XIIII. acre grave.
Modern name Standon, The Ridge in Standon, and Weston in Standon.

Hundred (Modern).
Pire-hill Hundred.
Parochial Acreage, 2570.

In the third chapter of this book will be found a continua-
tion from the time of Domesday, but I only give here the exact
account of Standon as given in Domesday, and a translation
in reference to Standon by the late Rev. Mr. Eyton, and some
explanation of the words and terms used in the Domesday
Book, which explanation is almost necessary to understand
the phraseology of that ancient record.   From this Domesday
period I hope to bring down to much later and modern times
an account of the manour and parish of Standon.   In many
places it will seem obscure, but 800 years is a long period in
our country's history; so also if we regard a small manour
and parish in that country it seems almost a longer and more
difficult period to account for, which, after all, in certain
years can only be accounted for by mere names of persons
and parish boundaries, and the state of the country at those
particular times as given us in history.

In this account we find, as I have mentioned, that Godwin
and Siward were the thanes (I take "Liber homo" to mean
thane), holding the manour of Standon before the Conquest.
That after the Conquest, the tenant in capite, the head or
supreme seigneur, was Robertus de Stafford, who also held
in capite other manours; under him comes, as tenant in
possession, Briend de Standon.

In Standon and the Rudge there was arable land sufficient
for eight ploughs, and in the lord's domain one would be .
used.   There is the priest holding as a tenant.   There are
two acres of pasture or meadow land, and fourteen acres of
wood, valued in Domesday at £2.

In Weston there were two ploughs used, and one of these
was for the lord's use, and so much wood.

We have a list of those dwelling on the manour, that is
to say, so many villi and so many servi.

I here introduce an account by Hallam, Vol. II., "Middle
Ages," chapt. viii., part ii., p. 310, which explains any error
we might be led into by supposing that the Norman estates
held in capite were held only by such, and the tenant in

fee or possession was not of importance and power. He says:—" In reading of a baron who held forty or fifty or one hundred manors " (Robert de Stafford, who was tenant in capite in Standon, held considerable possessions besides Standon as tenant in capite), " we are prone to fancy his wealth as something like what a similar estate would produce at this day. But if we look at the next words, we shall continually find that some one else held of him, and this was a holding by knight's service, subject to feudal incidents, no doubt, but not leaving the seigniory very lucrative, or giving any right of possessory ownership over the land.". So at Standon, Briend de Standon held of Robertus de Stafford.

I now proceed to review more generally the probable cause of the Domesday Book being made, and to give some explanation of the terms used in that book.

The year 1085 gives us the Domesday Book completed, and its direct origin arose from King William, in dread of an invasion from Denmark, boarding on the landholders a large number of Norman and Breton soldiers. On the first complaint of the landholders, an inquisition is held for the purpose of ascertaining what actual means existed with the landholders for supporting or not supporting such a burden. For carrying out this work and survey, Commissioners are appointed, named " Legati Regis," or the King's justiciaries. For the survey of this part of England we find the names of Remigius, Bishop of Lincoln ; Walter Giffard, Earl of Buckingham ; Henry de Ferrers, and Adam, the brother of Eudo Dapifer (the feast-bearer). These bore the name of Inquisitors, and their duties (very similar to those of Royal Commissioners) were—upon the oath of the sheriffs, the landholder, the presbyter (priest) of each church, the reeves (stewards) of every hundred and the bailiffs, and six villans of every village—to find out and enrol the name of the tenant ; both the present possessor and the possessor in the time of Edward the Confessor ; the exact number of hides in each manour ; the number of carucates (land under tillage) ; to inquire into the number of dependants on each manour, and what their particular office was; how much land in each demesne was given up to pasture; what to meadow; whether on that demesne a mill stood; what fish ponds existed; what possession each freeman or sochman had when Edward the Confessor reigned; to whom it was bestowed by King William; and also at what value the demesne stood at the actual time of the survey. The survey commenced by entitling the estate to the owner, always beginning with "Terra Regis" (Land of the King). Then the hundred was specified; next the tenant who held, and the measurement and kind of property. Thus throughout each estate the whole number of dependants were classified, and from their different names we obtain their peculiar service. It is to the late Sir H. Ellis we are really indebted for the careful classification of each person on the estate. Those who held the highest place under the King were the bishops and abbots. We learn from the "Constitutional History of England," by the present Bishop of Chester, Dr. Stubbs, that the very early bishops of England held their sees to the same extent of possession as the kingdom was heptarchically divided, and the capital of each division was as a rule the site of the cathedral. Abbeys within the sees were mostly of Royal foundation, and were ruled by persons of noble birth, both male and female. After the bishops and abbots, the Norman barons would come next in rank; in possessing manours these barons would be the King's immediate freeholders, tenants in capite. Occupying a similar position amongst the Saxon nobility would be the " Taini," " Tegni," " Teigni," " Teini," or " Teinni " (thanes),[4] who were the nobility or barons of the Saxon times. These thanes were divided into three orders—" Thani Regis " (thanes of the king), " Thani Mediocres " (thanes of the second order or middle order), and

---

[4] "By Sinel's death I know I am Thane of Glamis."—Shakespeare, "Macbeth," Act 1, Scene 3. The thaneship of Glamis was the ancient inheritance of Macbeth's family

" Thani Minores " (thanes of the lower order or class). The " Thani Mediocres " would have been equal in rank to the lesser barons or lord of the manour, and the "Thani Minores" would have been the lowest class of freeholders. The name thane or thanes continued after the Norman Conquest, as we find archbishops, bishops, abbots, and even great barons are called thanes. Next, or almost equal to the " Thani Mediocres," were the " Vavasours " : they would rank directly under the barons and higher thanes, and might be termed the minor barons. In succession to the vavasours would come the "Aloarii," " Alodarii," tenants of "Allodium," *i.e.*, freehold or manour, which term denotes possession before the Conquest : it also denotes a free estate that could be disposed of by gift or sale, but subject to the common tax of hidage (military service). The term " milites," which we often meet with, is difficult to distinguish as to whether it meant merely soldiers, or whether persons of a higher rank. All milites under bishops held larger allotments of land than under other tenants.

Before we pass to others in rank on the manour we meet with the class called " Liberi Homines." This class of holders seems to include both freemen and freeholders of a manour, and also men who hold the rank of those mentioned above. Another rank of landowners in the survey remained —the " Sochemanni " and " Socmens," and " Rachenistres " or " Radmans." Both these classes were smaller landowners, holding land in the " Soc "[5]; that is to say, the franchise of a great baron. We come next to those who were not landowners. The principal class would be the villani : the name must be derived either from " Viles " (Lat.), worthless, or else from " Villa " (Lat.), a village, because they lived in villages, and their occupation was principally connected with rustic or sordid work. Judge Blackstone traces their tenure from a Danish origin. As they were connected with " heriots," fines paid to the lord of the manour at the death

[5] See Chapt. I

of a landowner, so we may probably presume that the villani
often passed at the death of the landowner to the lord of the
manour.   We have a graphic description of a villanus, or
rather "Porcarius," swineherd, in the story of "Ivanhoe,"[6]
though at the same time we may suppose "Porcarius" was
higher than "Villanus."   These villani were under the
Saxon government treated as slaves, subject to the most
servile labour, and they and their children passed in the same
way as stock or chattels passed from landowners to landowners.   They were passed in this way as annexed to the
manour, when the term "regardant" might be used ; or else
they were in "gross," at large, or merely annexed to the
person of the lord of the manour.   If they decamped, they
could be recovered by action at law, just as cattle or goods.
They held in some cases small holdings, of which they could
be dispossessed at the lord's own will.   And there was no
law as to the time or hours of their labours, nor as to the
baseness of their labour.   General the Hon. G. Wrottesley,
one of the greatest authorities on this time, does not hold
with villani being so servilely used.   (See Hist. Collections
of Staffordshire, Vol. V., part p. 17.)   "Villanus, in fact, was
really a well-to-do tenant, with fixity of tenure, for though he
could not remove from his holding, the lord could not dispossess
him so long as he performed his accustomed service."   The
Bordarii, " Boors," cottagers (from Bur, a cottage, a shady
spot, and from which derivation we get the word " Bowers "),
seemed to have held a less servile place than " Servi " and
" Villani."   They sold poultry and eggs and other small provisions to the lord, for his table.   Similar to the Bordarii
would be " Cottarii," " Cotmanni," " Coscets," or cottagers
holding small parcels of land.   " Servi " (slaves) would be the

---

[6] "Ivanhoe," Vol. I., Chap. I.   In the description of Gurth,
Scott says :—"One part of his dress only remains ; it was a brass
ring, soldered fast round his neck.   On this was engraved in Saxon
characters, ' Gurth, the son of Beowulph, is the born thrall (that is,
one with the ear bored) of Cedric of Rotherwood.' "

lowest in rank, dependent on the lord, beneath " Villani."
Female servants passed by the name of " Ancellæ," and were,
in circumstances of their lives, similar to the " Villani " and
" Servi." " Censarii," " Censores," terms that are met with,
were occupiers of land, free, and paid a tax or tribute
("reddentes censum"). Two other classes remain " Porcarii "
—swineherds : they were probably free occupiers renting
woodlands for feeding their pigs, some for money, some for
payment of kind; and " Homines," feudatory tenants, men
who claimed the right of having their causes heard in their
lord's court, and who nevertheless owed submission to him.

We now pass to the land. A manour would be divided
into " Terra," land under the plough; " Silva," wood; and
" Pastura" and " Pratum," pasture and meadow land. The
account of woods given at that time is of interest. " Silva,"
"nemus," and " silvula " (woodland) are always mentioned ;
not that the value was measured, as now, by good timber in
the square foot, but by the extent of foliage which produced
the greatest expanse for the pigs to lie under, and which
shed the greatest amount of acorns and beech mast; this use
of the tree had its own name, " Pasnagium," or " Pannage,"
which meant either the feeding of hogs or the price paid for
so doing. The Domesday return is most minute in its
descriptions of wood. It gives : Wood that could be cleft ;
" Silva ad clausuram," wood for an enclosure, and wood that
would be used only for repairing fences ; "nemus " (a thick-
planted wood) " ad sepes reficiendas," for repairing hedges ;
" Silva ad sepes et domos," timber for fences and houses ;
" Broca," [7] brushwood ; " grava," a grove ; " Fraxinetum,"
a grove of ash trees ; a furlong, four squares ; " Spinetum,"
a thorny wood or young wood, whence our common word " a
spinney ;" salictum, an osier or willow bed. From the
Saxon word " orceard " we obtain our English word orchard,

---

[7] " Broca": There is little doubt we get the name of the place
" Brocton " in different places from this word. Brocton : The township of Brushwood.

but in the early days it meant only a plantation of herbs. "Hortus," "Pomarium," and "Vinea"[8] give the garden, the orchard, and vineyard in Domesday.

We now allude briefly to words used in more particular parts of England. "Essary," from the French, "Essertir," to make plain, would be an open space in a forest, a clearing. "Mersc," "Mora," would be a marsh or fen, as in Cambridgeshire. Amongst the many assistants in labour, husbandry, and other occupations, we find "Fabri," carpenters or smiths; "Apium custos," beekeeper; "Arantes Homines," ploughmen; "Bovarii," neat herds; "Caprarum Mediator," a goatherd; "Granatarius," keeper of granaries; "Tonsor," the barber; "Joculator" and "Joculatrix," the minstrels.

The measurement of land at that time has remained a difficulty. A hide of land, from the Saxon "Hydan," to cover, might mean 100 acres,[9] or 120 according to our measurement; or else only the knight's fee—land held to a certain extent. "Carracuta"[10] was as much land as could be managed with one plough. A "Virgate" would be either thirty, twenty-four, or fifteen acres. An acre[11] would be forty perches long by four perches wide. Perch (Lat., "Pertica") would be sixteen feet and a half—but sixteen feet according to the Register of Battle, in Sussex. "Quarantena" (Lat.), forty perches, was used in measuring woodland. The hundred in a shire might mean a hundred hides, or a hundred villages, or else a district with a hundred men, which is hardly probable.

---

[8] "Vinea." There is little doubt of the existence of vineyards at this time and earlier. In A.D. 282, Probus, the Emperor, allows them to the "Hispanni, ac Britannis." King Alfred, about A.D. 888, brings in a law for damage to vineyards.

[9] Hide. See Kelham on Domesday.

[10] In Domesday Book we find this occurs in the return—"Terra est ii. carra." There is sufficient land for two ploughs.

[11] "Acre," in Saxon, a field; "Ager" (Lat.), a field; and "Akoro" (Heb.), a field.

Most ancient castles in our country are of Norman origin, rather than Saxon. Roman castles can still be pointed out. On a manour would be the "castle," or "aula," the hall. The "curia" would be the court room, or large entrance hall, where justice would be carried out, and would be existing on most manours, though it may mean a house, as now the "court." Different law terms are met with. Tenure in "frankalmoign" was the tenure of a religious house, a monastery, over land. As religious houses they were discharged from secular service, but had to repair bridges, build castles, and repel invasions. "Saca" was the power of hearing causes. Soca was the place or territory where the causes were heard. "Presbyter," the priest, is found owning land as other tenants. "Capellarii," "clerici," would be probably domestic priests or private chaplains. And we have also the Latin word "sacerdos," a priest.

In conclusion, we find from the late Sir H. Ellis an abstract of the population for each county. We give that of Staffordshire: this may not be quite exact as to the total population, but as regards the agricultural population it is a good record:—Tenants in Capite, 32; Under Tenants, 138; Ancilla, 1; Angli,[12] 10; Bordarii, 912; Burgenses in Tamworde (Tamworth), 12; in Stadford, 86; Canonici Lecefelle (Lichfield), 5; "Presbyteri" (Priests) in Statford (County), 18; Francigenæ, 6; Homines Mercati (Merchants) de Tuteberie (Tutbury), 42; Liberi Homines, 18; Milites, 5; Servi, 212; Servientes, 2; Teini (Thanes), 6; Villani, 1,728; in all, three thousand one hundred and seventy-eight.

---

[12] Angli often occurs, generally as under-tenants.

CHAPTER III.

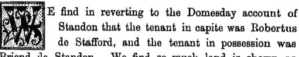E find in reverting to the Domesday account of Standon that the tenant in capite was Robertus de Stafford, and the tenant in possession was Briend de Standon. We find so much land is shown as being cultivated by the lord of Standon, and so much land cultivated by tenants. This is the case in Standon, Weston, and the Rudge; also there is so much land (two acres) in meadow, so much land in wood (40 acres), in Standon; and in Weston, so much also in wood (120 acres); the former smaller acreage of wood being more valuable, no doubt, on account of the pannage (acorns), which was thought of so much when a great number of swine were kept. When we revert to this state of Standon we should like, if possible, to picture the fields or wild commons, the woods and trees. We know only certain owners and dwellers at this early date by name, as again and again their signatures have been deciphered from some ancient deed, or they have had to appear at some court of justice, or have gone forth on some expedition, as in the year 55 of King Henry III., A.D. 1271, when Robert de Standon went in the crusade of that year

under Prince Edward. And there is nothing more than historic descriptions of other writers to give us any idea of the country at that early time.

It will be remembered in Lord Macaulay's " History of England "[1] what a picturesque description he gives of England two hundred years ago. What must, then, our country have been like a thousand years ago, and also our own village? In all probability the larger house or houses would be more or less square, with steps to the upper rooms from outside; and one large fireplace would be the almost only means of heat; the offices outside, such as kitchen, &c., being connected by a passage. Any castle would, however, be on a larger or more exalted scale.

I have little doubt the present manour house of Standon stands on the exact site of the old hall or court, for it is very evident the large room in Standon Hall was the court room in later times. Our trees and woods were more frequent and extensive, taking the Domesday acreage; and we should have met with, if we had lived in those days, those open spaces which are still to be found in our large forests, and which Sir W. Scott, in his opening chapter of " Ivanhoe,"[2] so beautifully describes:—" The sun was setting upon one of the rich, grassy glades. Hundreds of broad-headed, short-stemmed, wide-branched oaks, which had witnessed perhaps the stately march of Roman soldiery, flung their gnarled arms over a thick carpet of the most delicious greensward; in some places they were intermingled with beeches, hollies, and copsewood of various descriptions, so closely as totally to intercept the level beams of the sinking sun."

The roads or lanes would be best described, by a phrase which we meet with in the Stone Chartulary, as " virides viæ," greenways,—in a dry summer, no doubt, soft and pleasant to traverse; in winter and bad seasons, muddy and heavy.

---

[1] Lord Macaulay, "History of England," Vol. I., chap. III., p. 290.

[2] "Ivanhoe," Vol. I., p. 7. R. Cadell's Ed., Edinburgh.

And so, when we look back to these early days, we can only imagine and fancy, even if we know the names of families and people.

It is greatly owing to the W. Salt Arch. Soc. that names have been more fully given, or rather deciphered, in connection with Standon.

When it is known that these names are often written only on most ancient deeds, with fading ink, and ancient nomenclature, it can be understood then, that the task of interpreting these names has been by no means one without the employment of skill and labour.

We have, before this society existed, the Walter Chetwynd MSS.,[a] which give an excellent cursive description of many

---

[a] I have copied this from a MS. in W. Salt Library, of which MS. I find the following note in my uncle's writing, the late Mr. W. Salt :—" The following pages were written probably at the time the Rev. S. Shaw was compiling his history of Staffordshire, as they came into my hands with the rest of his collection, and were then loose sheets, wrapped in brown paper, thus endorsed, ' Loose copy by a boy, intended for the work.' The original volume, eighteen inches in height, and twelve in breadth, is beautifully written. I examined it at Ingestre, 8th April, 1836, and made up this volume in the following month. Signed, W. M. Salt." In the book of Shaw, " Staffordshire," Preface vii., printed 1798, by J. Nichols, Red Lion Passage, Fleet Street, London, we find this : " It is said Mr. Chetwynd had the additional collections of Mr. Ferrers, of Baddesley, and Mr. William Barton, the Leicestershire historian, besides very large ones of his own. These excellent MSS. continued in obscurity till a few years since, but all these upon the repairing of Ingestre Hall, though carefully put up in a box by the Rev. James Milnes, rector there, were unhappily lost, since found at Rugge (That is, Rugge in Standon.—E. S.), and restored to Ingestre. I have since been most kindly favoured with the use of them by Col. C. Talbot and the Rev. G. Talbot, uncles and guardians of the present earl. They consist of two folio volumes, beautifully as well as accurately written : the one a vellum chartulary, containing copies of all the records of the Chetwynd family, &c., with elegant drawings of monuments, seals, &c., and the church and house of Ingestre ; the other a clear and concise account of most of the parishes, with pedigrees of families in the hundred of Pyrehill." It is this latter from which the MSS. in W. Salt Library are copied. Walter Chetwynd, the author of these MSS., was descended from a long line of ancestors, seated at Ingestre from the time of the marriage of Sir John Chetwynd with Isabel, daughter and heiress of Philip de

parishes in Staffordshire, and which the antiquarian, Erdeswicke, has (I believe) fully used ; but the present W. Salt Arch. Soc. fills in, by giving different names and incidents, the more general outline or sketch of W. Chetwynd, Erdeswicke, and others. I propose first to give, in Walter Chetwynd's own words, the account of Standon, and return to the W. Salt Arch. Soc. for fuller details. He (W. C.) says:—"The rectory is valued in the king's books at Lb10 : s2 : d4=£590 (present money). The patronage having ever belonged to the lords of ye manour of Standon.

" The manour and parish contains (vulg., Staune) Bowers, Rugge, Walford, and Weston, all which were, at ye time of the general survey, held by Brian, descended of Rob. de Stadford (Stafford) ; there being then a church there, and a mill valued at 5 sol. That the family of the Standons (who afterwards residing here assumed that for their surname,) descended from ye aforementioned Brian, is, I think, not to be doubted, in regard they did not only succeed him in all his inheritance in this county, but were also anciently possessed of Ditchford, in ye county of Warwick, which was likewise held by Brian in the time of the Conqueror of Rob. de Stadford. In the time of Henry II. (A.D. 1154 to 1189), Adam de Standon was Ld. of Standon and Ditchford. He had issue Roger de Standon, or de Ditchford (for he wrote himself both ways), whose son, Vivian de Standon, was certified, Tempore (in time of) Henry III., to hold 2 knights' fees in Standon, Weston, and half a knight's fee in Ditchford, of Henry de Stafford. This Vivian[4] had issue Philippa, his only daughter, who, by her husband, Sir Thos. Dutton,

Mutton, who inherited that estate in the reign of Edw. III. He (W. Chetwynd) introduced Dr. Plot (Plot's " Natural History of Staffordshire ") into the county. A portrait of W. Chetwynd, by Sir P. Lely, is at Ingestre. This Walter Chetwynd died in London, 1693, and was buried at Ingestre.

[4] A note is found in the MSS., by a high authority, mentioning that Vivian was succeeded by a son, Robert de Standon, who was succeeded by a son Vivian. (I prove this further on.—E.S.)

Knight, had issue Sir Hugh Dutton, Knight, of Dutton, co. Chester. Sir Robert, who was lord of this manoure, and Thomas, to whom his father, with the consent of Philippa, his wife, gave ye villages of Great and Little Rownall, in this county. In 24 Edward I., A.D. 1296, Sir Robert de Standon claimed a Court Leet[5] and free Warren in all his desmaine lands here, which were then allowed. He bore for his arms, i.e., his shield, Dutton's coat, charged with a labell of three points (azure), and married Agnes, the daughter, and, as I take it, at last the heir of Sir Will Mere (of Mere juxta (near) Standon), Kt., by whom he had Vivian, Ld. of Standon, E. II., A.D. 1807 to 1827; and Robert and Thos., to whom he gave severall lands within Mere.

"Vivian[6] had issue Vivian, who, altering the arms used by his grandfather, gave quarterly ermin and gules fretted, i.e., (red fretted, or {gold}); leaving Elizabeth, his daughter and heir, the wife of Gilbert de Shotesbroke, of Berkshire, Knight, by whom she had issue John de Shotesbroke, who was certified to hold a knight's fee here (King Henry VI., A.D. 1422), but died soon after; for 10 year of King Henry VI., A.D. 1432, Thos. Rogers, of Bercott, in Berks, in the right of Elizabeth his wife, was seized of this manoure, which descended to Thos. Rogers, their son, who had issue,

---

[5] There were two Courts held at that time: (1) Court Baron, which had to do with copyholds, civil cases, &c. (2) Court Leet with criminal cases.

An account of Free Warren is given in Chapter IV.

[6] There is an ancient deed seen, with those arms mentioned above on the seal, at W. Salt Library, Stafford. The words of the deed are:—" Vivianus dominus de Standon Miles dmo Joh de Hawkeston militi quem habeo in feudo de Onley test Jacob Pype Johes Chetwynd, Miles, Nicho Synnerton, Rector Ecclesiæ de Muckeston, Rob. and Tho. Dutton, &c. Vivian, Lord of Standon, Knight, to Lord John de Hawkeston, Knight, whom I have a hold in fee farm at Onley. Witnesses: Jacob Pype, John Chetwynd, Kt., Nicolas Synnerton, Rector of Mucklestone, Rob. and Thos. Dutton." This deed may be about 1320 A.D. as to its date. The Gloucestershire family of Dutton, Lord Sherborne, still bear "fret."

another Thomas, whose only daughter, Elizabeth, brought this manoure (together with Bercott and divers other lands), in marriage to Sir William Essex, Lambourn, co. Berks, Kt., from whom it came by descent to Sir Essex, who, 6 year of Elizabeth, A.D. 1594, passed away ye manoure house and severall lands here to Humphrey Vyse, of Walford, Gent., selling the rest at the same time among the tenants in Free Farm, reserving the old rents, heriotts, and services, and in 12 year of James I., A.D. 1615, Sir William Essex, of Lambourne, Bart., sold the Royalty to Andrew Vyse, grandson to Humphrey."

" The advowson or patronage belonged to the Lords of Standon till Sir William Essex before mentioned conveyed it to Sir William Harcourt of Ronton (Ranton), Knight, his father-in-law, who in 4 year of King James, 1606, sold it to Andrew Vyse, whose posterity,[7] set down in the preceding pedigree, are now patrons of the church and lords of the manour, A.D. 1680.

" *Walford.*—Walton, or rather Walford,[8] is not mentioned in Domesday Book, being then included in Standon, of which it is a member. In this small place lay ye ancient freehold of the Vyses (now heirs of ye manour), ye inheritance of which is by descent come by Vyse of Standon, Gent. Weston (juxta-Standon) in 20 Conqueror (William I., A.D. 1086) Brian held one yard land in Weston of Rob de Stadford (Stafford), with woods half a mile in length and two furlongs in breadth, all valued (*i.e.*, the wood) at 20 shillings. In[9] ye time of Henry II. (A.D. 1154 to 1189) Adam de Standon

[7] The pedigree of the Vyses comes in the chapter on the Church and Registers.

[8] Walford is far more appropriate as a name for the place than Walton, a small brook running at the bottom of Walford Hill giving it a definition as to the latter part of its name.

[9] From an extract in possession of W. Chetwynd. I believe from what I gathered from H. E. Chetwynd Staplyton, Esqre., &c., &c., that the Chetwynds resided occasionally at Weston in Standon, also at the Rugge.

was seized (possessed) of this place, and soon after it came (as I think in Frank's marriage) to the family of the Chetwynds of Chetwynd. Henry III. (A.D. 1216 to 1272) it was in the possession of Sir John de Chetwynd, Kt., and Edward I. reign (A.D. 1272 to 1307) Reginald de Chetwynd was certified to hold a knight's fee here of Sir Robert de Standon. Reginald, whose daughter was Joane, was married to Sir Rich. Peshall, Kt., and had issue by him Sir Thomas Peshall, father to Richard, Henry VI. reign (A.D. 1422 to 1461), and he having only two daughters his inheritance was divided betwixt them, to the elder, who married Pigott, having Chetwynd and other lands in Shropshire, and Isabell, the wife of Tho. Grosvenor, which descending to Randolf Grosvenor, their great grandson, he in the time of 2nd of Queen Elizabeth (A.D. 1560) sold it to Francis Roos, of Loxton,[10] county Nottingham, Esq. (a gentleman of an ancient family and fair estate), who some time resided here, and purchased divers lands in this county, and he died 20 of Queen Elizabeth (A.D. 1578) seized of this manour or village, half ye manour of Mere, with divers lands and tenements in Cherleton, Chaveldon, and Bowers, together with ye Grange of Elaston, Bachacre, Clanford, and Knighton (all of which granges formerly belonged to the Monastery of Ranton), Peter Roos, his son and heir, being then forty years of age, who by Bridgett, ye only daughter and heir of Robt. Roos, of Ingmanthorpe, co. Nott, had issue Gilbert, who sold all his lands both in this county and Nottinghamshire. His mother, being by his wretched unthriftiness and her own misfortunes reduced to so great poverty, that she is reported to have gleaned corn among other poor people in Laxton fields, this village (and almost all his Nottinghamshire lands) being purchased by his kinsman, Peter Broughton, younger son to Mr. Thos. Broughton, of Broughton, who dying unmarried left it to his nephew, Thos. Broughton, Esqre., father to Sir Brian Broughton, Kt. and Bart., the present owner of it, A.D. 1680.

[10] See Chapter V. on the Church.

PEDIGREE OF THE CHETWYNDS OF THE RUDGE.

Circa (about) de Rugge (Rudge).

William Chetwynd   m.   Eliz. (d.) John Ferrers Mil
de Ingestre, obiit   de Tamworth Castle.

Anthony s. of William,   m.   Cath. (d.) Radulphi Thikness de Batterley.

Thomas s. of Anthony, m. Dorothy, d. of Thos.   John Chetwynd m. Maria, fil. of Humphrey Willes
Madeley de Denston.   de   de Hoarcross.
Rugge

John Chetwynd (s. of John and Maria Chetwynd), m. Susanna, d. of Johannes
obit 1674, A.D.   Broughton de Whittington.

Walter   Brien   and John Chetwynd   of which
Thomas   William   de Rugge   (the said)
sons of John and Susanna,   John Chetwynd   m.   Lucia, d. of Rob. Reane de Tolworth,
Walter,   John,   Lucia,   and   de Rugge (A.D.1680)   co. Surrey.
William are sons of John and Lucia.

"In ye time of Henry II. Ivo de Mutton held Rugge of Adam de Standon; he had issue Sir Philip de Chetwynd, Kt., younger brother to Sir John de Chetwynd of Chetwynd (as hath been made declared in Ingestre) this place was possest by ye heirs of that family till 32 Henry VIII. (A.D. 1541) when Will. Chetwynd of Ingestre, Esqre., settled a part of it upon Anthony, his younger son, whose great grandson, John Chetwynd of Ingestre, sold another part to Sir Gilbert Gerrard, Kt., Master of ye Rolls, which is by descent come to Digby Ll. Gerrard, who gave it to John Gerard of Hilderston, Esqre., his younger son, in whose posterity[11] it still continues."

I now come to the account of the early inhabitants of Standon, from the time of Domesday. The earliest record after the Domesday Survey is that which can be found in the two books called the Liber Niger (black book) and the Liber Rubens (red book) which were evidently written during the reign of Henry III. (A.D. 1266 to 1272), and which contain the knights' fees[12] in the time of Henry II., A.D. 1154 to 1189

---

[11] Rugge is now in the possession of the Hon. Mrs. Meynell Ingram. (E.S.)

[12] As soon as William the Conqueror had subdued England he found it necessary to govern it by the sword, by military tenure; hence, he introduced a more perfect principle of land tenure by knights' service, which may be known by the name of free services. Of this free service but few were exempt, some instances of freedom being granted to monastic houses who had held before in free alms, or francalmoigne. This free service consisted in affording for the king so many horsemen fully armed; but as the chief tenant held by this service, so also the tenants under him held of him. The oath taken was as follows:—"Hear, my lord. I become your liege man of life and limb and earthly worship, and faith and truth I will bear to you to live and die. So help me, God." The lord was, on his part, to protect his vassal, and give him a warrant of holding; and the vassal, on his part, was to promise subjection and reverence to his lord. The greater tenants, who may be called barons, had to appear at court. But also we find that on the fee granted to vassals there were certain charges, such as, when a son came of age and came into possession, he had to pay a certain sum which was called 'heriot' among the Saxons, and 'relief' among the Normans; also, there was a sum paid to the

(these books are now kept in the new Record Office, Fetter Lane, London). Coeval with these are the Pipe Rolls, to which I allude later. The writs for these returns were sent out about 12 King Henry II., A.D. 1166.

The sheriff would address his writ to the " tenant in capite," and thus each " tenant in capite " would make his return out with the tenants under him; so we find Robert de Stafford sends in the names of his sub-tenants, and we are enabled in many manours to obtain the names of owners from Domesday; this is the case with Standon. It is very probable that the writ sent out in A.D. 1166, was " for fiscal [13] purposes connected with the levy of scutage.[14] " Scutage (scutum, Lat., a shield) was a compounding on the tenant's part in money for not attending the king in military service for forty days, and in 5 Henry II. (A.D. 1159) it was levied on Henry's expedition to Toulouse, France. It is believed that Henry II. raised this tax at the suggestion of Thos.

lord when the lord's son was made a knight, or his eldest daughter was married, or when he was in custody in the hands of his enemy. When, again, the vassal's heirs were females, they were not allowed to be married without the lord's consent, though this could not be refused without some strong excuse. When the father died the lord became guardian of the daughters, which is called wardship; when she became fourteen he could compel her to marry the man of his choice; and her husband did homage. From this we can gather how all lands held in fee—that is to say, subject to a higher lord—were constantly the occasions for law suits (inconvenient as they must have been at the time, they are interesting to us of later date for giving names of ancient families). I give this sketch from the graphic account in Dr. Lingard's Hist. Eng., Vol. I., chap. viii. See also note by him, p. 242, Vol. I. :—" The quantity of land constituting a knight's fee was regulated by the custom of the manour, whence it differed in different manours according to the arrangement made by the original tenant in capite. Some knights' fees contained five carucates, others went up to forty-eight (Lib. Niger, Scac. 1; 294, 306). It is supposed by some that a barony consisted of thirteen knight fees and one-third; on this point there is some difference."

[13] All sentences placed in inverted commas, unless otherwise specified, are copied direct from the Staff. Hist. Collec. W. Salt Arc. Soc.

[14] Blackstone, Vol. I., p. 309.

à Beckett, Lord Chancellor, &c.[15] " Robert de Stafford, who
makes this return of his knight's fees at this time, was third
in descent of the first line of the Barons of Stafford." This
same Robert de Stafford held, amongst other knights' fees (I
think fifty-one in all) seven knights' fees which were made
up from ten different manors, to which amount Standon con-
tributes, with part of Wolverton, in Warwickshire, two-thirds
of a knight's fee. This same Robert de Stafford held in suo
dominio (in his own possession as demesne lands), $\frac{3}{4}$ f.m.
(knights' fee) Standon, in Stafford, and part of Wolverton,
in Warwickshire. In Weston, near Standon, Ricardus de
Mara (Richard of Mere) held two-thirds of a knight's fee,
which was also part of the seven knights' fees mentioned
above. It appears, as already mentioned, that Brien de
Standon held Stantone (Standon), Rigge, Westone (Weston)
in Standon, also Levedale in Staffordshire, Dicford in Warwickshire, and a double manor at Roscebi in Lincolnshire.
Brien no doubt was the founder of the family of Standon
or Staundon.

" Radulphus filius Brieni (Ralph, son of Brien) is a
frequent witness to deeds of Nicolas de Stafford, in the reign
of Henry I. (A.D. 1100-1135) in the Stone and Kenilworth
Chartularies," as also is Brien, Ralph's father, the Domesday
tenant. In A.D. 1088 (this is from a deed, now at Wrottesley,
of a grant in the year 1088, of Robert de Stafford—grant of
Wrottesley and Loynton to the Abbey, Evesham—written on
parchment, in a hand of the fourteenth century) is found the
signature of Brien, viz., " Ego Brien concessi " (I Brien have
agreed), after which is the sign of the cross. This Brien is
Domesday tenant of Standon. His son Radulphus[16] filius
Brientis, Ralph, son of Brien, is a witness to a deed in which
Nicholas de Stafford concedes Idlicote to Kenilworth Priory
(Harleian MSS. 86, 50) in the 23 to 26 Henry I. (A.D. 1122-

---

[15] Dr. Lingard Hist. Eng., Vol. II., p. 57.

Radulphus. See about Radulphus in Chapter V. on Church.

1125). In a deed of Stone Chartulary, 31 Henry I., A.D.
1130, Radulphus filius Brieni (Ralph, son of Brien), is again
a witness. Again much later, 5 to 15 King Stephen (A.D.
1140-1150), the name of Ralph, son of Brien de Standon,
appears in a deed. He evidently was now advanced in years.
The grandson of this Brien, I take it, is Radulphus or
Robertus de Standon, who pays half a merk in a recognizance
(a bond) for his father's death. In 27 King Henry II., A.D.
1180-1181, this Radulphus or Robertus is dead, for in 31
King Henry II., A.D. 1184, there is a lawsuit between Adam
de Standon and Roger de Dicford about the service of half a
knight's fee. Later on, 28 King Henry III., A.D. 1289,
"Fraricus de Dicheford is sued by Vivian de Standon to
acknowledge a fine levied at Oxford in the reign of King
Henry II., between Adam de Standon, grandfather of Vivian
and Robert de Dicheford (Warwick), father of Fraricus,
respecting half the manour of Dicheford, held by the service of
one knight's fee and four merks annual rent; the jury find in
favour of Vivian.

To return to Adam de Standon. He is witness to a deed,
30 King Henry II., A.D. 1184, of Robert de Stadford (Stafford),
Ivo de Mutton (Mytton) appearing also as a witness. This
Adam de Standon is succeeded by Robert de Standon or
Roger de Standon (Chetwynd MSS.). This Robert de
Standon[17] appears in an assize 1 King John, A.D. 1199, as
under age, claiming that the assize should not be held, as it
would be to his detriment if Reginald de Burghton, who
held the land in question at Burghton, was to lose,
"inasmuch as Ralph de Mutton, to whom the said Reginald
rendered 11s. annually, paid 10s. of it to his father and to
him."

[17] Robertus de Standon : Robertus quidam filius Adamæ de Standon
qui infra ætatem est, venit et dicit quod assisa inde capi non debet,
quia si capiatur et Reginaldus perdat hoc erit ad detrimentum
servicii sui quod inde habere debet, &c., &c.

Ralph is representative of Ivo de Mutton or Ivo de Staundon (Chetwynd MSS.).

In the pipe roll[18] of 2 King John, A.D. 1208, Robertus

[18] The Pipe Rolls bring us in connection with the exchequer. The Bishop of Chester, Dr. Stubbs, in his Const. His. of England, p. 579, gives a full account of these Pipe Rolls. I give verbatim what he says to make clear the meaning of this tax :—"Two chambers were used for this purpose in the palace of Westminster : The upper one or exchequer of account, was that in which the reports were received, and all the legal negociations were transacted ; and the lower one or exchequer of receipt, in which the money was paid down, weighed, and otherwise tested. The record of the business was preserved in three great rolls ; one kept by the treasurer, another by the chancellor, and a third by an officer nominated by the king, who registered the matters of legal and special importance. The rolls of the treasurer and chancellor were duplicates ; that of the former was called from its shape the great roll of the pipe, and that of the latter, the roll of the chancery. These documents are mostly still in existence. The Pipe Rolls are complete from the year of Henry II. (A.D. 1154 to 1189). And the chancellor's rolls nearly so. Of the preceding period only one roll, that of 31 King Henry I., A.D. 1130, is preserved, and this, with Domesday Book, is the most valuable store of information which exists for the administrative history of the age. The financial reports were made to the barons by the sheriffs of the counties. At Easter and Michaelmas each of those magistrates produced his own accounts, and paid into the exchequer such an instalment or proffer as he could afford, retaining in hand sufficient money for current expenses. In token of receipt a tally was made : a long piece of wood, in which a number of notches were cut, marking the pounds, shillings, and pence received ; this stick was then split down the middle, each half contained exactly the same number of notches, and no alteration could of course be made without certain detection. At the Michaelmas audit these tallies were produced, and the remainder of the accounts made up. If the sheriff were able to acquit himself entirely, he began the new year without arrears ; if not, a running account was kept by the same primitive method. The particulars accounted for by the sheriffs afford us a complete view of the financial condition of the country. The first item is the firma or ferm of the shire. (N.B.—The ferm of Staffordshire was not a large ferm, the king's dominions not being large.) This is a composition for all profits arising to the king from his ancient claims, &c., &c. This was estimated at a fixed sum which was regarded as a sort of rent, at which the county was let to the sheriff, and recorded in the Rotulus Exactorius ; for this, under the name of ferm, he answered annually : if his receipts were in excess, he retained the balance as his lawful profit, the wages of his service ; if the proceeds fell below the ferm, he had to pay the difference from his own purse. If lands fell out in waste, he was

Lupus[19] owes forty merks for having the custody of the land and heirs of Robert of Standon and his wife; he pays sixteen merks. This, I think, must be the widow and children of Robert, grandson of Brien, and not Robert, son of Adam de Standon, as Robert de Standon is only dead in A.D. 1185, and this Pipe Roll is A.D. 1208.

In the "Testa de Nevill, King Henry III. (A.D. 1216 to 1272), Vivianus (Vivian) de Standon, grandson of Adam de Standon, held two knights' fees in Standon, Weston and Sarden, in Staffordshire, and in Warwickshire he held one third of a knight's fee in Wolvardinton, and half a knight's fee in Dicheford, which Fraricus de Dicheford held of him."

On the Fine Roll of 25 Henry III., A.D. 1241, the Sheriff of Staffordshire is ordered to deliver 3 virgates of land (see Chap. II.) in Fenton to Vivian de Standon, on his paying his relief for the same, Vivian being heir to Philippa Fenton, who held the land in capite.

Owing to this small tenure in chief, and in accordance with feudal rule that all lands of a tenant in capite, under whatever tenure they might be held, fall into the king's hands on the occasion of a minority, on the death of Vivian de Standon shortly after this date his lands were bestowed by the king upon Philip Luvel.

On the Coram Rege Roll of 34 Henry III., A.D. 1150, Robert de Stafford sues Philip Luvell, for the wardship of Isabella (see note on Knight's Fees, Chap. III.), daughter and heir of Ralph de Mutton; Philip claiming her because

excused a proportionate amount under the head of waste, if new land was brought under tillage, he had to account for the profit under the title of increment. Before rendering this account the sheriff discharged the king's debts in the shire, paid the royal benefactions to religious houses, provided for the maintenance of stock on the crown lands, the expenses of public business, the cost of provisions supplied to the court, and the travelling expenses of the king and his visitors incurred within his district."

[19] Robertus Lupus (Wolf) reddit compositionem de XL marc pro habenda custodia terræ et hæredum Roberti de Standon et uxoris ejusdem Roberti.

Ralph held his lands of Vivian de Standon, the custody
of whose lands had been given to him by the king.
Robert stated in reply that Ralph held of him by knight's
service Ingestre Gratewick, and Rule ; and that Ralph's
ancestor had been enfeoffed (put in possession) by his
ancestor.   By fine levied in the following year, Robert
de Stafford acknowledges the marriage of Isabella, daughter
and heir of Ralph de Mutton, to be the right of Robert,
son of Vivian de Standon."   This is all interesting as
giving us the date of Vivian's death, and mention of his
son Robert de Standon (about whom see later on).

It is necessary here to take notice of the Courts of Justice.
Up to Henry II., A.D. 1154 to 1189, most of the issues at
law were administered by local and manorial courts.   Each
lord had an authority in civil as also in some cases in
criminal cases.   This was not the rule in every manour, but
no doubt when it did occur it was a continuance of a right
granted from earlier times than the Norman Conquest, as,
for instance, we remember Robert de Standon, son of Vivian,
claims a Court Leet (Chetwynd MSS.).   And though all may
seem changed now, the old principle of frank-pledge[20] was
favourably viewed by the people.   Frank-pledge consisted
in a certain number (ten) agreeing amongst themselves for
the good conduct of each other, and bound to produce any
member of that number if he committed a crime ; if these
could not produce the offender, the association was in misericordia,—that is, " at the mercy of the king for any fine
imposed by the justice."

When anyone was in misericordia, or amerced—a term
which we often meet with—it would be understood " that
further pledges would be needed for his appearance."   In the
reign of Henry II. an Assize[21] was instituted, in which the

---

[20] Frank-pledge means in deeds, " a surety."

[21] The following is an exact description of the new institution,
copied from Vol. III. " Hist. Coll. Staff.":—" The great assize is a royal
benefit conceded by the king, whereby the lives of men and safety of

jury consisted of twelve. This Assize, no doubt, was partly
intended to do away with the danger of losing a right by a
challenge to a duel, which challenge was constantly offered,
and partly to simplify the administration of justice.

On the occasion of non-appearance, excuses could be made,
called "essoins" The three principal "essoins" were: (1)
De servitio Regis—on service with the king abroad; (2) De
malo veniendi—detained on the road; (8) De malo lecti
—illness. In the assize, John I., A.D. 1199, Osbertus de
Standon stands as giving pledge. So, also, in the same
assize Ralph de Mutton essoined himself (malo veniendi), by
delay, from appearing against the Dominam (lady) of
Standon, and Robert her son. This Robert has been
mentioned before, he is the son of Adam de Standon. The
Royal Courts, in the time of King Henry III., A.D. 1216-
1272, were the Curia Regis—the Court of the King; the
Supreme Court of Justice: the Court Coram Rege—in
presence of the King; the Court de Banco at Westminster—
which was separated from the Court of the King; and the
County Court.

I return now to Vivian de Standon, in the time of
Henry III., A.D. 1219:—"In Plea Rolls of 16 Henry III.,
A.D. 1232, at Coventry, Warwick (the justices heard cases out
of their counties, when they could not arrive at a conclusion
through absence of one of the parties), Walter, son of Ralph,
and three other knights summoned to elect twelve to make a
recognition of a great assize between Hervey de Stafford,
plaintiff, and Vivian de Staundon, deficiant (one who keeps
another out of possession) of the service, which the said
Hervey claimed of Vivian for the free tenement which he held

their estates is so carefully guarded that, for the right which any man
possesses as his freehold, he may, in order to preserve it, decline the
ambiguous event of the duel, and by this means an untimely death is
avoided, or the opprobrium of perpetual infamy consequent on the use
of that disgraceful word in the mouth of the vanquished." "Craven"
was the word uttered by the vanquished when he yielded, and his life
was preserved.

of him in Dicheford, and respecting which Vivian, who is
tenant, had put himself on a great assize of the king, and
asked for a recognition to be made as to whether he owed to
the said Hervey the service of half a knight's fee for all
service as he alleged, or the service of a full knight's fee
which Hervey claimed from him, came and elected these
James de Bissegham, &c., &c.

"A concord was made. Vivian gave a mark for license of
concord by the pledge of Fraricus de Dicheford."

Again Vivian appears, in issuing a writ against Fraricus
de Dicheford, for paying a fine. Fraricus acknowledges the
fine. In the 34 King Henry III., A.D. 1250, the decision
already mentioned of Vivian's son Robert having the right
of the wardship of Isabella de Mutton, confirms the lordship
in the family of the Staundons. In the final concords, in the
time of King Henry III., A.D. 1248, at Lichfield, " Felicia,
daughter of Adam de Bures, Thomas de Chatkulum, and
Sarra his wife, Richard de Boys and Basilia his wife, Nicholas
de Chatkulum and Alice his wife, John de Suggenhull and
Alditha his wife " are complainants against Viviau de Standon for twelve acres in Standon.

They gain their suit, and they, the wives, are allowed the
land as their own for ever. In the year 1248 John de
Swynnerton and his wife Margery are complainants against
Vivian de Staundon as tenant ; Vivian claiming with his
heirs common pasturage in Swynnerton Heath (most likely
Swynnerton Old Park)[22] for cattle, but not for swine ; that
Vivian and his heirs and his villeins at Standon would pay
4s. at Swynnerton yearly, John and Margery de Swynnerton
having the rest of the common towards the north : the result
is that John and Margery de Swynnerton agree to this.
Vivian again appears in a Final Concord at Coventry

[22] No doubt, in old days, Swynnerton Old Park reached down to
the stream, the Meece ; for part of Swynnerton Parish borders Standon
at that point. The greater portion of Swynnerton Old Park is quite
due north of Standon.

(A.D. 1232: King Henry III.), with Hervey de Stafford, in which the result is that Vivian agrees to Hervey having the right of service of half a knight's fee at Dicheford, and Vivian gave to Hervey 12 marks of silver. Again, in A.D. 1239, at London, Vivian, as complainant, agrees that Fraricus de Dicheford has the right in the manor of Dicheford to be held of Vivian and his heirs for the service of a knight's fee and 4s. annual rent. I now come to Robert de Standon, the Crusader. I conclude that Vivian de Standon, his father, died between A.D. 1248 and 1250, as in A.D. 1250 Robert de Standon, his son, is acknowledged as being in possession; this Robert, the Crusader, joined Prince Edward in the last crusade, A.D. 1270, two years before the death of King Henry III. (Prince Edward's father). The proof that Robert de Standon was in the crusade is found in the Pleas of the Forest, in A.D. 1271. These pleas were heard before special justices. (An account of the forest I reserve for the fourth chapter.) It seems that Robert de Standon, with others, had taken, before Christmas Day, 48 King Henry III. (that is, 1264), some venison in Kanock (Cannock) Forest (ten does, three bucks), and carried them to the house of one Ralph Basset, at Drayton. Some of Robert's companions are some time afterwards caught and imprisoned, but Robert de Standon is respited, being in the Holy Land as a crusader. This action on Robert's part may seem illegal, but at the same time the forest laws were very despotic, and the cause of the greatest abhorence to the people (see Chap. IV.). As a crusader,[28] Robert de Staundon must receive the respect of those who may live in later times in the parish of Standon. I think it not improbable that our Robert de Standon was cotemporary with Sir Roger Swynnerton, who either did undertake the crusade with Prince Edward, or else intended to go in the crusade of A.D. 1288—Pope Nicholas's crusade—which fell through. The

[28] It is not without interest that a son of Colonel Howard Vyse lately fell bravely in battle in the Egyptian War, his ancestors, the Vyses, being for centuries the Lords of the manour of Standon.

beautiful monument in Swynnerton Church (the monument of a crusader) is to Sir Roger Swynnerton. As at this time the crusade could be taken up, and a scutage paid for not going, the actual proof that Robert de Staundon did go to the crusade is a sufficient assurance of his bravery.[24]

This crusade, which commenced A.D. 1270, was the last actual crusade, Pope Nicholas's falling through. Prince Edward sailed from England in the year 1270, and arrived at Tunis, in Africa; from thence he continued his voyage to the Holy Land.

Matthew Paris, in his history, gives us the Latin expression, "Signatus est cruce."[25] He is sealed with the cross, or rather he took up the cross, which no doubt was the term then, A.D. 1258, historically used for entering a crusade. Amongst a vast amount of information about the crusades, there is in existence the MSS. of Pierre de Langtoft, who evidently wrote in the 14th century. Among these MSS. is an account of the reign of Edward I. These MSS. have been most carefully edited by Mr. T. Wright, M.A., F.S.A., &c., &c., and, from his English translation, I give some portion in connection with this crusade of Prince Edward, A.D. 1270 :—

"In the fourth year after King Louis went
Towards the Holy Land with very great equipment;
Counts, dukes, barons, and knights he took thither,
As became such a prince in such a business.

---

[24] Malmesbury Sharpe Ed., p. 415. Urban (Pope), on the first crusade, says:—"Those who may die will enter the mansions of heaven, while the living shall behold the sepulchre of the Lord. Blessed are they, who, called to these occupations, shall inherit such a recompense; fortunate are those who are led to such a conflict, that they may partake of such rewards."

[25] See Malmesbury, Sharpe Edit., p. 413. Urban (Pope) says:— "Let such as are going to fight for Christianity put the form of the cross upon their garments, that they may outwardly demonstrate the love arising from their inward faith." This alludes to the first crusade, A.D. 1095.

When he came to the sea he had good weather.
He arrived against the King of Tunis in his land,
Began very well to conquer and ravage ;
Great was the misfortune that he could not live,
Death took him, alas, his life he ended.
Sir Edward, son of the King of England, provides
That in August following after his way he takes thither.
At Rome, on his way, he spoke with the Pope,
And then remained that winter in Sicily.
As soon as the fair weather of summer approached
He put to sea towards Tunis, the land where he entered
He found the rich King of France, Louis, dead.
Sir Edward passed from Tunis to Acre, &c., &c.
Much was the pagan people frightened
That the Christians had so numerous a chivalry
They feared Sir Edward more than any man alive.
Wherefore the Soldan studies night and day
How he may kill Sir Edward by treason, &c., &c.
The Soldan sends a Saracen to murder Prince Edward.
And he the Saracen is to say :
" Sir, the Soldan salutes thee as a friend—
Alone in a room without other company
I will show thee secrets."
Now is the Saracen come to Sir Edward
In very rich cloths of gold is he clad ;
Beneath he bore poisoned knives.
As he was instructed, he has said his salutation, &c., &c.
He has wounded Sir Edward ; his blows are known
Each is mortal ; Sir Edward, strong and prudent,
Has slain the traitor, has vanquished him by the hand."

Here King Edward slays with a trestle the Saracen who
came to him on a message in treason from the Soldan.

Of Sir Edwards' wounds many a man is in grief ;
His surgeon examines them, tells him certainly

If he wishes him to save him, rest is necessary for him.
It was a very great misfortune, great injury
To Christian people in the Holy Land.[26]

It is with this crusade of A.D. 1270 that Robert de Staundon is connected. Before this period, A.D. 1265, " Odo de Hodinit (Hodnet, Salop) appeared against (by attorney) Robert de Knightele and others, amongst whom is Robert de Staundon, in a plea that they had entered the manour of Odo during the disturbances in the kingdom, and taken away his goods and chattels. The defendants did not appear." In A.D. 1272, Henry III., " Geoffrey de Greseleg sued Robert de Staundon in plea that, he should give up to him Henry, the son and heir of Henry de Verdun, the wardship and marriage of whom belonged to him, inasmuch as Henry held his land of him by knight's service. Robert did not appear."

In the year A.D. 1272, 56 Henry III., the year Henry died, Robert de Staundon appears as one of the jury chosen to decide a case of Nicholas de Overton and Agnes his wife against William de Evenewyk, the Master of the Hospital of St. John, of Lichfield. The verdict, about some land, was given in favour of the Master and Knights of St. John. It is seen by this that Robert de Staundon had returned to England. This is in accordance with the length of the crusade, though not with Prince Edward's return to England. Robert obtains in the same year charge of the heir of Henry de Verdun; this comes through knight's service in Levedale. It seems that the wife of Vivian de Standon was Roes de Standon ; she seems to have lived up to A.D. 1279. She

---

[26] The French original runs thus :
Au quarreme après, le ray Lauys alait
Devers la Terre Saynte of molt graunt coplait
Countes, duks barouns, chuvalers i menait
Cum entel mester à tel prince appendait.
In the fourth year after King Louis went towards the Holy Land, &c., &c.

appears in A.D. 1272, 56 Henry, by her attorney, against Ralph, son of Roger Reyner, and two others for breaking open a chest of hers at Roger Reyner's house, in Salop, and taking 39 marks from it. She also appears " as putting in her place as attorney Gervase de Levedale, or John de Hopes, against Adam de Chetwynde, in a plea of trespass." In 34 Henry, A.D. 1250, Thomas (the parson) of Staundon is mentioned. This seems to be Thomas de Mere. From the year A.D. 1301 I have a consecutive list of the clergy at Standon, which I give in the fifth chapter of this book. In 2 Edward I., A.D. 1274. Robert de Staundon, Thomas Dytton, who now appears as interested in Standon; Thomas, the parson of the church of Standon (N.B.—The way this church is mentioned is a proof of its prior existence.) are mentioned in the Plea Rolls of having disseised (dispossessed) John de Kokfield and Philippa his wife of their free tenement in Mere and Aston. It is said John de Kokfield had never had fees in possession of the tenement. Also Thomas de Dutton, Robert de Standon, and Thomas, parson of the church of Standon, " are accused of unjustly disseissing John de Cokefeud and Philippa his wife of free tenements, of Philippa in Great Roughenhale (Rownall) and Little Roughenhale, viz., of a carucate of land, a water mill, etc." Thomas appears for the defendants, but the record is not concluded.

Robert de Staundon appears, 4 Edward I., A.D. 1276, in the Plea Rolls, Banco Roll, sueing John de Swynnerton that he must carry out the agreement respecting the common pasturage at Swynnerton, as agreed upon by Robert's father, Vivian, and John de Swynerton and Margery his wife. The sheriff is ordered to distrain on John de Swynnerton.

In A.D. 1278, Edward I., Magister de Vernay sues, amongst others, Robert de Staundon for £10. None of the defendants appeared. In A.D. 1280, a convention is made between Sir Robert de Staundon, knight, and Magister Walter de Mare, by which Magister Walter was " to prosecute at his own cost the right of Sir Robert to the lands which

D

belonged to Sir Henry de la · Mere, knight, in ˙Alingscote,
Pighmundecote, Burmarcote and Ashcote, in Oxon Co., which
should revert to Sir Robert as his escheat.[97]   The said Henry
had committed a felony, and died a felon.   Robert agrees that
he would enfeoff (put into possession) Walter de la Mere of
them, to be held by the same service as Gunnora de la Mere
was accustomed to pay." . . .   Robert de Staundon sues
Emma, the widow of Griffin, son of Madoc de Bromfeld, in
A.D. 1282, for a messuage and carucate of land in Boer
Sardun (Bere Sardon).   Emma had no entry except by
Henry de Audedeleye.   Emma called to warranty William de
Audedeley; a jury is summoned to try the case.   In A.D.
1279, an assize held in the matter whether Robert de
Staundon had rightly disseissed Roes, widow of Vivian de
Staundon (and probably mother of Robert) about her free
tenement in Staundon, "one third of two mills[98] and twenty-
six bushels of hard wheat annually."   Robert de Staundon
acknowledges the claim.   In 21 Edward I., A.D. 1293, Alice,
widow of Robert de Wystanswyk, gains back an acre of land
from Robert de Staundon in Mere.   Before this, in A.D. 1281
and 1282, Edward 1st (this mention is made in the expenses
of Edward 1st), we find to three shoeing smiths of the king,
returning to the king towards Staundon, for their expenses,
£0 s8 d0.   It is probable that the Welsh road that runs
through Cotes and Swynnerton was used for the conveyance
of the king's troops.   The king seems to have assembled his
knights and their attendants in Cheshire and Salop, in
A.D. 1279 ; this date, then, must show no doubt it was a rein-
forcement going to him.   In A.D. 1293, 21 Edward I., Robert
de Staundon is on a jury of sixteen.   He is also named at this
time as justiciary of North Wales.   In the same year Robert de

[97] The escheat here was the right of possession to the lord, on
account of Henry de la Mare's death as a felon.

[98] Two mills : One mill only now remains, and there is no proof
except this, of two on the manour of Standon.   This second mill might
be either Hatton or Mill Meece ; unless there was a mill at Weston.

Staundon, with three other knights elect a jury in a case in
connection with the Prior of Stanes (Stone). Again, in the
same year, " William, son of Griffyn, acknowledged he owed
Robert de Staundon £33 : this is a settlement respecting the
case of the manour of Bere Sardon, Emma and William
Griffin, mentioned before. He is also mentioned at this time
as a coroner. The following is an account of his acting as
coroner :—"Thomas de Wyshawe and Alexander his groom,
coming from the market of Newcastle, overtook Ralph le
Frend and John his groom, and a quarrel arising between
them, the said Thomas struck Ralph with a sword on the side,
so that he died on the following day, and Thomas and
Alexander returned to the manour of Madeley, and were
apprehended there by Robert de Staundon the coroner, and
John de Norton the king's bailiff, and were delivered into the
custody of the vill of Madeley, in order to be taken to the
king's prison of Bruges (Bridgenorth), when a number of foot-
men and horsemen from Chester, whose names are unknown,
rescued the said Thomas and Alexander from the hands of
the said vill and beheaded them, and they carried their heads
into Cheshire. The chattels of the said Thomas were worth
s16, for which the sheriff answers. It afterwards appeared
by the coroner's Rolls, that Margaret de Whyshawe, the sister
of Thomas, had appealed in the county court, Adam Brun,
Richard his brother, and Thomas Cotey, of Madeley, for the
death of her brother : and the said Margaret did not appear
before this court. She and her sureties, viz., Philip de
Mutton and Robert Teverey, are therefore in misericordia (at
mercy), and Adam Brun and Thomas Coty appeared and
appealed to a jury : and the jury of the hundred and four
neighbouring vills, say they are not guilty, and they do not
suspect Richard Brun : and the jury testify that William Frend
living at Hunstreton in co. Chester, John, son of William Frend,
Robert de Lee and Roger his son, and thirteen others named,
had rescued the said Thomas and Alexander from the hands
of Adam Brun and others of the vill of Madeley, who

were conducting them to prison and had beheaded them. The justiciary of Chester is therefore commanded to arrest them and produce them before this court on the Octaves of the Purification. A postscript states that three of the accused appeared before the court and appealed to a jury, which acquitted them, and the justice of Chester returned that the others could not be found. They are, therefore, to be out-lawed. It was afterwards testified that Robert de Lees and two others named were dead." This shows the unpleasant state of the neighbourhood and country at this period.

In the year A.D. 1298, Robert de Staundon has a free warren in Standon, Fenton (Vivian). (See Chap. IV.)

Again, in the same year, Robert de Staundon is on the jury in the case of William de Bagenholt receiving two men who were robbers. William claims exemption as being a clericus. The Prior of Stone proves that is so, and he is acquitted on the part of the jurors.

In the same year it is recorded that " Some unknown malefactors broke open the mill of Staundon, and killed Roger de Dereslowe, and they immediately fled, and it is not known who they were. Afterwards[20] a hue and cry was raised, and they were pursued by the men of Eccleshale, so that one of them, by name Robert de Porcher, fleeing from the king's peace, was beheaded. He had no chattels, and Philip, son of Hamon, the first finder, did not appear, but is not suspected, and he was attached by John, son of Robert de Swynnerton, and Robert Overey, of Waleford. They are therefore ' in misericordia,' at mercy." This extract gives us a clear account of the outlawry of that age.

At this very early date we get the name of Gervase (Jervis), of the same family as the present owner of Chatcul, and that of Lord St. Vincent, in the person of Thomas, son of Gervase de Staundon. The mother of Warine, of Standon,

---

[20] A horn was used for the hue and cry, hence a horn was a symbol of jurisdiction.

seems to be Roysia. Before concluding the further accounts
of Robert de Staundon, I mention that we get the name of
Vivian de Staundon in a Plea Roll, in 3 Edward I., A.D. 1275.
Also, about the same time, the names of Dytton or Dutton,
appear more generally. Thomas de Dutton is mentioned
about land in Great and Little Rownall, and in 10 K. Edward I.,
A.D. 1282, Thomas de Dutton and Philippa his wife are
coparceners[30] in the vill of Mere, with three others. Evidently
Philippa de Dutton had been put in possession of Great and
Little Rowenhale by Sir Vivian de Staundon. See deed
14 Edward I., A.D. 1286, in consequence of which there was
a law suit between her and Robt. de Dytton, brother, I take
it, of Thomas de Dytton. Robert de Dutton serves as a juror
in A.D. 1293. In the same year Robert de Dutton appears as
knight.

The names of others of the Dytton family at this date are
William and Roger.

To return to Robert de Staundon, Magister[31] Thomas
and Warine seem to be his brothers, and William his son.

Robert de Staundon is summoned for a foreign expedition
of the king, to recover his Continental dominions, in A.D.
1297. The justices receive a writ that Robert de Staundon,
with others, John de Swynnerton, Roger de Swynnerton, are
under protection as about to go to lands beyond the sea.
(" Profecturi sunt ad partes trans marinas.")

Sir Robert de Staundon, in a deed, A.D. 1292, appears as
signing as knight. Robert appears again by attorney against
William de Clebury, parson of Forton, about some land
transaction at Overton, near Wolverhampton ; this is in A.D.
1301. Robert is sued as custos (custodian) for land of
Thomas, son and heir of Robert de Halghton, in A.D. 1305.
In the next year " John de Chetewynde sued Robert de

---

[30] Coparceners : Having equal portion in the inheritance of the
ancestor.

[31] Magister : See Chapter V.

Staundon for causing waste and destruction in houses, woods, and gardens, which he held in custody of the inheritance of John, in Weston, near Standon. Robert did not appear." In A.D. 1807, Robert de Staundon's name appears as a juror, and in the same year John de Chetwynde withdrew his writ against the said Robert respecting tenements in Standon.

This Robert de Staundon, who plays such a large portion in the early history of Standon, is succeeded by Vivian. In 18 King Edward II. (A.D. 1820), Vivian, son of Robert de Staundon, is mentioned as complainant against Roger, parson of the Church of Blumenhal. In A.D. 1298, Vivian de Staundon had stood as surety to produce Margaret Bagenholt, who had harboured her outlawed son. In an original deed, which is at the Wm. Salt Library, Stafford, " Thomas de Halthton, John de Chetewynde, Robert de Dutton, John Ipstones, Vivian de Staundon, Roger (parson of Blumenhall), Vivian de Chetwynde, William de Weston Jones, Robert, son of Robert de Dutton, Jordan de Penvelesdon, and James de Toddemore are bound to Sir Roger de Swynnerton, Chivaler, in a sum of 500 marks, by a recognizance made in Chancery, 15 Edward II., A.D. 1822, of which 500 marks the said Sir Roger de Swynnerton now grants, for himself and his heirs, to the said Vivian de Staundon, that if the said Vivian shall keep the peace towards him and do him no manner of wrong, that the said recognizance of 500 marks shall be void, and no effect. Witnessed by Monsr. James de Audeley, Monsr. Robert de Knytheley, Monsr. Thomas de Oyle, Geoffrey de Wasteneys, and John de Bromley. Dated at Swynnerton, A.D. 1822."

In 17 Edward II., A.D. 1824, Vivian de Staundon, with William de Chetwynd, Vivian de Chetwynd, John de Ipstones, " stand as bail for the good behavior of those " who, on the side of the Staffords of Bromshull and Sandon, had attacked the Swynnertons. In the Exchequer Subsidy Roll of A.D. 1827 (this subsidy roll was levied to meet the expense of King

Edward III.—expense in the Scotch war—in the taxation) the commissioners are ordered to summon the most loyal men of each vill who were to carry out the taxation. In Staundon we find Vivian de Staundon heading the list ; in Weston, John de Chetwynd. The lists at Staundon and Weston are as follow :—

STAUNDON.	s.	d.
De Viviano de Staundon	vj.	
Roberto filio Prepositi (aforesaid)		xv.
Stepho Medico (the doctor)		xij.
Henrico de Aston...........................		xx.
Adam Bercario (the shepherd)		xviij.
Thoma Carettario (the carter)		xvi.
Rickardo Batkoc		xij.
Adam Carpentario (carpenter)		xviij.
Adam Bercario de Cherlton (shepherd)		xvij.
Willm Capellano[93] (the chaplain)		xviij.
Adam de Walford		xviij.
Thoma Herberd	ij.	
Johne Overey		xij.
Johne Frauncheterre		xx.

WESTON.		
De Johne de Chetwynde	v.	
Willmo le Motere...........................		xxj.
Galfrido de Weston..........................		xij.
Thoma Molendinario (miller)		xviij.
Ricardo de Offylege........................		xx.
Robert filio Thome		xvj.
Johnne Bercario (the shepherd)		xvij.
Thoma Bercario		xvj.
Henrico de Rugge		xviij.
Johne Attelowe		xviij.
Henrico filio Ranulphi		xiij.

In 19 K. Edward II., A.D. 1325-26, John de Staundon, Richard Vivian de Chetwynd, Philip de Ipstanes, and others are ordered to be arrested with Isabel, Lady of Ingestre, for a controversy about the possession of the Church, Eyton juxta Gnousale (Gnosall). The matter had caused in these troublesome times a great deal of disturbance and partizanship.

---

[93] William de Pulteneye was rector at this time, A.D. 1322 to 1333.

This Vivian, who succeeded his father, Robert de Staundon, and lived in the reign of Edward II., A.D. 1307, is succeeded by Vivian dominus de Staundon, who, it is said in the Chetwynd MSS., changed his shield—it is the same shield that Lord Sherborne quarters now—leaving a daughter, Elizabeth, who married Gilbert de Shotesbroke, of Berkshire, Knight, who held a knight's fee at Staundon, K. Henry VI., A.D. 1422; but in A.D. 1432, 10 Henry, Thos. Rogers, of Bercott, is in possession, in right of Elizabeth his wife, who was succeeded by Thomas Rogers, who was succeeded by Thomas Rogers, the daughter of the last named Thomas, Elizabeth (by name), brought the manour into the family of Sir W. Essex, who, in Queen Elizabeth's reign, A.D. 1564, passed by sale the manour to Humphrey Vyse, of Walford.

Side by side with Standon go the lands of Walford, Weston, and The Rugge, and we already see, as almost collateral with the interests of Staundon then and later, the families of Chetwynd, of Jervis, of Broughton, of Vyse, and Shrimshere.

These all fill a considerable page in the history of the parish of Staundon, or in adjoining villages; and it would be interesting to see how each came into connection with the whole parish of Staundon, but I must be content now with the more distinct family of Staundon and its successors, reserving for after chapters any general account that can be obtained of these families at the different periods which this account of Standon parish and manour may extend over.

I trust, between the time of Edward III., A.D. 1327, and Queen Elizabeth, A.D. 1558, more light will be thrown on our Staffordshire manours. Luckily, I am in possession of the Standon Court Rolls from the time of Edward III., and we have the Chetwynd MSS., also the list of the possessors of the advowson of Standon from A.D. 1301. These give additional help, but, no doubt, in time we shall hear more fully about our parish and manours during these periods.

I believe the pedigree of the Staundons to be as follows:—

Brien de Staundon. (Domesday Ten., A.D. 1086.)
Radulphus de Staundon.
Robertus or Radulphus de Staundon.
Adam de Staundon.
Roger or Robertus de Staundon.
Vivianus de Staundon.
Robertus de Staundon, Knight, the Crusader, A.D. 1270, and who, according to the Chetwynd MSS., took the Dutton arms.
Vivianus de Staundon.
Vivianus de Staundon, Dominus, who took the arms mentioned secondly in the Chetwynd MSS., and which are now quartered by the Duttons—Lord Sherborne—of Gloucestershire.

Thence by female line into the family of Shotesbroke.

CHAPTER IV.

COURT ROLLS OF THE MANOUR OF STANDON FROM A.D. 1338
TO 1773: AND THE GENERAL SURVEY OF THE PARISH FOR
A.D. 1818.

E find that Robert de Standon is granted a free
warren in Standon in the reign of King Edward I.,
that is to say, sporting rights over his lands in
Standon. We may remember that the same Robert de
Standon had escaped appearing, on account of his absence
on the crusade wars, to a summons against him for taking
venison. This grant of free warren introduces us to the
forest laws, and also the extreme harshness of the Norman
kings in all their hunting laws. William II. made it a capital
offence,[1] or the loss of eyes, to take a stag or boar. It has
been also said that William the Conqueror, for the sake of
acquiring hunting ground, had destroyed numerous churches
in Hampshire, where he extended the New Forest.[2] (The
ancient name of the forest was Ityne.) The forest laws were
not in their extreme cruelty restricted till the reign of John.

[1] Sharpe's translation of W. Malmesbury's "History of Kings of
England," p. 389. Hallam, "Middle Ages," Vol. II., p. 312.

[2] Sharpe, Malmesbury's "Hist. of Kings of England," p. 348.

Matthew Paris[8] describes the cruelty of Geoffrey of Langley, as bailiff and inquisitor of the king, for trespasses in the king's forests, in A.D. 1250, 34th year of King Henry III.

In Vol. V., Part I., of W. Salt's "Historical Collection of Staffordshire," the rights of the king in his forests are most fully described. We find the forest was considered the most important hunting ground; then came the chace—(Cannock Chace was a Royal forest, not a chace)—then came the park; and, last of all, the free warren.

The charter of free warren contained the clause, dum tamen terræ illæ non sunt infra metas forestræ nostræ—*i.e.*, " So long as these lands may not be within the limits of our forest."

" The beasts of the forest seem to have been the hart, the hind, the hare, the boar, and the wolf.

" The beasts of the chace were the buck, the doe, the martin, and the roe.

" The beasts and fowls of the warren were the hare, the coney or rabbit, the pheasant, and partridge."[4]

We get in names of lands in Standon the coney-gree, or coney-grave, evidently derived from the word coney.

The deer was held, as now in Scotland, the highest species of game.

As Standon Manour has been, no doubt from the date of the granting of the free warren and before, more or less connected with sporting rights, I give some of the old woodman's terms, as quoted by Guillim in his Book of Heraldry[5]:—" Terms of footing or treading of all beasts of venery and chase: That of the hart is termed slot; buck and all fallow deer, view; fallow deer, tract; boar, treading.

---

[8] Matthæi Pariensis, Mon St. Albans, "Chro. Majora," edited by Dr. Luard, Vol. V., p. 136.

[4] Copied from the work on Forest Pleas, by General the Hon. G. Wrottesley, &c. W. Salt, " Hist. Collec. Staff."

[5] Guillim's " Heraldry," Ed. 1724 A.D.

That of an hare is termed according to her several courses, for when she keepeth in plain fields and chaseth about to deceive the hounds, it is said she doubleth; but when she beateth the plain highway, where you may yet perceive footing, it is said she pricketh. The fat of all sorts of deer is called suet. Also it may be very well said, This deer was a high deer's grease. The fat of a roe is termed bevy grease. Boar and hare, grease. You shall say: Dislodge buck, start hare, unkennel the fox, rowse the hart, and bowlt the coney. Terms used by foresters: A hart belloweth, a buck groaneth, a roe belleth, a hare and coney beateth or tappeth, a fox barketh, a wolf howleth. You shall say a litter of cubs and a nest of rabbits. Skilful foresters and good woodmen do use to say: A herd of harts, a herd of all manner of deer, a bevy of roes, a sounder of swine, a rowt of wolves, a riches of marternes, a brace or lease of bucks, a brace or lease of foxes, a brace or lease of hares, a couple of rabbits or coneys. Skilful woodmen, describing the head of a hart, do call the round roll next the head the burr, the main horn the beam, the lowest antlier the brow, antliers next above thereunto the bey, antliers next above that the royal, upper part of all the surroyal top. And in a buck's head they say first a burr, then a beam, then a braunche, then advancers, then a palm, then spellers. The buck is in the first year a fawn, second year a pricket, third a sorel, fourth a sore, fifth a buck of the first head, sixth year a buck or great buck. A doe in the first year is a fawn, second a pricket's sister, the third a doe. A fox in the first year is a cub, second a fox, and afterwards an old fox. You shall say that a hart harboureth, a buck lodgeth, a roe beddeth, a hare seateth or formeth, a coney sitteth, a fox knelleth."

This same Robert de Standon, who claimed a court leet and a free warren, appears by name in a charter of the date of 14th year of Edward 1st, A.D. 1286. By which John, lord of Wetemor (Whitmore), releases and quits claim to the Lord Robert de Standon. Witnessed by Master Thomas, rector of

the church of Staundon, Robert Gerveis, Adam de Swines-
heved (Swineshead), Thomas de Wetindon. There is another
charter by which Robert, lord of Staundon, confirms to
Vivian de Staundon certain lands in Fenton, and also gives a
dower to Maude, Vivianus's wife, daughter of Sir W. Boydell.
Witnessed by Master Thomas, parson of Staundon, John
Coyney, &c., &c.

From this Vivian family we pass to the different landowners and lords of the manour, whom we meet with further
on, in the Court Rolls. A recent book by Professor Rogers,
&c., &c.—" Six Centuries of Work and Wages "—gives us a
descriptive account of the state of many of our villages during
the thirteenth century.   He says : " A thirteenth century
village contained some sixty to eighty inhabitants, most of
them were constantly engaged in husbandry, all, indeed, for
certain periods in the year. The most important artificer,
indeed, was the smith, but it is plain from the records which
have been preserved, that the smith's work was not sufficient
to maintain a smith in any manor; and that the same person
served the needs of three or four." At the court house or
hall the court baron would be held, and the writer goes
on to say, " Such manor houses are still to be found, the
building of which goes back nearly to the thirteenth century.
Many have been expanded into larger houses, or been partly
razed for the building of country houses."

" The manor house was generally near the church. Sometimes the church and churchyard were within the private
grounds of the lord.[6]

" The most important lay tenant of the manor was the
miller; every parish had its watermill. The mill was the
lord's franchise, and the use of the manor mill was an obligation on the tenants. The lord therefore repaired the mill,

---

[6]Broughton, Maer, and Swynnerton, are good instances of how
this may have been. Standon Hall (evidently the present house, is
placed on the old site) is some distance from the church, but we have
mention of chaplains.

the wheels, and found, often a most costly purchase, the mill
stones." All this is a true picture, as may be found further on,
on turning over the pages of the Court Rolls of Standon.
Before, however, entering directly on that subject, some of
the readers of this book may like to know how the parish of
Standon lies. Eccleshall, with its large parish, surrounds
Standon on the south, the town itself being distant more than
four miles. Standon has never been part of Eccleshall.
The stream of the Meece or Sow bounds and divides Standon
from Cotes (Eccleshall) on the east. On the north-east
and north of Standon lies the parish of Swynnerton and
Chapel Chorlton, which former parish is divided from Standon
by the Meece, and the latter by a brook that runs down from
Maer.

The parish of Maer lies at the west of Standon. And
again on the south a brook, which runs by Shortwood,
Standon, and Walford, divides Standon from Chatcull (Eccleshall). Apart from Standon, with Chatcull, Broughton, and
Bromley between, lies The Rudge or Rudge, adjoining Ashley.
This evidently had been brought or given into the lord of the
manour's possession from the Norman times or earlier, and
held from that time as a part of the parish of Standon and
the manour.

The old Park of Swynnerton, the wooded hills of Maer are
pretty features in the view from Standon ; but Standon, not
having the same elevation as Swynnerton, cannot command
such extensive views. Still, Stafford Castle can be seen from
Walford, Bowers, and Standon ; and also from parts of the
manour, the Chace of Cannock and the Shropshire Hills are
seen.

A manour constituted like Standon, with Court Rolls,
gathers from them a considerable light for the more obscure
times of history and parochial life. Two courts were held by
the lord of the manour—the court leet and the court baron.
The court leet was granted to the lord of the manour by the
king ; but not every lord of a manour had the power of a

court leet. We find that a court leet was granted to Robert de Standon, the crusader, for he claimed such in 24th year of King Edward I., A.D. 1276.

Judge Blackstone, in his "Commentaries on the Laws of England," gives us this description of the Court:—"Court leet or view of frank pledge, which is a court of record held once in the year, and not oftener, within a particular hundred, lordship, or manor before the steward of the leet, being the king's court granted by charter to the lords of those hundreds or manors. Its original intent was to view the frank-pledges, that is the freemen within the liberty. Besides this, the preservation of the peace and the chastisement of divers minute offences against the public good are the objects both of the court leet and the sheriff's tourn. It was anciently the custom also to summon all the king's subjects, as they respectively grew to years of discretion and to strength, to come to the court leet, and there take the oath of allegiance to the king. The other general business of the leet and tourn was to present by jury all crimes whatsoever that happened within their jurisdiction." All this business at last developed into the quarter sessions.

The court baron, on the other hand, had to deal with civil matters. And in the present day in some manours a court baron is still held. I take from Judge Blackstone's "Commentaries on English Laws" a definition of the court baron : "The residue of the manor being uncultivated was termed the lord's waste, and served for public roads and for common of pasture to the lord and his tenants. Manors were formerly called baronies, as they still are lordships ; and each lord or baron was empowered to hold a domestic court, called the court baron, for redressing misdemesnors and nuisances within the manor, and for settling disputes of property among the tenants. This court is an inseparable ingredient to every manor ; and if the number of suitors should so fail as not to leave sufficient to make a jury or homage, that is two tenants at the least, the manor itself is lost."

In the 18th year of Edward I., A.D. 1290, an Act was passed that no fresh manours should be created, so that all manorial rights exist only as prior to that date. This Act was introduced to prevent a multiplication of manours. The rights of the Standon Manour, then, are necessarily ancient. And the court rolls and court barons in the following pages throw a vivid light on the different periods which have passed over the manour and parish of Standon.

COURT BARON, HELD 12 KING EDWARD III., A.D. 1338-1339.

This court baron was held in the time of Vivian[7] (probably the third lord of that name) of Standon, but as the accounts of the courts baron from this date to the last held— for Mr. J. Stevenson[8] by Mr. W. Keen, A.D. 1773—are not complete, we must trust to the names of the patrons of the living, also the Chetwynd MSS., as a means of filling in the probable names of the lords of the manour of Standon, though in some cases the names are given in the rolls. However, we now arrive at other names in connection with the manour. These court rolls, as ancient deeds, are beautifully written, in the early part in Latin and with abbreviations. When in English they are very quaint. The Latin deeds have been translated, and with great care, for my uncle, the late Mr. W. Salt, evidently for the purpose of being made known. It is, therefore, with no small satisfaction I put them in print :—

Court of Staundon, holden on Wednesday next after the Feast of St. Augustine, in the 12 year of the reign of King Edward the Third from the Conquest.

---

[7] In the deed, mentioned in the 3rd chapter, in which Vivianus Dominus Staundon appears, one of the witnesses was Nicholas Swynnerton, rector of Mucklestone, who was dead A.D. 1350. This gives a pretty clear estimate of the period of Vivian's life. The name of Vivian appears also on the Court Roll, though not in it.

[8] From John Stevenson are descended my cousin, Mr. T. Salt, M.P. (the present lord of Standon manour), and myself. (E.S.)

William de Boures, chaplain, did fealty, and he has a day to acknowledge his service, and he gives the lord one ox and one horse (fealty).

Thomas de Hatton did fealty, and he acknowledges to hold one messuage and the moiety of one virgate of land by knight's service, and he gives to the lord 12d. (fealty).

John de Brikhul did fealty, and he acknowledges to hold one messuage and one virgate of land, and he will render yearly 7s. 2d., and suit of court, and he will be the fourth to find, at his own cost, one horse, iron shod in front, at Oswaldestre (Oswestry in Salop), to carry the lord's shield (on this shield probably would be the arms mentioned in the 3rd chapter as belonging to Vivian on his seal), and he gives to the lord 40d., one moiety at the Feast of St. John and the other moiety at the Feast of St. Michael.

Robert de Chattoulne (Chatkiln) did fealty, and he acknowledges to hold one plot of meadow for the term of his life, and he will render yearly 18d. at the Feast of St. Michael, and another moiety at the Feast of St. Michael, and he gives to the lord 12d. at the Feast of St. John (fealty).

Roger de Cavereswelle (Caverswall) did fealty, and he acknowledges to hold two parts of the part of Levedale[9] by the service of two parts of one knight's fee, and suit of court every three weeks, and he has to do homage.

Dionisia de Offyley took from the lord one messuage and the moiety of one virgate of land (except four acres and a half of land) for the term of 20 years; and she gives to the lord 15s., viz., 10s. at the Feast of St. John the Baptist, and 5s. at the Feast of St. Peter ad Vincula (in chains), and suit of court and a heriot and 4s. yearly (fealty).

Distraint: Still as at first they present that they distrain John de Chetwynd for his service, John de la Pole, James de Audeley, and the Lady of Rugge (Rudge).

[9] We must remember that Levedale is mentioned as possessed by Brien in Domesday account.

E

Amercement 1d. (That is, he is in misericordia for that sum) see Chapt. III. John de Bromleye, of Mees (Meese), is attached (that is, has a writ served on him) for two colts in the lord's meadow.

Pledge, Roger Aleyn. Robert Sweckyns for one colt in the same.

Ditto Amerce. 2d. Adam the Miller is attached for one swine in the enclosure.

Amercement 1d. Hugh de Coten is attached for one colt in the meadow. Pledge, Henry the Smith (Lat., Faber).

Ditto Amer. 2d. Avice de la Lowe is attached for the swine in the meadow.

Ditto Amer. Adam de Boures is attached for four oxen in the enclosure.

4s. The inquest say that William de Boures, chaplain (this may mean merely the name given, which would be Capellanus; or else William was chaplain to the lord— [William de Boures, however, is not rector of Staundon.— E.S.]), and Adam de Boures took from the lord one messuage and two nooks of land (small angles in a field`, in Boures, for a term of years: and they say that the said messuage is deteriorated 8s. to the damage of the lord: and the dilapidations of the said Adam exceed those of the said William by 4d.

They say also that the vill of Boures has destroyed the hedges of Rousiche: and that the vill of Standon has likewise destroyed the hedges at the head of Rousiche

Taxors Robert Jerveys. Henry le Mareschal. Total 8s. 8d. Geoffrey de Weston took of the lord three acres of open land in Boures, which Adam, son of Robert the Reve, held at the will of the Lord: and he is to render yearly 2d., at the Feasts of St. Michael and the Annunciation of the Virgin Mary.

Memorandum.—That Henry le Mareschal undertook to make the ironwork of one plough belonging to the lord, and of his own iron and at his own furnace, and the fastenings of the same plough, for two heifers, in front and behind, for 4s. 4d., from the Feast of the Ascension to the same feast for one entire year : and he may take it from his ingress.

Herbage.—Stephen de Rugge took from the lord a certain plot of pasture, which is called Lynacre, and he will render for the same 16s. at the Feasts of St. John and St. Michael.

Thomas de Dutton took the herbage of the Schertewode (no doubt Shortwood, but I think Scherte from the Dutch, Skoerte: Skirtwood; Shortwood being at the extreme west of Standon manour and parish) for 18s. 4d. at the same feasts.

Henry le Mareschal gives for the herbage of Wyvenhull 12d. at the Feast of St. John.

Richard, son of Robert the Reve, and Andrew his brother, William the chaplain, 12d. Adam the Miller, 8d. Adam Berc, 12d. : (see Chap. III.). Nicholas de Boures, 10d. John Faunchetre, 8d. Margory Cut, 6d. Roger Aleyn, 16d. John Overeye, 7d. Adam le Hayward, 12d. John Bockard, 8s. Richard le Reccherg, Thomas Cut, 5s. Richard de Swynnerton, 18s. 4d. Henry le Mareschall took of the lord the moiety of one messuage and one virgate of land for the term of 20 years, and he is to render yearly 11s. and to carry mill stones : and he gives a heriot and 12d. to the lord, and four colts for his entry : and he did fealty, and he is to pay at the Feasts of St. Michael and the Annunciation of the Virgin Mary. Roger, son of the smith, took of the lord the other moiety of the aforesaid messuage.

The Court of Staundon, held on Wednesday next after the Feast of St. Barnabas in the year above mentioned :—Adam del Borne sues Thomas Cout in a plea of debt. Ellen, who was the wife of William Atthate, sues Adam Bercar. The lady of the Rugge was distrained to do fealty, and came and did fealty,[10] and she claims to hold Ruge and Mutton of

---

[10] Fealty: An oath of fealty was required by the feudal lord to be taken by all tenants to their landlords. (Blackstone, Vol I., p. 867.)

the lord of Staundon by fealty and scutage, viz., by knight's service.

Still they are commanded to distrain James Daudeley and Thos. del Polhuses, because it is testified that John de la Pole demised his tenements to the said Thomas.

Also John de Chetewinde for his services, because the bailiff returned that he did none therefore.

Amercements.—Adam del Berne prosecutes not Thomas Cout, he is therefore in mercy 6d. Ellen, who was wife of William Atthate, prosecutes not, and is therefore in mercy 2d. The Lord Henry the Chaplain (Dominus: see chapter on Church), is attached for destroying timber, and is therefore in mercy 80d.; pledge, Robert the Chaplain. Robert the Chaplain, is attached for six swine in the lord's orchard (pomerarium), amercement 4d.; pledge, Robert Jerveise. Henry Mareschal is attached for six cattle in the lord's enclosure, amercement 4d.; pledge, the bailiff. Adam le Haiwart is attached for two cattle in the lord's meadow, amercements 1d.; pledge, Thomas Cout. The common shepherd is attached for one ox, amercement 1d.; pledge, the bailiff. Stephen de Ruge is attached for two mares in the lord's corn; he came, and therefore is distrained. Adam le Shepherde is attached for destroying the hedges of Rousick. Cecilia de Swineshed is attached for the same, amercement 8d. Thomas Cont is attached for the same, and he is in mercy 1d.; pledge, Roger Alerhus. Adam Mulewart as above for the same is in mercy 8d.; pledge, the bailiff. Avice del Lode as above for the same is in mercy 8d.; pledge, the bailiff. Adam le Haiwart as above for the same, and he has a day to plead in the next court, and because he found not pledges he is in mercy 1d. Adam de Hatton as above for the same is in mercy, and pardoned. William, son of Walter, is in mercy for the same 8d.; pledge, the bailiff. Nicholas de Boures for the same, 2d.; pledge, the bailiff. Richard, son of Robert the Reve, for the same is in mercy 1d. Henry le Mareschal as above for the same is in mercy 1d. Henry le

Mareschal as above for the same, and he says that he committed no trespass, and therefore he demands trial; pledge, John Brinhul. Adam Bercon for the same is in mercy 1d. John Bret as above in mercy 1d.; pledge, the bailiff. Adam, son of Robert the Reve, as above is in mercy; pledge, the bailiff; he is pardoned by the lord.. William de Madeley as above is in mercy 1d.; pledge, the bailiff. Robert the Reve as above is in mercy 2d.; pledge, the bailiff. Richard le Hare as above is in mercy 2d.; pledge, the bailiff. Taxors: John Breet, Adam, son of Robert. Adam de Chatculne has a day in the next court to show his charter.

The Court of the Manor of Staundon, holden on the Wednesday, the Feast of St. Oswald, in the year above mentioned. Suits :—Thomas Balle sues Nicholas de Boures and Thomas le Carter in a plea of debt; pledge, the bailiff. Adam, son of Robert the Reve, sues Henry the Smith, and Roger, his brother, in a plea of trespass; pledge, the bailiff. Amercement, 2d. Henry came, and they are by licence agreed.

Adam de Chatculne has a day to do fealty, and he came and did fealty, and he acknowledges to hold one plot of meadow in Staundon for 2d. yearly, at the Feast of St. Michael, for all services, and he gives the lord 6d., and he has a day on the Feast of St. Michael.

Stephen de Ruge, for two horses in the lord's corn, is amerced 3d.; pledge, the bailiff.

Thomas Ball offers himself against Nicholas de Boures and Thomas le Carter in a plea of debt, and he seeks 18s. by the pledge of William Attehate; and they come and say that they owe nothing to him, and thereupon they demand a trial. Pledges, John Brinhull and Thomas Cutt; and thereupon he has a day at the next court.

Henry le Mareschall has a day to do fealty, and he does not find a pledge, therefore he is in mercy. Pledge, the bailiff. Amercement, 3d.

Henry le Mareschall is attached for one labouring beast in the lord's corn, and he is in mercy. Pledge, the bailiff. Amercement, 4d.

Avice de la Loue, for two sheep in the lord's enclosure, is amerced 2d. Pledge, Henry le Mareschal.

Adam le Shepeherde, for six sheep in the lord's enclosure; he is therefore in mercy, 2d. Pledge, the bailiff.

Robert Cot, for ten sheep in the lord's enclosure, is in mercy 2d. Pledge, Henry the Smith.

Robert Chaplain, for six swine in the lord's garden and meadow, is in mercy 8d. Pledge, the bailiff.

Thomas Cut, for one labouring beast in the lord's meadow, is in mercy 1d. Pledge, Roger.

William Freeman gives 6d. for suit of court.

The Court of the Manour of Staundon, holden on Wednesday next after the Feast of Saint Bartholomew, in the year abovesaid.

Robert Jerveyse, concerning common, by Adam Ball and Thomas Ball, offers himself against Thomas Ball, Nicholas de Boures and Thomas le Carter, in a plea of debt; and the said Nicholas and Thomas now come and plead that they owe no money to him; therefore it is considered that the said Thomas is in mercy.

Meadows sold.—The Lady of Swynnerton, for the meadow of Caldewall, 8s. Adam le Warde, for the meadow near Brode Medewe, 6s. Thomas de Dutton and Richard de More, for Brode Medewe, 10s. Also the tenants of Staundon give to the .   .   .   . 9s. for (obliterated).

Adam the Miller, for the meadow which is called Stockyng, 5s. 3d.

29TH EDWARD III., A.D. 1855-1856.

Staundon Court, holden on Tuesday next before the Feast of the Apostles Philip and James, in the 29th year of the reign of King Edward the Third after the conquest.

Adam le Smythe is in mercy because he was convicted at the suit of John le Swyneshed in a plea of trespass, 3d. Richard Alwyn prayed in the last court to wage law; he did so, and therefore he is aquitted (acquit). The plaint touching John de Swyneshed plaintiff, and Adam le Smyth defendant, in a plea of trespass, because the aforesaid John alleges that the aforesaid Adam entered his garden and destroyed his meadow to the damage of the same John of 40d., and the said Adam denies it, and therefore he wages law; pledge Richard, son of Robert. Afterwards they are agreed by license, and the said Adam is in mercy. Roger de Gaywode, 3d. Thomas, son of Geoffrey, 1d. Thomas Pere, 3d. Thomas the Miller, 3d. Adam Smyth, 4d. Robert Gaywode, 2d. Henry Bercar, 1d. William Alwyne, 4d. Adam, son of Robert, 18d. John Bragge, 3d. Richard, son of Robert, 18d. Robert Adam, the bailiff, 6d. Adam, son of William Wattes, 1d. Thomas le Mettire, 1d. Richard Gerveyse, Chaplain, 1d., and Henry le Smith, 1d., are in mercy for their cattle found divers times in the lord's corn, as appears in a certain schedule remaining with the bailiff.

Adam le Smythe is in mercy because he did not prosecute against John de Swyneshed in a plea of trespass. The inquest say that the mill has stood still since the Feast of St. Peter in Cathedra, until the present day, on account of the defect of the mill. Richard, son of Robert, 3d. Adam, his brother, 3d. Henry le Sheperde and John Brag, 3d., are in mercy because they were convicted at the suit of Thomas Pere, in a plea of trespass, as it appears in the preceding court. Total, 6s. 9d.

The Court of Staundon, holden on Thursday next, after the Feast of the Translation of St. Thomas the Martyr, in the 29 year of the reign of King Edward the Third after the Conquest. Thomas de Weston, chaplain, plaintiff, offers himself in a plea of trespass against Henry le Shepeherde, of Walford, in a plea. Pledge to prosecute, the bailiff.

John le Beysin, for 18 horses in the lord's corn, pledges Adam le Bailiff and Henry le Smith.   The same Adam, 2s. and 1d., for 25 oxen in the lord's corn ; pledges as above. The same John, 14d., for 14 colts in the lord's corn ; pledges as above. Alice de Broughton, for 11 oxen in the lord's corn; pledge, William Cot. Thomas, son of Geoffrey, for labouring beast in the lord's corn, 1d. ; pledge, the bailiff.   The same Thomas, 8d., for 20 sheep in the lord's corn ; pledge, the bailiff. Richard, Rector of the Church of Staundon (this is Richard de Brompton), 6d., for 2 oxen in the lord's meadow ; pledge, the bailiff.   Thomas de Bachaker, 4d., for 2 oxen in the lord's corn ; pledge, the bailiff. William de Wirley, for 2 oxen in the same; pledge, the bailiff. Thomas Pere, 8d., for 2 oxen in the same ; pledge, as above. Thomas, son of Geoffrey, 8d., for 2 oxen in the lord's corn; pledge, the bailiff. William Fayrchilt, 2d., for 2 labouring beasts in the same; pledge, Adam, son of Robert. John Hicoun, 2d., for 1 labour- ing beast in the lord's corn ; pledge, Adam, son of Robert. Thomas de Bachaker, 1d., for one labouring beast in the lord's corn ; pledge, the bailiff.   Richard, son of Henry, 2d., for 2 labouring beasts in the lord's corn; pledge, Philip, son of David. Roger de Gaywode, 2d., for 2 heifers, in the lord's herbage ; pledge, John Brigge. Adam, son of Robert, for 8 cattle in the lord's enclosure, 8d. ; pledge, the bailiff. The same Adam, for two colts in the lord's corn, 8d.; pledge, the bailiff. Richard, son of Robert, for one colt in the lord's corn, 2d. ; pledge, the bailiff. The same Richard, for one colt in the lord's corn ; pledge as above. Adam del Lowe, for one labouring beast in the lord's corn ; pledge, Thomas, son of Geoffrey. Adam, the bailiff, for three cattle in the lord's corn ; pledge, the bailiff.   Richard, the rector of Staundon (Richard de Brompton), for four swine in the lord's meadow, 2d. The same Richard, for thirty cattle in the lord's pasture. The same Rector, for sixteen swine in the same pasture, 4d. ; pledge, Adam, son of Robert. Adam le Smethe, for four oxen in the lord's corn, 6d. ; pledge, the bailiff. John de Dotton, for four oxen in the lord's corn and herbage; pledge, Thomas Cutt. Yevan de Mere, for five cattle in the lord's corn, 6d.; pledge, the bailiff. John de Dotton, for two colts in the lord's corn, 2d.; pledge, Roger, the bailiff's servant, and John Brag. Adam, son of Robert, for two cattle in the lord's corn, 4d.; pledge, the bailiff. Richard, son of Robert, for one colt in the lord's corn, 2d.; pledge, John Brag. Thomas de Bachaker, for one labouring beast in the lord's corn, 2d.; pledge, Roger, the bailiff's boy.

Adam, son of Robert, offers himself in a plea of convention against Thomas Loukters, and the said Adam puts himself, &c. Total, 18s. 7d.

30TH YEAR OF EDWARD III., A.D. 1356-1357.

Court of Staundon, holden on Monday next after the Feast of St. John before Port Latin, in the 30th year of the reign of King Edward III. after the conquest.

Adam le Smethe complains of Richard, son of Robert, in a plea of trespass, 3d.; pledge, the bailiff. The aforesaid Adam alleges that the aforesaid Richard, by his cattle, destroyed his corn growing in his fields to his damage of half a mark (6s. 8d.) And the aforesaid Richard comes into the court, and he is not able to gainsay it. He is therefore in mercy by the taxor of the court. The damages are taxed at 18d.

The same Adam complains of Adam, son of Robert, in a plea of trespass, 3d.; pledge, the bailiff. And he alleges that the same Adam, son of Robert, destroyed the corn belonging to him, the said Adam, and growing in his fields, to the damage of half a mark; and the said Adam, son of Robert, is not able to gainsay it, therefore the same Adam recovers damages by the taxor of the court, and the aforesaid Adam, son of Robert, is in mercy, and the damages are taxed at 18d.

The same Adam complains of John Brag in a plea of trespass, 8d.; pledge, the bailiff. And the said John is not able to deny having committed the trespass, therefore it is considered that the aforesaid Adam shall recover damages; and aforesaid John is in mercy by the taxor of the court, and the damages are taxed at 12d.

John, the bailiff of Staundon, offers himself in a plea of trespass against Thomas Longcors, and he says that the aforesaid Thomas took the mill of Staundon that he might answer to the lord for the profit arising from the same. He answered for no profit by the testimony of the bailiff; but he damaged the same to the amount of 20s. The aforesaid Thomas came and acknowledged that he had for himself one bushel of malt worth 8d., and did damage to the amount of 20s., and he puts himself upon the lord's grace; pledges of the same Thomas, Adam Smethe, Thomas Pere, and Thomas, son of the miller. The jurors present that Christiana le Moder is a common malefactor, and burns houses; and that Adam, son of Robert, is attached for one colt in the lord's corn, amer. 1d.; and that Richard, son of Robert, amer. 2d.; Adam, his brother, amer. 8d; Adam, the bailiff, amer. 2d.; and John Brag, amer. 8d., are attached for nine cattle in the lord's corn. Mill demised: Memorandum that John de Chaldon took of the lord the lord's mill and farm (ad firmam) for one year, viz., from the Sunday next after the Feast of the Purification of the Virgin Mary last past unto the same day then next following, rendering therefore yearly eleven quarters of toll corn (tol korn) and two strikes of oatmeal, by the mainprise (security) of John de Swyneshed.

Thomas de Bachaker is attached for one labouring beast in the lord's corn. Ralph, son of Henry, is attached for two labouring beasts in the same; pledge, Philip, son of David. Roger de Gaywode, for one heifer in the lord's close, 2d.; pledge, ... Adam, son of Robert, for one colt in the lord's corn, 2d. The same Adam, for one cow

and two calves in the lord's close, 2d.; pledge, the bailiff.
The same Adam, for two colts in the lord's corn, 4d.;
pledge, as before. Richard, son of Robert, for one colt in
the lord's corn, 2d.; pledge, John Brag. The same Richard,
for one colt in the lord's corn, 2d.; pledge, John Brag. Adam
del Lowe, for one labouring beast in the lord's corn, 3d.;
pledge, the bailiff. Adam the bailiff, for three cattle in the
lord's corn; pledge, the bailiff. Richard, the rector of
Staundon (the same Ric. de Brompton), for thirty-three swine
in the lord's close; pledge, the bailiff. Geoffrey de Weston,
for two colts in the lord's corn, 4d.; pledge, Henry le
Shepeherd. Richard le Mason, for three colts in the lord's
close, 4d.; pledge, Richard, son of Robert. Also the whole
vill of Staundon for all their cattle in Lee Meadow and the
Rabbit Warren; pledge, Richard, son of Robert, and Adam
his brother. Henry le Shepeherde, for four cattle in the
lord's meadow, 4d.; pledge, Adam, son of Robert. William
Aylwyn, for three cattle in the lord's meadow, 3d.; pledge,
Adam, son of Robert. Also, Robert de Walford is attached
for nine cattle in the lord's meadow, 9d.; pledge, Thomas de
Bachaker. Also, Thomas, son of Geoffrey, for nine cattle in
the lord's corn, 12d.; pledge, the bailiff. William de
Weston, for eleven cattle in the lord's corn, 12d.; pledge,
the bailiff. The whole vill of Weston, for twenty cattle
in the lord's pasture, 8d.; pledge, Adam the bailiff. Also,
Adam the bailiff, for sixteen cattle in the lord's corn, 4d.;
pledge, the bailiff. Also, Richard, son of Robert, for two
cattle in the lord's corn, 3d.; pledge the bailiff. Adam, son of
Robert, for two cattle in the lord's corn, 4d. Henry le Smyth,
for three cattle in the lord's corn and meadow, 3d.; pledge, the
bailiff. John Chaldon, for one labouring beast in the lord's
corn, 2d.; pledge, Thomas Pere. Thomas le Meter, for
one cattle in the lord's corn; pledge, Thomas Pere.
John le Here, for thirteen heifers in the lord's close; pledge,
John Bragg and Adam, son of Robert. Robert de Walford,
for forty wethers in the lord's meadow, 6d.; pledge, the

bailiff. Roger de Hakedon, for eighty sheep in the lord's meadow, 12d. Richard, son of Robert, for thirty sheep in the lord's meadow, 4d.; pledge, ... John Brag, for two cattle in the lord's meadow, 4d.; pledge, the bailiff. William de Weston, for ten cattle in the lord's oats; pledge, the bailiff. Total, 17s. 7d.

Court of Staundon, held there on Thursday, on the morrow of the Feast of the Apostles Peter and Paul, in the 30th year of the reign of King Edward III. after the Conquest.

Roger de Gaywode, 3d.; John de Chaldon, 3d.; Robert de Weston, 2d.; John de Dutton, 1d.; Richard de Podmore, 7d.; John, son of Thomas, 2d.; Thomas, son of Geoffrey, 2d.; and John Hykenes, 1d., are amerced for their cattle in the lord's corn, as appears in the schedule remaining with the bailiff. Giliana, formerly the wife of Henry le Sheperde, surrenders into the hands of the lord all the lands and tenements which she held in dower in Rugge, to the use of Thomas, son of the aforesaid Henry, to hold according to the custom of the manour, who gives for having his entry therein [11] . . . . . . and he did fealty.

. . . . . . distrains Margery de Oneleye, to show her charter, by what service, &c., &c.

It is to be inquired what tenements have been leased and not enrolled, in order that they may be enrolled; and what tenements remain in the hands of the lord, and through whose death, and what each tenement is accustomed to render, and . . . . . it is to be examined, and where necessary amended.

. . . . . . has taken into the hands of the lord one . . . . . meadow, which Robert de Walford still holds of the lord . . . . . and it is to be ascertained whether he or Henry le Shepeherde has the greater right thereto. Total, 2d.

[11] This deed is much obliterated.

34 AND 35 EDWARD III., A.D. 1361-1362.

Court of Staundon, held on Saturday next after the Feast
of St. Denis, in the 34th year of the reign of King Edward
the Third after the Conquest.

Richard Gerveyse gives for pasture in the lord's fields
and woods, for his swine, 2s. 6d. Also, Thomas, son of
Geoffrey, gives . . . . . 5 swine, in the same, 4d.
Also, the tenants of Walleford (Walford) give for their swine
6d. Also, John de Barnevill is in mercy for oxen in
Bradmedewe. Also, John, son of Roger, is in mercy 3d., for
3 oxen in the same. Pledge as above. Also, Henry de
Chaldon is in mercy 6d., for 6 oxen in the same. Pledge,
Thomas, son of . . . . . Also, John le Parmenter is
in mercy for one ox in the same. Pledge, Thomas, son of
Richard. Also, Howell de Chatculne is in mercy for 2 heifers
in the same. Pledge, John Brag. Also, John, son of
Thomas, is in mercy for 5 swine in the lord's severalty (land
apart from the rest), 3d. Also, Henry le Smithe is in mercy
for 2 swine in the lord's barley, 2d. Also, John Brag is in
mercy for one labouring beast and one colt in the lord's
barley, 2d. Also, John Hare is in mercy for one labouring
beast and one colt in the same, 2d. Also, the Rector of the
Church of Staundon is in mercy for the sheep of two-teeth in
the lord's corn, 8d. Also, Adam, son of Robert, is in mercy
for 8 oxen in the lord's oats; pledge, Richard, son of Robert.
Also, Adam de Staundon is in mercy for two oxen in the
lord's oats, 2d. John Brag, for 2 oxen in the same, 2d.
Also, Henry le Smithe, for one cow in the same, 3d.
William de Chetwynde, Knight, 6d. ; Margaret de Oniley and
Adam, son of Henry de Swynnerton, 2d., who ought to
appear and came not, therefore they are in mercy and
distraint to come, &c., &c.

Inquest.—Thomas the Miller; William Cut, John Brag,
William Aylwyn, Henry Bercar, Henry le Smith, Robert
Gerveise, Adam Smithe, Adam le Bailiff, William Chapmon,
John Hare, Nicholas Prés, jurors.

Increment, 8d. The lord has granted to Adam, son of William, son of Walter, one plot of ground, called Oweynes-heth, to hold at the will of the lord. Total, 8s. 2d.

In expenses of the steward 18½d., for two attendances for the increased rent of 8d.

Court of Staundon, held on Monday the eve of the Feast of St. Chad the Bishop, in the 35th year of the reign of King Edward the Third after the Conquest.

Adam, son of Henry de Swynnerton, essoins himself (but it does not lie because he owes two appearances) on a common essoin by John de Charnes (see Chapter III.).

Laurence de Penlesden gives 6d. to the lord for releasing his suit of court till the Feast of St. Michael next ensuing, fine 6d. Geoffrey de Weston complains of Adam Smethe for detaining one wine measure (algie, algia). Pledges to prosecute John de Swynesh and the bailiff, and he seeks from him the said wine measure price 12d., and damages for unjustly detaining it 16d., and he comes and answers nothing, there-fore it is considered that the said Geoffrey shall recover the said wine measure with the damages aforesaid, and he is in mercy for the unjust detention.

John Pecok, of Podmor, is in mercy for six cattle in the lord's enclosure 4d.; pledge, the bailiff. William Fairchild is in mercy for two cattle in the same, 2d.; pledge as above. Also the same William is in mercy for one beast in the same, 1d.; pledge as above. Also Richard del Lewe de Mere is in mercy for twelve two-teeth sheep in the lord's inclosure, 2d.; pledge, the bailiff. Also John de Charnes is in mercy for twelve cattle in the lord's corn, immediately after the feast of St. Michael, 6d.; pledge, Adam de Staundon and the bailiff. Also Thomas, son of the miller, is in mercy for cutting the lord's hedges, 3d. Also Margery, wife of Stephen de Blorton, is in mercy 2d. for carrying away firewood from the lord's orchard. Also Agnes de Somersete is in mercy for the same, 2d.

Richard de Peshale, knight, lord of Weston, who owes suit at court and came not, therefore he is distrained to come at the next court to do suit of court, and afterwards to do fealty : and he did fealty and he has a day to acknowledge his service at the next court, and he acknowledged suit of court. (This seems to be cancelled.) Richard de Peshale, knight, did fealty, and acknowledged to hold of the lord the vill of Weston[12] near Mere, for one knight's fee, rendering therefore yearly 12d. at the usual terms, and doing suit at the court of Staundon.

The tenants of Walford have taken from the lord Le Ruding (Rough Reading) with Le Gorses (may be Gorsey Field in Standon), to hold for the term of four years next ensuing, rendering therefore yearly 7s. at the terms of the Annunciation of the Virgin Mary and St. Michael, by equal portion.

Memorandum.—That John de Hatton has taken from the lord the mill of Staundon for the terms of four years next ensuing after the Feast of SS. Peter and Paul, in the 34th year of the reign of the present king, rendering for the first year nine quarters of multure (ground corn), and for the three years then next following ten quarters of multure annually ; and rendering the said farm (firmam) every three weeks ; and keeping in repair two new wheels for carrying the lord's timber and malt ; and at the end of the said term he is to leave the mill in a good state in all things except the mill stones.

The tenants of Boures hold the arable lands in the Common fields (Standon Common) until the lord shall have tenants for those tenements. Rendering therefore yearly 4s., at the terms of the Annunciation and St. Michael.

Richard, son of Robert, and Adam his brother, have taken the arable lands, with the meadows adjoining in Rousiche ("Rousage in Standon"?), to hold for the term of six years next ensuing, rendering therefore 6s., at the terms of the

---

[12] This seems to prove that the manour included Weston, and there were not two manours, Standon and Weston.

Annunciation and St. Michael. by equal portions. Total
2s. 7d.; expenses thereupon 15d.

Court of Staundon held there on Tuesday next, after the
Feast of St. Mark the Evangelist, in the year above said:—

Lord Richard de Peshale essoins himself by Thomas
Clerk. Thomas de Boures excuses himself from appearing by
Thomas de Weston. It does not lie because the essoiner did
not keep the day. William Cut essoins himself by the Rector
of the Church of Staundon (Richard de Brompton). William
Feyrchild was attached for two heifers in the lord's pasture in
le Shertewode (Shortwood), 2d. Also the same William
for one colt in the lord's corn, 2d. Also Adam Pecok for one
colt in the lord's corn, 2d. Also John le Thatcher for one colt
in the lord's corn, 2d. Also Thomas, son of Geoffrey, for one
colt in the lord's corn, 2d. Also Thomas, son of Juliana, for one
colt in the lord's corn, 2d. Also Adam, son of Robert, for four
cattle in the lord's corn, 4d. Thomas, son of Geoffrey, for two
oxen in the lord's corn, 2d. The same Thomas for one colt in
the lord's meadow, 2d. Thomas Pere for one colt in the lord's
corn, 2d. Richard, son of Robert, for one beast in the
Shertewood (Shortwood), 2d. Adam, his brother, for one beast
in the lord's corn, 2d. Adam le Baillie for one beast in the
same, 1d. Henry le Smith for one beast in the same, 2d.
Hugh de Chalden, of Mere, for one colt in the lord's pasture,
1d. Richard, son of Roger, for one colt in the same, 2d.
Richard del Lewe for one colt in the same.

The tenants of Walleford have taken the meadow of
. . . . . for one croppe (crop) 21s. Also the Rector of
Staundon (Richard de Brompton), has taken " le Conin-
grave" (Rabbit Warren), with the meadows adjoining, for one
crop—11s. Also the tenants of Boures have taken the
meadow of Whewell? (Mewell), " . . . ." for one
crop, and they give 7s. Also John de Hatton has taken " le
Mulne Medewes " (Mill Meadow) for one crop, and he gives
6s. 8d. The tenants of Boures have taken "le Mylne?" in

" le Lowe feld " (Lower Field, Bowers ?) for the herbage for one croppe, and they give 5s.

Also the Rector of the Church of Staundon, Richard de Brompton, has taken the orchard of the ancient manour (pomerarium de antiquo manerio de Staundon) for one crop, and he gives 2s. 6d. Also Thomas, son of Geoffrey de Weston, has taken the pasture del Shertewode for one crop, and he gives . . . . . Richard de Walford and his neighbours have taken the pasture of the lands of . . . . . . of Walford for one crop, and they give 2s. John Hare has taken one wick (vicū)—a bend (probably by the stream)— which belonged to Henry le Smith, for one crop, and he gives 6d. Also Adam, son of Robert, has taken one wick which belonged to John Everge for one crop, and he gives 4d. Also Adam, son of Robert, has taken one wick near Le Brode mark . . . . . . And he gives for one crop 6d. Also John . . . . . . one plot of meadow called Le Akeresmede, rendering for one crop 12d. (In Walford we get the Broad Meadow fields). Robert Gerveyse, a suitor, 3d. William de Chetwynde, Miles, (kt.), Adam, son of Henry de Swynnerton, freeholders, came not, and are therefore in mercy.

It is found by the inquest that Christiana le Meter, Matilda, daughter of Simon, and Amy, daughter of John, are common hedge breakers by their mainpernors (sureties). And the inquest has a day until next court to prosecute further. Also they present that Richard, son of Robert, 4d. Adam his brother, 4d. Adam, son of the bailiff, 4d. Robert Gerveyse and John Larasete have not repaired the gaps by the day allowed, therefore they are in mercy.

The essoin of Thomas de Boures . . . . there-fore the said Thomas is in mercy, and he is distrained to be at the next court.

The Lord has granted that Alice le Soustere may take three waste lands adjoining her cottage, rendering for the said waste lands 12d., at the terms of the Annunciation and

F

St. Michael, beginning to pay rent at the Feast of the
Annunciation of St. Mary last past, at the will of the lord.
Total of the pleas and perquisites of court, 5s. 10d.   Total
. . . . . . pasture and meadow, 61s. 9d.   Total,
67s. 7d. Increase of rent, 12d. Expense of the steward, 14d.

40, EDWARD III.: A.D. 1865-1866.

Court of Staundon, held on Thursday next, after Feast of
Saints . . . . . . Martiny in the 40 year of the reign
of King Edward III., Richard, son of Robert, was attached
for twenty-four oxen in the lord's oats, 1s. 4d. Adam Smethe
was attached for three calves in the lord's oats, 2d. John
Parsones for a calf in the lord's oats, 2d.; pledge, Alice Cotte.
Henry Bercar, Robert de Weston, John Nicolas, for thirty
two-teeth sheep in the lord's meadow. The Rector (Richard
de Brompton) for two horses in the lord's oats. The same
Rector for one horse in the same, and again two horses in
the same. Richard Hobbesone for one heifer in the lord's
oats. William de Schesturchur for two heifers in the lord's
corn; pledge, Adam, son of Walter. Thomas de Weston for
one colt; pledge, Richard Burgeyse. The Rector of the
Church, the same Richard de Brompton, with his ploughs and
horses, for treading down the lord's corn.

Alice Coutte for six geese (sex ancas) in the lord's oats.
Total 6s. 8d.

The lord seeks against Richard the Rector (R. de
Brompton) in a plea of trespass for divers trespasses. Robert
Jerveise offers himself by William Jerveise. Margaret de
Onyley made her appearance on that day, in what manner
she holds it is not known, therefore it is said to her that she
may have her charter (carta). Hugh del Berne did fealty,
and agreed to hold of the lord one plot of ground in Le . .
. . . . . estad, in the vill of Scherla (this may be
Chorlton), and he has a day to show his charter until the
next court. It is presented that the bailiff shall take into
seizin (seisina, possession) of the lord . . . . , . . .

which belonged to Philip le Drapur on account of the minority of Agnes, daughter and heir of the said Philip. (See Chapter III.)

Fines for suits of court in this year.

Richard de Pessat gives to the lord for this year 12d. ; Alice Fremon, of Rug (Rudge), gives to the lord for suit of court 6d. ; Elianora, who was the wife of Thomas, son of Henry le Scheppeherd (Shepherd), gives the lord for suit of court 4d. Taxors : A. and B. Total, 15s. 6d.

John Nouweres[13] and Isabella, his wife, and Philip de Staundon, have given to John de Dutton half a virgate of land in Mere to hold to him and the heirs of his body issuing of them, for 4s., at the usual terms and one appearance at the Court of Staundon, and he owes a heriot (Saxon)—relief (Norman)—after death ; but he renders to the said donors until the full age of the said Philip.

1 AND 2 KING HENRY VI., A.D. 1422-1424.

Staundon.—Account of William Vyse, from the Feast of St. Michael the Archangel, in the 1st year of the reign of King Henry VI., to the same feast next following, in the 2nd year of the same king's reign, for one whole year.

The same account for 65s. 8d. from rent of all tenements, as well free, as . . . . . (Rents of Assize there). Total, 65s. 8d.

And for 57s. 2d. of rent of Assize of all tenements in Walford, alone as above. And for 58s. 6d. from rent of all tenements . . . . alone as above. And for 5s. from rents in Aston, alone as above. And 5s. from rent in Audelee (Audley), alone as above. And for 25s. 1½d. of rent in Chorleton, by the year, alone as above. And for 11s. 4d. from rent in Mere, alone as above. And for 2s. from rent in

[13] John Nouweres (knight) is the patron of the living of Staundon, A.D. 1369. Philip de Staundon no doubt is a descendant of the Staundons, not improbably son of Vivian, as we find Elizabeth, probably his sister, carries the estates into the family of Shotesbroke.

Polhouson, yearly, alone as above. And for . . . . .
from rent in . . . . . yearly, alone as above. And
for 12d. from rent in Weston, yearly, alone as above. And
of 4s. 6d. from rent in . . . . . yearly, alone as above.
Total, £8 8s. 7½d. And for 40s. from the farm of the mill
. . . . . alone, to John Burywode, for the term of
two years (Farm of the Mill). Total, 40s. And for £6 from
the farm of demesne lands, closes, meadows . . . . .
of the Manour of Staundon, so granted to William Vyse for a
term of years. Total, £6 0s. 0d.

Perquisites of Court.—And for 5s. 9d. from perquisites of
one court held within the year. And for 10s. arising from
the heriot on the death of William Amysone. And for 11s.
from one ox, arising from the heriot[14] on the death of
William de Shylton. Total, 26s. 9d.

And for 88s. from rent in Rugge, arising to the lord from
wardship, being in his hand by the death of Richard
Chetewynd, and during the minorage of the heir of the said
Richard, whose marriage pertains to the lord, and he is of
the age of . . . . paying the rent thereof . . . .
Chetwynd, the widow, for her dower, for the term of her life.
Total, 88s. Sum total, £22 18s. 0½d. From which account
there is paid in rents resolute for the lord's tenements, at the
Hundred of Stone, this year 4s., and in rent resolute[15]
. . . . . for the lands and tenements lately belonging to Richard Shelton, and this year being in the hands of
the lord, 8d. Total, 4s. 8d. And in deficient rent of one
messuage and half a virgate of land, now in the tenure of
Richard Wolseley, in Boures, which were accustomed to pay
7s., now demised to the same at 6s. yearly. And so in
reduced rent 12d. And in deficient rent of one messuage,
with certain lands and tenements in Cherleton, late in the

---

[14] Heriot.—The heriot would be originally paid to the lord by
means of the chattels of the tenant, and in kind rather than money.

[15] Resolute: in resolucione—by resolution.

tenure of Richard . . . . . which used to pay yearly
5s., but now in the hands of the lord. And so in deficient
rent 5s. And in deficient rent of one tenement, with certain
lands, late of John Elkyn, in Mere, which used to pay yearly
5s., but are now in the hands of the lord, and land thereof
sold for 2s. . . . . . And so in deficient rent 4s.
And in deficient rent of one messuage, and half a virgate
of land in Staundon, being in the hands of the lord, which
used to pay yearly 7s., now holden on lease of Ralph Bery at
6s. yearly, and so in . . . . reduced rent 12d. And in
deficient rent of two messuages and two virgates of land in
Staundon, late of Thomas Adison . . . . which used
to pay yearly 18s., now demised for half a year at 9s., and so
in deficient rent 9s. Total, 20s.

And to one man for rebuilding the lord's mill, 40s. . .
. . 30s. to the same before allowed. And to other men for
the full repair of the lords . . . . And in carriage of
timber and clay to the same, 5s. 4d.

Expenses of the steward this year nothing.

And paid to William Lee, the lord's steward, for his wages
of the office of steward, 26s. 8d. Total, 26s. 8d.

In money delivered to Henry, the lord's servant, for the
term of the Annunciation of the Virgin, without deduction,
£7. And to the same Henry, for the term of St. Michael,
without deduction, £9 2s. 5d. Total, £16 2s. 5d. Total of all
the expenses, &c., £20 19s. 1d. And so . . . . . 11½d.
From which in allowances to the same for the sale of wax,[16]
paid to the lord. Thomas de . . . . . of the lord, 7s.
And to the same for one meadow, called Brad Medee (Broad
Meadow, in Walford) 1d., given to the lord of Swinerton
for . . . . . . for 18s. 4d., and he is to have it in the
year to come . . . . . and there is due clear 13s. 7½d.,
from which . . . . (obliterated) of the Lord of
Weston for lands and tenements which he holds in Weston,
because they are ignorant . . . .

[16] Cera, wax.

18TH YEAR OF HENRY VI., A.D. 1484 TO 1485.

Staundon Court, holden there on Saturday next before the Feast of St. Thomas the Apostle, in the 18th year of the reign of King Henry VI., after the Conquest of England.

Thomas Amyson, Ralph Frere, Thomas Martyn, William Bromley, Thomas Filly, William Bishop, Richard Chesterton, Thomas Mason, Richard Manchester, Nicholas Bromley, Henry Swyneshed, John del Lowe, John Fox, jurors.

The jurors present that Richard Peshale, Hugh White, 2d., Lord of Charnes; the Prior of Ronton, 2d.; Hugh Dutton, 2d.; Thomas de Endon, 2d; the Lord of Lechdale 2d.; and Thomas Gerveis (pardoned) 2d.; owe suit at this court, and came not, therefore they are in mercy. And that Thomas Amyson 2d., Thomas Martyn 2d., have fished in the lord's several waters (piscatores fuerunt), therefore they are in mercy. And that Thomas Amyson, 6d., felled three ash trees in the lord's wood without licence (in bosco dni. sine licenc), therefore he is in mercy. And that Richard Chesterton, 1d., felled one ash in the lord's wood, therefore he is in mercy. And that John Fox felled one other ash, 1d., therefore he is in mercy. Richard Manchester, 1d., felled one other ash, therefore he is in mercy, And that the Parson of the Church of Staundon (this is either John Lutte or John Wollaston) destroyed the lord's rabbit warren of Staundon with his swine, and is therefore in mercy 4d. And that Nicholas de Bromley felled another ash, therefore he is in mercy, 1d.; and Mabel de Boures is a common stealer of the hedges of the neighbourhood, therefore she is in mercy 1d.; and Lœtitia de Wolley does the same. And that Richard Wolley, who held of the lord one messuage and half a virgate, is dead, and there falls to the lord in the name of a heriot one saddle mare, and it is in the hands of the bailiff (unam doseam equam—dorsuarium, a pack saddle). Afferers (afferatores, officers who set fines on the offenders) of the court: Ralph Frere, Thomas Amyson, jurors.

To this court came Henry Swyneshed, and took of the lord one toft (toftum) with the land adjoining, late in the tenure of John Shelton, for the term of twenty years, rendering annually to the lord during the aforesaid term 8s., and if he should wish to let the aforesaid land within the term aforesaid he shall agree with the lord for his heriot.

Staundon Court, held on Wednesday next before the Feast of Pentecost, in the 18th year of Henry VI., after the Conquest. Prior of Ronton and Thomas Pikkyn essoin themselves from suit of court. Ralph Frere, Thomas Amyson, John Fox, William Bromley, Thomas Martyn, Richard Chesterton, Nicholas Bromley, Thomas Filly, William Byshop, William Wolveley, Thomas . . . , John Brewood, jurors, who being sworn present that Richard Peshale, of Chetewyn, 2d. Hugo White, lord of Charnes, 2d. Thomas Gerveis, pardoned. Hugh de Dutton, 2d. Thomas de Endon, 2d. John de Astbury, 2d. The Lord of Lechdale, Philip Chetewyn, owe suit at the court and came not, therefore they are in mercy. Afferers of the court—Thomas Martyn, John Fox. At this court Thomas Manchester acknowledged and agreed to repair the house in his tenure before the next court; and if he be in default in the said reparation at the day fixed, he agreed that 6s. 8d. shall be levied on his goods and chattels by the bailiff there for the use of the lord.

14TH YEAR OF HENRY VI., A.D. 1485-1436.

Staundon Court holden there on Saturday next after the Feast of St. George the Martyr, in the 14th year of the reign of King Henry VI., after the Conquest.

Richard Frere, John Brewood, John Fox, Thomas Martyn, William de Bromley, Richard Chesterton, Nicholas Bromley, Thomas Filly, William Byshop, William Wolveley, Thomas Mason, Hugh Dutton, jurors, who being sworn present that Richard Peshale, of Chetwynd, 2d.; Philip Chetwynd, 2d.; Hugh White, Lord of Charnes, 2d.; the Lord of Lechdale,

2d.; the Prior of Ronton, 2d.; Thomas Endon owe suit of court, and came not, therefore they are in mercy.

Afferers of the court — William Bromley, Richard Chesterton, jurors.

23RD YEAR OF HENRY VI., A.D. 1444-1445.

Staundon, the great Court held thereon Wednesday next after the Feast of St. Michael, in the 23rd year of the reign of King Henry the Sixth, after the Conquest.

Hugh Dutton, Thomas Gerveys, William Bramley, Thomas Martyn, John Voxe, Thomas Amyson, Nicholas Bromlegh (Bromley), Richard Chesterton, Ralph Hykoc, John Wylkys, William Byshopp, John Ravold, jurors, who come and present that the lord of Rugge, 8d.; the tenants of the lands and tenements of John Couper, of Rugge, 4d. The Lord of Weston, 6d. Walter Stafford de la Dale, 8d., John Knightley, 4d. The Prior of Ronton for his lands in Walford, 8d   Roger Swyneshede, John Fletcher, freeman, who owe suit and have made default on this day; therefore, they are in mercy, 2d. And they present that John Voxe, 1d., unjustly felled two ash trees worth 4d., in his close which he holds of the lord, according to the custom of the manor, therefore, he is in mercy; and, nevertheless, it is ordered that the price aforesaid be levied to the use of the lord.

Also they present that William Bramlegh 2d., unjustly felled one ash tree worth 2d., in his close which he holds as aforesaid; therefore, he is in mercy, and, nevertheless, it is ordered that the price aforesaid be levied to the use of the lord. And they present that Thomas Amyson, 2d., entered on the lord's pool in front of the mill (ante molendinum), and there unjustly fished, and took fish there without the lord's license (injuste piscavit et cepit pisces sine licencia); therefore he is in mercy. And they present that Thomas Martyn unjustly entered upon the demesne land of the lord at Shortewode, and there unjustly broke the lord's hedge, on the Feast of the Invention of the Holy Cross in the 22nd year of the said king's reign, and there his six oxen and three steers unjustly commoned and consumed the pasture there ; which said Thomas, present in court, thereupon put himself upon his charter granted of ancient time by the lord for his justification, or otherwise he throws himself upon the lord's grace by the pledge of Thomas Gerveyse. And they present that the tenure late of Agnes Cheterton is injured and deteriorated by the default of the said Agnes, to the damage of the lord 2s. which he delivered to Philip Snokstone, tenant of the lord, to repair the aforesaid tenement before the next court at the sum aforesaid. He offers in money 2s. And they present that Thomas Endon, late of Aston, is dead, who held of the lord by knight's service, one tenement in Aston aforesaid, within the fee of Mere, with its appurtenances : therefore it is ordered that one heriot be taken from the aforesaid tenure ; and moreover it is ordered that a distress be levied before the next court upon the lands and tenements lately belonging to the said Thomas, sufficient as well for the homage due to the said lord as to satisfy the lord for his relief for the land and tenements aforesaid, saving the right, &c.

To this court came Hugh Dutton, and claimed to hold of the lord in the right of Joan his wife, daughter of William Boydell, the moiety of the lands and tenements lately belonging to the said William, in Oneley, at the yearly rent of 2s. 6d., at the Feast of St. Martin ; suit of court twice a year, and by knight's service ; and he did fealty to the lord and is admitted tenant. It is nevertheless ordered that he be distrained before the next court as well to do homage to the lord, as to satisfy the lord for his relief due for the lands and tenements aforesaid.

And they present that Thomas Amison still allows the hall with the north side to be in ruin and unroofed ; the sheep pen to be badly roofed, and the timber thereof at the east end to be utterly destroyed, and the stable to be nearly fallen down for two feet, and the new grange to be not fully roofed, and the bakehouse to be wholly open.

That John Voxe allows the hall, with the chamber on the north side, to be in ruin; and the little house at the east end of his chamber to be in ruin, and the stable to be badly roofed, and the mud walls thereof to be broken, and the sheep pen to be nearly fallen down.

That Richard Chesterton allows the hall with the chamber to be in ruin, the walls on the south side to be broken, and the bakehouse to be badly roofed.

That William Bromley allows the hall with the chamber to be badly roofed, and the east end of the same to be nearly fallen down, and the grange there in part to be unroofed.

That Nicholas Bramlegh allows nearly the whole of his tenement to be nearly fallen down.

That William Bysshopp allows his grange to be badly roofed, and the said grange to be without a door, and the east end thereof to be almost fallen down.

That Ralph Hethcok allows his tenement to be in ruin on the south side, and his grange in like manner as above said.

That John Ravolde allows his bakehouse to be almost fallen down.

That William Vyse allows the wall of his tenement, opposite his freehold,[17] to be broken, and the whole of the aforesaid tenement to be badly roofed and almost fallen down. Upon which they seek a day before the next court, and each of them undertakes well and faithfully to sustain and repair them, under a penalty of 3s. 4d., by the assent of the parties to be paid.

A distraint is ordered against the next court upon Thomas Hutchyn, and Alice his wife, daughter of William Boydell, to do fealty to the lord for the moiety of the lands and tenements lately belonging to the said William, in Oneley, at the annual rent of 2s. 6d., at the Feast of St. Martin, and suit of

---

[17] William Vyse, holding freehold at this date, is probably one of the ancestors of the Vyse family who were afterwards lords of the manour.

court twice a year, and by knight's service, and to satisfy the lord for the homage and relief for the lands and tenements aforesaid.

To this court came Philip Snokstone, miller, and took of the lord the water-mill there, with the pasture of the same, the dams and their appurtenances, and one half a virgate of land, with one rood of land called "Hulleyerde" (Hill Yarde, in Bowers), late in the tenure of Thomas Martyn; and one messuage and one virgate of land with appurtenances, late of Agnes Chesterton, in Bouris (Bowers), to hold to him and his assigns for the term of 20 years next following, and fully to be completed according to the custom of the manour, rendering therefore to the lord yearly 56s. 6d., at two terms of the year, viz., at the Feasts of the Annunciation of the Blessed Mary and St. Michael the Archangel, by equal portions, with all other burthens to the same mill, and tenure pertaining, which were accustomed to render 53s. 4d. And so there is an increase of 3s. 2d. of rent. And the aforesaid Philip shall find the braces, spindoles, and goynger (ley braces, spindoles, et goynger), with their support, and the repairs of the said mill and messuage and the damages of the same with their appurtenances, from year to year during the said term. And toward the costs and expenses of the said Philip, the lord and his heirs shall find large timber (mere-mium, timber) for the same, by the view and advice of the lord's ministers, to be assigned as well as for the aforesaid mill as for the said messuage. And he did fealty to the lord. And afterwards there was delivered to him one new horse millstone, of the value of 12s., with the old millstone, and so it is demised to the term. Afferers : Thomas Amison, John Ravold, sworn in the accustomed form. Total of this court 4s. 6d., and increase of rent 3s. 4d.

Staundon.—Court held there for the 23rd year of the reign of King Henry VI., after the Conquest. To this court, held as above mentioned, came John Fox, and took of the lord one messuage and one virgate of land in Walford, lately

holden by John Vyse, to hold for the term of his life according to the custom of the manour, rendering therefore to the
lord the yearly rent and the service thereupon due, and of
right accustomed, and he gives to the lord for a fine one calf
for use of the lord; and he did fealty to the lord and is
admitted as tenant.

To this court, held as above mentioned, came John Fox,
and took of the lord one messuage and one virgate of land in
Walford, late of Richard Chesturton, and formerly of William
Amyson, with its appurtenances, to hold to him for the term
of his life, according to the custom of the manour, rendering
therefore to the lord yearly 16s. 8d., which rent was accustomed to be 13s. 4d. yearly, and so there is an increase of
3s. 4d.   And he will give to the lord in the name of a heriot,
when it shall happen, 3s. 4d.   And licence is granted to him
to constitute a sub-tenant with a profit of the same upon his
death; and he did fealty to the lord.

23RD TO 25TH YEAR OF HENRY VI., A.D. 1444-1447.

Staundon.—The account of William Vise, bailiff there
from the Feast of St. Michael the Archangel, in the 23rd
year of the reign of King Henry VI., unto the same Feast of
St. Michael the Archangel, in the 25th year of the reign of
the said king, for two entire years.

The same renders account of £20 9s. 0¾d. of his arrears
of his last account as appears at the foot thereof. (Arrears
total, £20 9s. 0¾d.)   And of £4 6s. 8d. of rent of assize of
free tenants there for the aforesaid two years last past, viz.,
for each year, 43s. 1½d.; whereof from Thomas Gerves for
his freehold, with its appurtenances in Staundon, yearly
18d.; from William Vise, for his freehold there, with its
appurtenances, 2s. yearly; and from the procurators of the
church (procuratores) there for one tenement and three cottages adjoining with their appurtenances, granted to the
Church of God there, by the lord there long since (ex

antiquo) to find a light for the Blessed Virgin Mary, 2s.
yearly; and from the Prior of Ronton, for his certain lands
and tenements in Walford, yearly, 2s.; and from Thomas
Pykkyn, for his cottage and its appurtenances in Bowrys, yearly
5d. From William Vise, for one messuage and its appurtenances
there, yearly 1½d. From Thomas Martyn, for his one cottage
there, with its appurtenances yearly one halfpenny. And
from William Vise, for his freehold, with its appurtenances there, yearly 1d. And from Thomas Gokyn, for his
freehold in Aston, late John de Endon, with its appurtenances, yearly 5s. And from Hugh de Dutton, for his
freehold, with its appurtenances in Oneley, yearly 5s. And
from Thomas Shelton, for certain lands and tenements, his
freehold in Charleton (Chorlton), yearly 18d. From William
Vise, for one messuage there, with its appurtenances, yearly
4s. From the said Thomas Shelton, for one other tenement
there, yearly 28d. From . . . . Hare, for his freehold
lands and tenements, 8d. From Ralph Asshehurst, for his
freehold, with its appurtenances there, 2s. 1½d. From Ralph
Haymes, for one messuage, with its appurtenances, formerly
of William Walyssh, there, yearly 7d. From Humphrey,[18]
lord of Swynnerton, for his freehold lands and tenements
there, yearly 4d. From Stephen Bromley, for his freehold,
with its appurtenances there, yearly 11d.; and two hens
(Gallinis), value of each 2d., and in all 4d. And from John
Lowe, for his freehold lands and tenements there, yearly 6d.
And from William Boydell, for his freehold in La Mere, 4s.
From Isabella Fraunces, Lady of Polhousen, for certain free-
hold lands and tenements there, yearly 2s. And from
Margaret Yong, for her freehold in Charnes there, yearly 5s.
From Thomas Litylton and other coparceners, for their certain
freehold lands and tenements in Weston there, formerly of
Philip Chetwyn, Kt., yearly 12d. And from the lord of

[18] Humphrey, lord of Swynnerton. He was dead before A.D. 1463.
Staff. Arch. Soc., Vol. VII.

Rugge, for his freehold lands and tenements there, yearly 6d.
Total £4 : 6 : 4. And from £19 : 16 : 0 of customary rent
there arising, as appears by the rental there renewed on the
18th of the month of February, in the 20th year of the reign of
the king that now is for the two years above mentioned, viz.,
for each year £9 : 18 : 0. And from 4s. 8d. of the increased
rent of one tenement in the hand of John Fox, late of Richard
Chesterton, lying in Walford, as appears in the roll of the
court, there holden on Wednesday next after the Feast of
St. Mathew the Apostle, in the 23rd year of the reign of King
Henry VI., viz., for the 2 years above mentioned, viz., for
each year 2s. 4d. Total £20 : 0 : 8. And from £4 : 6 : 8 rent
from Philip Snokystone, from the farm of the water-mill, with
certain pasture adjacent to the said mill and its appurtenances.
To have and to hold to him from the Feast of St. Michael the
Archangel, in the 23 year of the reign of the king that now
is, for the term of 20 years then next following, fully to be
completed, viz., 48s. 4d., payable at the two usual terms of the
year, by equal portions. The rent previously paid by the year
being only 40s., and so there is an increase of 8s. 4d. of the
farm of the mill, and the said Philip is to undertake the
repairs of the said mill, as appears by the roll of the court
holden there in the 23rd year of the king's reign above said.
Total, £4 6s. 8d. And from £16 rent from William Vise from
the farm of the demesne lands for the said two years, viz.,
for each year, £8, for which the rent was not accustomed to
be more than £7 yearly, and so there is a yearly increase of
20s. for the farm of the demesne lands so demised to the said
William, for the term of seven years as appears on the back
of the account of the said William, in the 23rd year of the
reign of the king that now is. Total, £16. And from 4s. 6d.
from perquisites of the court thus holden on Wednesday next
after the Feast of St. Michael the Archangel, in the 23rd
year of the reign of King Henry VI., as appears in the roll of
the court there holden in the year above said. Total, 4s. 6d.
Sum total of the receipts with arrears, £65 7s. 1¾d. From

which accounts in rents resolute to the lord of Rugge for one messuage and certain lands adjacent thereto, with their appurtenances, which John Yremonger (Iremonger), by copy (copiâ): viz., for the two years above said, by the year 16d., in all 2s. 8d. And paid to the bailiff of the Hundred of Stone, for a fine for releasing the suit of court of the lord of this manour at the aforesaid hundred 4s. yearly, and so for the two years aforesaid contained within the time of this account, in all 8s. Total 10s. 8d. And he delivered to the lord by the hand of Richard Warneford the lord's receiver by one acquittance, dated 17th of the month of October, in the 23rd year of the reign of the king above said, upon this account restored and cancelled of the arrears contained in his last account, £10.

And he delivered to the aforesaid lord by the hand of the said Richard, the lord's receiver, as of the arrears of his last account, by one tally[19] before us shown, levied on the 26th day of the month of July, in the said year of the reign of the said king, upon this account restored and cancelled, £20. And he delivered to the aforesaid lord, by the hand of the said Richard, by one tally upon this account restored and cancelled, levied on the 19th day of the month of October, in the 23rd year of the reign of the said king, £8. And he delivered to the aforesaid lord by the hand of the said Richard, by one tally upon this account restored and cancelled, levied on the 25th day of the month of April in the 23rd year of the reign of the king that now is, contained in money, £10.

And he delivered to the aforesaid lord, by the hand of the said Richard, by one tally upon this account, restored and cancelled, levied on the 14th day of the month of November, in the 25th year of the reign of the king that now is, contained in money, 10s. Total £48. Sum total of all the expenses and deliveries, £48 10s. 8d., and so he owes £16 18s. 5¾d. Thomas Pykkyn, farmer, of Weston (Firmarius), from rents in arrear to the lord 12d. yearly for the two years within

[19] See Chapter III.

the time of the account and seven years next proceeding, in all 9s. Ralph Haymes from his rent in arrear for his tenement called Walshes Place, in Charleton (Chorlton?), yearly 7d.—viz., for the two years of this account and the seven years immediately preceding this account—in all 5s. 8d. Margaret Yong, late wife of William Yong, lady of the vill of Charnes, from the rent of her freehold in arrear for three years last past, yearly 5s.—in all 15s. Amounting to £15 7s. 2¾d. From which he paid to John Yong at the end of his account, by the command and assignment of the lord, 100s. And allowed to the same accountant for the expenses of the lord being there, with his servants and six horses in all, as appears in a certain schedule before us exhibited and cancelled, 12s. 7d.; and so he owes in clear £9 18s.

Indorsed—Staundon: Roll of Accounts there from the 26th year of the reign of King Henry VI.

Staundon—Vyvyan—Corte Rolle.

7TH YEAR OF HENRY VII., A.D. 1491-1492.

Staundon. The great court of William Essex, held on the 23rd day of September, in the seventh year of the reign of King Henry VII. John Bobilegh, Richard Schelton, John Brodoke (essoins). Jurors: Geoffrey Swynshed, William Marten, John Bromley, John Bradwall, Richard Beam, Robert Lovat, Thomas Stedeman, John Ameson, Robert Stonelaus, Roger Swynerton, John Marten, Thomas Sutton.

Who upon their oath present the Lord of Barnesse, 2d.; the Prior of Ronton, 2d.; Ralph Gravenor, 2d.; Herbert Michael of Swynford, 2d.; Herbert de Endon, 2d.; Richard Rogeres, 2d.; William Chetwyn, 2d.; and Herbert de Dutton, 2d.; for default in appearing. Also they present the death of John Vyse, who holds the manor, after whose death there fall to the lord three heriots. Also they present the death of John Wylkyn, who holds of the lord a messuage; after whose death there falls to the lord one mare worth 8s., in the name of the heriot.

Also they present Thomas Stedeman, for default in repairing one barn. Also they present one house, in the tenure of Robert Stanelands not properly repaired. It is therefore ordered to be repaired on this side the Feast of St. John the Baptist next ensuing, under a penalty of 6s. 8d. Also they present that a fine of 6s. 8d. put on the Lord Nicholas Hyde,[20] rector of the Church of Staundon, because he openly put divers parcels of land, viz., ye Bacchecroft and Evynsflat (Bachcroft and one of the Flatts, in Standon) as they were in field of ancient time. Afferers, John Brodoke and William Marten.

7TH YEAR OF EDWARD VI., A.D. 1552-1553.

The Manour of Staundon.—Court Baron of Sir Thomas Essex, Knt., holden there the 18th of March, in the seventh year of the reign of King Edward VI.

At this court the lord granted out of his hand, by his steward, to William Bednall and William, his son, one messuage, with all lands, tenements, meadows, feedings, and pasture thereunto pertaining, now in the tenure of the said William, the father, to have, to the same William and William for the term of their lives and that of the longest liver of them successively by the verge,[21] at the will of the lord, according to the custom of the manour, by the rent and services thereupon first due, and accustomed, and the heriot when it shall fall due, they pay to the lord a fine. The aforesaid William, the. father, did fealty, and is admitted tenant of the premises. The fealty and admission of the

---

[20] There is a monument in the chancel of Standon Church to Nicholas Hyde. He was dead, A.D. 1526.

[21] By the verge: The tenant, holding a rod or stick in his hand called verge, did fealty to his lord, who was called thus tenant by the verge.

G

said William, the son, are respited until after the death of his
father.   Agnes, his wife, 88s. 4d.   Memorandum : That this
copy is enrolled by the within named Richard Archdale, and
ingrossed up at the second court after the enrolment thereof.

7TH YEAR OF EDWARD VI., A.D. 1552-1553.

Manour of Staundon.—At the court holden there on the
18th of March, in the seventh year of the reign of King
Edward VI., and so enrolled.

At this court the lord granted out of his hand, by his
steward, to William Thorley and Thomas, his son, one water
mill, with all lands, meadows, and appurtenances within that
lordship which the aforesaid William now occupies (the
Milnefield, [mill field,] only excepted), to have to the same
William and Thomas for the term of their lives and that of
the longest liver of them successively by the verge, at the will
of the lord according to the custom of the manor by the rents
and services therefore due and of right accustomed.   They
pay to the lord a fine, and the aforesaid William did fealty,
and he is admitted as tenant of the premises.   The fealty
and admission of the said Thomas are respited until the
aforesaid William shall die.   By me : Richard Archedale,
steward.   Thomas and William, his sons, £23.

7TH YEAR OF EDWARD VI., A.D. 1552-1553.

The Manour of Staundon.—To the court there holden on
the 18th day of March, so enrolled.

On this day the lord granted out of his hands to Robert
Sutton and Matilda, his wife, one cottage, with all lands,
meadows, and their appurtenances within that lordship which
the aforesaid Robert now occupies, the Milnefield (mill field)
alone excepted, to have to the same Robert and Matilda for
the term of their lives, and that of the longest liver of them,
so long as the said Matilda (if she outlive the said Robert)
shall remain single and unmarried, by the verge, at the will of

the lord according to the custom of the manor by the rent and service thereupon at first due and accustomed, and they give to the lord a fine. And the aforesaid Robert did fealty, and they are admitted as tenants.—By me, Richard Archedale, steward, 26s. 8d.

1ST AND 2ND YEAR OF PHILIP AND MARY, 1554-1555.

Staundon.—Great Court of the manour aforesaid of Sir Thomas Essex, Kt., holden there on the 8th day of August, in the 1st and 2nd years of the reign of Philip and Mary, King and Queen of England, France, Naples, Jerusalem, and Ireland, Defenders of the Faith, Princes of Spain and Cicily (Sicily), Archdukes of Austria, Dukes of Milan, Burgundy, and Brabant, Earls of Hasburgh, Flanders, Tyrol, before John Iremonger, deputy of Richard Archedale, steward there.

At this court the lord, by his steward, granted out of his hand to John Sutton and Margaret his wife, two messuages, one of which is called Nycolles Yourde (probably name of possessor or tenant), with all lands and tenements, meadows, feedings, and pastures, with all and singular their appurtenances to the same messuages belonging or pertaining, lying in Bowrys (Bowers), within that lordship, now in the tenure and occupation of the aforesaid John. To hold to the same John and Margaret for the term of their lives, and the life of the longest liver of them, so long as the said Margaret (if she outlive the said John) shall remain single and unmarried, by the verge, at the will of the lord, according to the custom of the manour aforesaid, by the rent, heriots, reparations, and other services thereupon first due and of right accustomed. And they give to the lord a fine for their entry, and they did fealty, and are admitted tenants thereof. In testimony whereof to this present copy, the seal of the aforesaid John Iremonger is set on the day and in the year above said.—By me, the aforesaid, John Iremonger, £8.

1st and 2nd year of Philip and Mary, a.d. 1554-1555.

Staundon.—Great Court of the manour aforesaid of Sir Thomas Essex, Kt., holden on the 8th day of August, in the 1st and 2nd years of the reign of Philip and Mary, King and Queen of England, &c., &c., &c., before John Iremonger, deputy of Richard Archedale, steward there.

At this court the lord, by his steward, granted out of his hands to John Wetwood senior, and John Wetwood his son, one tenement, with all lands, meadows, feedings, pastures, with all and singular, their appurtenances to the same tenement belonging or pertaining, lying in Staundon aforesaid, now in the tenure and occupation of the aforesaid John Wetwood senior, Le Milnefield (Mill Field) excepted. To hold to the same John and John for the term of their lives, and the life of the longer liver of them, by the verge, at the will of the lord, according to the custom of the manour aforesaid, by the rent, heriots, reparations, and other services thereupon first due and of right accustomed. And they give to the lord a fine for their entry. And they did fealty and are admitted tenants thereof, by the aforesaid verge in the form aforesaid. In testimony whereof to this present copy the seal of the aforesaid John Iremonger is set, on the day and in the year aforesaid.—By me, the aforesaid John Iremonger.

1st and 2nd year of Philip and Mary, a.d. 1554 to 1555.

Staundon.—Great Court of the manour aforesaid of Sir Thomas Essex, Kt., holden there on the 8th day of August, in the 1st and 2nd years of the reign of Philip and Mary, King and Queen of England, &c., &c., &c., before John Iremonger, deputy of Richard Archedale, steward there.

At this court the lord, by his steward, granted out of his hands to Roger Broughton and his assigns, the reversion of one messuage,[22] and all the lands and tenements, meadows, feedings, pastures, with all and singular pertaining, lying in Walford, within that lordship, now in the tenure of Thomas Stedman. To have and to hold the reversion of the aforesaid messuage and other premises, with their appurtenances, to the aforesaid Roger, and his assigns, immediately after the decease of the aforesaid Thomas Stedeman, unto the end of the term of twenty-one years then next following, and fully to be completed, by the rent, reparations, heriots, and all other services thereupon first due and of right accustomed, upon this condition, that the aforesaid Roger and his assigns shall themselves dwell upon the premises, and that the aforesaid Roger shall not assign the premises, nor any parcel thereof, to any person or persons, neither to his wife nor his children. And he gives to the lord a fine for his entry; to have when it shall come, and he did fealty, and is admitted tenant thereof in the form aforesaid. In testimony whereof the seal of the aforesaid John Iremonger is set to this present copy, on the day and in the year above said.— By me, the aforesaid John Iremonger. Endorsed Roger Broughton and Mary his wife, and William Broughton his son, of the town of Cherteleg, " Cherteleg and of the parish Elilsowe." This is evidently indistinct. May it not be Charleton (Chorlton), in Eccleshall, in which place the Broughtons were landowners?

COURT ROLL, 13TH YEAR OF JAMES I., A.D. 1616.

Staundon, also Stawne.—Extract from the court baron of Andrew Vyse (Armiger), on the thirtieth day of March, in the thirteenth year of the reign of James, king of England.

---

[22] I am unable to say what house in Walford this is, and unluckily we have no field mentioned by name in this deed. In Standon Church there is a monument to Roger Broughton and his wife, date A.D. 1617. This is, I think, the same Roger Broughton of this deed. See also Chapter V.

Imprimis.[23] In the first place of the heires of Sir John Egerton, Kt., for not doeinge suite to this Courte, so they are in misericordia of the lord, vi*d*. Alsoe of James Skrimsher, Esqre., for the lyke, vi*d*. Alsoe of Tho. Skrimsher, Esqre., for the lyke, vi*d*. Alsoe of Thos. Broughton, Esqre., for the lyke, vi*d*. Alsoe of Peter Broughton, Gent., for the lyke, vi*d*. Alsoe of Raffe Bremer, for the lyke, vi*d*. Alsoe of Wllm. Badnall, for the lyke, vi*d*. Also of Wllm. Greene, for the lyke, vi*d*. Alsoe of John Highfelde, for the lyke, vi*d*. Alsoe of James Reade, for the lyke, vi*d*. Alsoe of Homfrey Mosse, for the lyke, vi*d*. Alsoe for the alyenacon (alienation—the act of transferring property) betweene Henry Addams and Rendle Wetwood the younger, xvi*d*. Also of Willm. Machin, for not removinge his hedge in Rowley field, in Bowers (Role Field, in Bowers?), so he is in mia. (misericordia dni) of the lord, iii*s*. iiij*d*. Also of Rendle Wetwood, for gettinge ston (without lycence of the lord) in Standon Lane, in mia. dni, ii*d*. Alsoe of Thos. Machin, for gettinge claye in Bowers, without lycense, so he is in mia. dni, ii*d*. Alsoe of Andrewe Bownd, for the lyke, ii*d*. Sum total, xxv*s*. iiij*d*.

John Chetwind, seneschal of the Court.

Court Roll. (This Court Roll is obliterated). Staundon, also Stawne, Court Baron of Andree (Vyse), of the manour of Staundon, also Stawne; in the thirtieth day of March in year . . . . . . of James, by the grace of God, King of England, Scotland, France . . . . . . in the thirteenth year of his reign in England, and in the forty-eighth in Scotland . . . . . . Armiger, Seneschal.

Essoins—John Broughton, gent., William Bad.· . . _ .

William Boughey, gent., Thomas Rowe . . . . . _ .

. · . · . · . · . · . · . · . · . · . · . · . · . _ . · .

---

[23] The Court Rolls are now written partly in Latin, partly in English. I give the original English spelling.

COURT ROLL, 18TH YEAR OF JAMES I., A.D. 1616.

Court baron of Andree Vyse (Armiger), lord of the manour of Staundon, also Stawne, held on the thirtieth day of March, in the 18th year of King James, King of England, &c., &c., in the presence of John Chetwind (Armiger). Seneschal of the court. Essoins—John Broughton, gen., William Badnall, William Boughey, gen., Thomas Rowe, jurors. Henricus Addams, John Thorley, Rawns Wetwoode, Willm Heathe, Willm Shorte, Andreas Brown, Thomas Martyn, Willm Coup, tenants holding under the lord, Andreas Martyn, jurors. The jurors after having adjourned from the different dates to the 18th day of September, on oath make return that every one oweth suite to this courte, and made defalte, is in mia. dni. vid. Also the jurors aforesaid doe lay a payne (pœna, penalty), that Randle Wetwoode shall rid and cutt up his hedge in Rowsich to the Auncyent Mere, betwixt this and oure Lady daie next upon payne of iiis. iiijd. Alsoe they lay a payne that Thos. Lightwood shall ridd, and cutt up his hedge in Bowers Lane to the Auncyent Mere, before oure Lady Day next upon payne of iiis. iiijd.

Also they lay a payne that Thomas Broughton shall ridd and take up his hedge in Over Field Lane (Over Field, in Bowers) in Bowers to the Auncyent Mere, before oure Lady daie next upon payne of iiis. iiijd. Alsoe, they present upon theire othes (oaths) that Henrie Addams hath alyened (alienated) and sold a messuage or tenement in Staundon, and certayne lands there belonging to Rendle Wetwood the younger, wherefore there ys (is) due to the Lord for the same aleyenacon xvis. Also they present Willm Martyn for . . . . . . not removed his hedge and enlarged the wa . . . . . . ilde in Bowers, so he is in mia. dni. iiis. iiijd. Also they present Rendle Wetwood for . . . (taking) of ston in Staundon lane (without lycense of the lord), so he is in mia. dni. iid. Also they present Thomas Machyn for gettinge clay in Bowers Lane (without lycense of the lord), therefore he is in mia. dni. ii*d*. Alsoe they present Andrewe Bownde for the lyke, therefore he is in mia. dni. ii*d*. Also they present that all the wast land within the said manor doth belonge to the lord of the said manour.

Court Roll, 14th year of James I.

Staundon, also Stawne. The extract of this court baron of Andrewe Vise, Esqre., of the said manor, holden there the 12th day of November, in the yeres of the raigne of our Soveraigne Lord James, by the grace of God of England, France, and Ireland, Kinge, Defender of the Faithe, &c., the fourteenth, and of Scotland the fiftythe. Before Willm. Iremonger, gent., steward of the said mannor. ii*s*., the Heires of Sir John Egerton, Knight; xviii*d*., James Shrimshere, Esqre; vi*d*., . . Hodgkins; xviii*d*., Thomas Broughton, Esqre.; xviii*d*., John Chetwind, Esqre.; vi*d*., Raffe Brimer, free suters of the said mannor, for default of apparence; vi*d*., Willm. Greene, a free farmer, and oweth suite unto the said courte and hath made defalt; iiij*d*., John Highfeild; iiij*d*., James Reade, the lord's tenants, for default of apparence; iii*s*. iiij*d*., Willm. Machin, for not removinge his hedge and enlardgeinge the waye in Rouley Field in Bowers; iiij*d*., William Shorte; iiij*d*., Edward Broughton; iiij*d*., Thomas Broughton; iiij*d*., William Marten; iiij*d*., Robert Aston; iiij*d*., William Machin, for anglinge and therewith takinge fisshe in the river within the said mannor. The whole sume of this extract is xiii*s*.—William Iremonger, Seneschal of the said manour.

Endorsed. Staundon, also Stawne. The extract of the court there in the XIV. year of King James I. Staundon, also Stawne, court baron of Andrew Vise, Esquire (Armige)r, held on the 12th day of November, in the fourteenth year of King James I., &c., &c., &c., before Willm. Iremonger, gent., Seneschal of the said manour.

Essoine, nil. Homage—Thomas Martin, Ranulphus Wetwood, Willm. Shorte, Willius Badnatt, Andreas Martin, Thomas Roe, John Thorley, Robert Tew, Willm. Heath, Willm. Cowper, Humfrey Mosse, Henry Caldwall, jurors.

The jurors present that the heir of Sir John Egerton, ii*s*., James Shrimshere (Armiger), xviii*d*., Thomas Broughton (Armiger), xvii*d*., John Chetwind (Armiger), xviii*d*., Rodulpus Brimer, vi*d*., and Ranulphus Hodgkins, vi*d*., are free tenants, and owe suit of court and have made default of appearance, and are therefore in mia. dni. They present that Willm. Greene, vi*d*., is a free farmer, and owes suit to this court, &c., &c. Also they present that John Highfield, iiii*d*., and James Reade, iiii*d*., are tenants of the lord of the said manour, and owe . . . to this court and are in default, therefore they are in mia. dni. Also they present that William Machin, iiis. iiii*d*., because he has not removed his hedge in the Rouley Field, near the highway, for enlarging the way, &c. . . . . . . They present that William Short, iiii*d*., Edward Broughton, iiii*d*., Thomas Broughton, iiii*d*., Willm. Martin, iiii*d*. . . . Aston, iiii*d*., et William Machin, iiii*d*., for angling in the enclosed fishery of the said manor, the right of angling of which belongs to Hamis. . . A payne laid upon Thomas Marten, Fraunces Heamishe, John Highfield, William Shorte, &c. . . . Martin, that every one of them, before the Feast Dey of the Nativitye of oure Lord God . . . called Christmas Day, shall sufficiently make their doles of haymt[24] betweene . . . the said Willm. Shorte and Andrew Marten, called the Beech Hills (" in Bowers ") under the payne of . . . . maketh default to forfeite iiis. iiii*d*., and soe shall mayneteine it from tyme to tyme . . . . like payne.

A payne layd uppon all th occupiers of the severall parcells of grounde at Boweis To . . (no doubt Town) . . . .

---

[24] Doles of haymt: boundaries of hedges; hay, a hedge; in Norfolk, a clipped hedge.

called the Hempe Butts (in Bowers   ) remove there
hedge or otherwise doe make their diches . . . . side of the
said hedge from the highe way there may be a . . . .
Maye Dey next under the payne of everye one of them
to forefeite . . . . 11.

A payne layd upon all persons within the said maunnor
that they shall hereafter keepe there swyne sufficiently ringed
under the payne to forfeite for every swynne vi*d.* And alsoe
sufficiently yoked between Maye Dey and Michaelmas yerely
under the payne to forfeite for every swynne vi*d.*

A payne layd upon Thomas Marten and Thomas Roe that
they and either of them doe before Candlemas Dey next
make there haymt. (hedge) sufficiently betweene the Little
Toune Meadowe . . . . and the Greate Towne Meadowe
(Bowers) . . . .   under the payne of either of them to
forfeite iii*s.* iiij*d.* ; and soe shall maynetaine it under the like
payne.

A payne layd upon all persons that ought to make any
haymt. (hedge) between the Bent and the grett Towne Meadow
(Bowers), that every ye one of them before Candlemas next
doe repare there partes of the same haymt. (hedge) under
the payne for every one of them to forfeite iij*s.* iiij*d.*, and soe
mayneteine it under the like payne.

A payne layd that all persons before oure Lady Day in Lent
next doe sufficiently repare there partes of the ringe hedge
belonginge to the Lowe Field (Lower Field in Bowers) under
the payne for every one to forfeite iij*s.* iiii*d.* and soe shall
mayneteine it under the like payne.

A payne layd that Thomas Hightwood, (Lightwood, no
doubt) and Fraunces Heamishe shall hereafter keepe there
diches (ditches) sufficiently escoured whereby the water
cominge from the Towne Walle (Bowers) maye passe away
without any lett under the payne of either of them to forfeite
iii*s.* iiij*d.*

   . . . . (Obliterated) . . . the wall of Bowers.

A payne layd upon Andrewe Bownd that he shall before Candlemas next make a sufficient reyles (rails) or other fence to his cattell from the same wall under the payne to forfeite iis. Sum total of perquisites to this court, xiiiis. Afferers of the court, Thomas Martyn Ranus We . . d (Wetwood).—William Iremonger, Seneschal of the manour. Endorsed, " Staundon," also Staune.

COURT ROLL. 17TH YEAR OF JAMES I., A.D. 1620.

Account of the free tenants, who owe suit to the court baron.

The heir of John Egerton, Knight (deceased) for lands in Onneley, in the holding of Ranulphus Malpas.

John Skrymshere (Armiger), son and heir of James Skrymshere (Armiger, deceased), for lands in High Ockley (? High Offley), lately in the holding of Edward Lecke. The same John, for lands in Onneley, now in the holding of John Paile.

Thomas Broughton (Armiger), for lands in Chorleton.

John Chetwind (Armiger), for lands in Rudge.

Peter Broughton (Armiger), for lands in Weston.

The same Peter Broughton (Armiger), for lands in Bowers, in the holding now of Frances Heymys and William Martin. Ranulphus Hodgkin, for all lands lately belonging to Thomas Skrymshere, Kt., in Meare (Maer). Ralph Breuner, for lands in Aston. Franciscus Martin for lands in Bowers.

Fee Farmers, namely:—John Broughton, gent., for lands in Walford. The same John for lands in Staundon, lately belonging to William Stonyland and William Hill. He, John Broughton, accounted for Robrt. Tomkinson, his tenant in Stawne, Robert Wetwood, Ranulphus Wetwood, for lands lately belonging to Henry Addams, in Staundon.

Willm. Shorte, Willm. Badnall, Willm. Martin, Thomas Roe, Henricus Thorley, Willm. Greene, tenants by lease. Walter Aston, Thomas Lightwood, Willm. Heatheverte,

Andreas Bownd, Willm. Cowp, John Heighfeild, Robert Reathe, Homfray Mosse.

Staundon, also Stawne, court baron of Andrew Vise (Armiger), in the 17th year of King James 1st, &c., &c., A.D. 1620, before John Iremonger (gent.). Essoins, nil. Homage to the lord of the said manor:—Willm. Badnall, Willm. Aston (gent.), Ranulphus Wetwood, sen., John Heyfield, Willm. Shorte, Willm. Cowper, and Henry Heathe ; William Martin, in the place of Thos. Martin, his father, Thomas Roo, John Thorley, John Wetwood in the place of Ranulphus Wetwood, jun., Robert Tomkinson in the place of John Broughton (gent.), jurors.

A day is given for the jurors to render their verdict, viz., to the vigil of the Epiphany, at midday, at the hall of Staundon.

To which place, and at that time, the said jurors, before the Seneschal, and say on their oath that the heir of John Egerton, Kt., ii*s.* John Skrymsher (Arm.), xviii*d.* John Chetwind (Arm.), xviii*d.* Thomas Broughton (Arm.), xviii*d.* Peter Broughton (Arm.), xviii*d.* Ranulphus Hodgkin, vi*d.* Radulphus Brewner, vi*d.* Frances Martin vi*d.*, and William Greene vi*d.* are free tenants of the lord of the manor, and owe suit of court at this day and have not accounted, but made default, therefore they are in mia. dni. as named.

The same jury say on their oath that Henry Addams and Elizabeth his wife, daughter and heir of Thomas Amyson, late of Staundon, also Staune, deceased, who were tenants of the lord of this manor in fee farm of one messuage, with all the buildings, gardens, lands, pasturage, herbage, with their heriditaments pertaining to the messuage existing in Staundon, also Stawne, by an indenture given . . . . in the year of the reign of the lord King James, now King of England, has given, granted, and bargained (bargauizavit), and sold all and each part to Ranulphus Wetwood, jun., de London, to hold these severally and together his heirs and assigns, &c., &c.

And he holds all these premises from the lord by suit of fealty to the court, and by payment as relief of 16s., the lord already having been paid through John Wetwood, brother of the said Ranulphus Wetwood, &c., &c.

Also the jury present that Walter Hill and Elena (Ellen) Hill, his wife, only daughter of William Stonyland de Staundon, have themselves sold and bargained one messuage, field, and pasturage in Staundon to John Broughton de Waulford (Walford). gent., his heirs and assigns, for which a relief is due to the lord of the manner for this of 18s., now paid by John Broughton, &c. A relief is due from William Shorte, son and heir of Thomas Shorte, for having sold a messuage while he lived in Bowers, within the manor, to William Hawkins for the sum of 18s. 1d. (partly obliterated). The lord seems to have to distrain for the amount.

A pain is laid because Thos. Lightwood iii*s*. iiij*d*., Andreas Martin iii*s*. iii*d*., Packet Woodbourne iii*s*. iiij*d*. . . . . . because they have not repaired the hedges between le Bent and the large toun meadow, of Bowers, called in Anglice the Great Toune Meadowe . . . .

The jury present that they lay a pain on Thomas Roo iii*s*. iiij*d*., and Thomas Martin iii*s*. iiij*d*. because they have not repaired the hedges sufficiently between the Little Towne Meadow and the Great Toune Meadowe at Bowers, and thus they have to maintain them, &c., &c. (a day being given) . . . . . Therefore, &c.

The same jury present that a pain (pœna, penalty) is laid on John Heighfeild iii*s*. iiij*d*., Thomas Marten and William Shorte iii*s*. iiij*d*., because they have not made their doles (divisions) of hedges between the land of the said Willm. Shorte and Andrew Marten, called the Beech Hills, at Bowers, and they must maintain them from time to time (a day is given). Therefore, &c.

At the same court the jury present that Willm. Heathe iii*s*. iiij*d*., Packett Woodbourne iij*s*. iiij*d*., and Frances Heymys iii*s*. iiij*d*., have incurred a pain because they have not removed their hedges or otherwise made their ditches on the side above by the hedge of the high way at Bowers, in a certain place called the Hempe Butts, because the way is convenient for a passage of people (a day is given), therefore they are in mia. dni.

They also lay a pain because William Shorte vid., because he has not ringed his pigs, therefore he is in mia. dni.

The jury present on the death of James Skrymshere,[25] (Arm.), who held of the lord in High Offley, a heriot is due of ii*s*. And the executors of the said James Skrymshere, Richard Barnefield, and Henry Hocknell have paid the same, John Skrymshere, his son, being under age.

The same jury present that Humfrey Vyse (gent.) ii*d*., John Greenwood ii*d*., of Staundon. Walter Aston ii*d*., clericus. (This may be Robert Aston, who was Rector of Staundon, but I think his date is earlier, as he came to the living in 1570, Dec. 20.) John Wetwood ii*d*., Roland Allen ii*d*., William Cowp ii*d*., Ranulphus Wetwood, sen., ii*d*., and Robert Tomkinson, ii*d*., have dug on the waste of the land of the lord for a foundation for a mill,[26] and have carried away the same land at their own will without licence of the lord, therefore they are in mia. domni.

The same jury present that Willm. Shorte iiij*d*., Willm. Marten iiij*d*., Edward Broughton iiij*d*., Thomas Broughton iiij*d*., gent., and Robert Aston iiij*d*., have fished in the rivulet of the lord of this manor, commonly called Stawne ryver, without licence, therefore they are in mia. dni. . . . . . .

. . . . . . layd by a payne upon all the enhabytors of this manor, that they nor any of them, from after the publishinge of this paine, doe harbour or lodge any comon

---

[25] I think this James Skrymshire married Eleanor, da of . . . . Hocknall, of Hocknall, co. Chester. See W. Salt Hist. Collec., Vol. V., p. 2 and p. 268.

[26] This may be putting up a new mill on the foundation of the old one. The mill in that day would stand probably near or on the common ground. The mill existed from the Norman time.

begger, rouge (rogue), or other wanderinge person in his or their howses or barnes above the space of one night, under the paine to forfeite for everye tyme soe harboringe, vid.

A paine layde upon all the said inhabitors, that they nor any of the̓m shall from hencefourthe carrye any wood or broome (other than their owne), nor suffer any others to bringe unto their howses (houses), there to be spent, without lycence of the owner thereof, shall forfett to the lord of this mannor, for every tyme offending, vid.

A paine laid upon all psons that have any doles of hedges or fences belonginge or adjoyninge to any parte of the Great Towne meadowe and Little Toune meadowe, in Bowers, that they and every of them yerely shall well and suffycyentlye make and repare there own severall doles of hedges and fences, before ye Feast Day of ye . . . . . of oure Blessed Ladye St. Marye ye Virgin next cominge after the date of this courte, and so to repare . . ⌐ . . suffycyentlye, from tyme to tyme, untill the Feast Day of St. Michael . . . . followinge, and so yerelye after, and from yere to yere, under the paine of . . . . .

 . . . . . all persons within the said mannor, that they shall before the Feast Day . . . . of this Courte shall suffycyentlye keepe their swyne ringed . . . . . . goe unring . . . . . dayes together (except it bee in their owne severall grounds) under . . . . . . unring . . . vid. And alsoe yoked betweene the said Feast Day of St. Mathia . . . . . . the Archangell . . . . . next followinge, yerelye, and not suffer them to goe unyoked above the . . . . . in their owne severall grounds), under the paine for every swyne un-yoked to forfe . . . . . .

A payne layd upon all persons that have any haymt. (hedge) belonginge to the little Caldwall (. . . . . . .) . . . . . . make the said hayment well suffycyentlye before the Feast Day of the Annunciation St. Marye the Virgin next now ensuinge, and soe maynteine the same from tyme . . . . . .

Sum total of perquisites of this Court, two reliefs, one heriot, after the death of James Skrymshere (Armiger) paid to the lord . . . . . .

6TH SEPT,, 1664: MANOR OF STANDON. CHARLES II., 4TH YEAR.

Mannor of Standon.—An extract of ye court baron of ye mannor of Standon aforesaid, held att Bowers.

Sir John Egerton, knt., Sir John Bowier, kt. (of Mere), Sir Bryan Broughton, knt., John Skrimshere, Esq., Robert Picken, gent., Mathew Morton, Esqre, John Chetwind, gen., Thomas Greene, free suitors of ye court aforesaid, and att this day have made default of appearance, therefore in mercy vi*d*. a peece. Thomas Wootton, John Badnall, John Thorley, Widow Horsley, Thomas Briscoe, John Arnett, Willm. Dickenson, John Peake, Widdow Wood, Wm. Launder, Thomas Hearins, John Martin Webster, John Martin (Waggoner), Richard Snelstone, Thomas Launder, jun., Willm. Yardley, Robert Walter and John Wright, Widdow Levitt, William Bibby, Arthur Glover, Andrew Coop, John Machin, Humfrey Mosse, William Holland, Robert Gregory, Robert Lynn, Thomas Cooke, John Aston, for default of appearance in mercy, vi*d*. a peice.

Ralph Eardley, John Martin, Thomas Hearins, Edward Read, Robert Boone for incroacheinge on ye commone in mercy, vi*d*. a piece. Robert Boone, J. Martin, cunstable, Ann Martin vi*d*. (vidua, widdow), Thomas Nayler, for wateringe hempe in ye running water in mercy, i*s*. iiij*d*., iiijd. a peece. John Martin of ye Bunke (Bank), Robert Lynn and John Alstin for angleinge in ye river in mercy iiij*d*. a peece.

For a releife due William Dickenson, Thomas Key for ye like. Edward Barnes for ye like Thomas Nayler for ye like, William Tompson for ye like.—William Smith, Seneschal for the said manour.

FIRST JUNE, 1669 : STANDON. COURT BARON, HUMFREY VYSE, LORD OF THE MANOR, IN THE IX. YEAR OF CHARLES II.

John Serjeant, Seneschal, William Yardley, W. Tompson, Rob. Wetwood, Richard Roberts, John Badnall, William Roe, John Hardinge, Ralph Yeardley, Andrew Coop, Jo. Martin of ye Banke, Tho. Nayler, Andrew Heath, John Edwards, jurors.

Wee present all that have made default of appearance for the free suitors xviii*d*. a peece, and for other the tenants iiij*d*. a peece.

Homage. Present John Skrimsheire his death since the last court seised, as appeareth by a former jury, of lands in Highersley, by reason thereof there happened to the lord of this mannor, a herriett agreed by the lord of ye manour to accept £3 *vs*. viii*d*., or otherwise his best beast was due, and it was satisfied by the Widdow Skrimsheire of the Hill. The jury present Richard Roberts and William Tompson for releifes due. The jury present Tho. Key, nephew to Tho. Key, formerly presented for a releife. The jury presents Wm. Dickenson for a relife decease of his father.

The jury present Geo. Peake for a releife due to the lord.

The jury present John Harding, Robert Wetwood and Ralph Yardley for releifes due to the lord, but to bee censured by Mr. Milward or other able councell, how many releifes, whether one, two, or three, are due to the lord of the Manner.

The jury presents Brigett Thorley for a releife due att her husband's decease. The jury laie a payne that if the highe waye called the Swichway Lane[37] bee not sufficiently amended by the inhabitants of Bowers before St. James' Day they shall forfeit to the lord of the mannor the some of 8*s*. iiij*d*., to be levied by the lord upon anie inhabitant aforesaid. The jury lay a payne that if the pinfold of Staundon bee not

[37] Swich Lane : This lane ran from Mr. Wright's house, as it now stands, to the footpath from Bowers to Standon. (Note from Mr. W. Wright).

H

sufficiently amended by the whole parish before the Feast of
St. James next, that everie one of them that made defalt
shall forfeit severally iij*s*. iiij*d*. a peece to the lord of the
mannor. The jury present . . . . . . Lynn for erectinge
a cottage since the last court. Thomas Launder for an
encroachment upon the common, iiij*d*.

The jury present Henery Baddiley for forstallinge the way
into the fould of Tho. Nayler, and William Thompson from
the streete.

It was agreed by the lord of the manner, and being
present, that John Hardinge shall sett a gate betwixt the
leaneinge crab tree straite over against the well yard, he
payinge yearly the frith silver (small) of the towne, and
mainetayneinge the way within himselfe. It is agreed by
the lord of the manner and the jury and inhabitants of
Standon, that Robert Lynn shall or may enclose an ould pitt,
keepinge the water downe the ould hollow way, and maine-
taineinge the way.

1st June, 1669. It is agreed that John Hardinge, Richard
Roberts, and William Yardley doe veiw a supposed engage-
ment betweene John Edwardes and Robert Wetwood, and to
sett downe the meare stakes or stones betwixt them, and to
bee done on or before midsomer next.

1st June, 1669. Standon Verdict.
Mannor of Staundon.

An extract of the Court Baron of Humphrey Vyse, Esqre,
lord of the mannor of Staundon aforesaid, held att the 1st of
June, 1669. Sir John Egerton, Kt., the heires of Sir John
Boyer (Bowyer), the heires of John Skrimsheire, Esqre, Sir
Bryan Broughton, Mathew Moreton, Esqre, John Chetwin
(gent.), the heire of Robert Pickin. They are in mercy
xviii*d*. a peece, everie one.

Robert Linn, Humphrey Mosse, William Lander, Thomas
Heamies, Widdow Martin, Edward Martin, John Forde, John

Martin (constable), Thomas Lander the elder, Richard Shawe, Thomas Lander, jun., William Yeardley, Robert Walter, John Wright, John Chetwynd (gent.)., William Holland, for makinge default of appearance in mercy everie one iiii*d.* a peece. The jury present the death of John Skrimsheire by reason thereof there happned a heriott to bee due to the lord of this mannor. Jury present a releife due from Richard Roberts and William Tompson, Thomas Key, of Ashley, nephew unto Thos. Key, William Dickenson, for a releife due att his father's decease ; George Peake, John Hardinge, Robert Wettwood, and Ralph Yeardley, every one for a releife due to the lord of the mannor. Jury presents Bridgett Thorley for a releife due att her husband's decease.

The jury have laid a paine that if the highway called the Swichlane bee not sufficiently amended by the inhabitants of Bowers before St. James next they shall forfeite to the lord of the mannor iii*s.* iiij*d.*, to be levied uppon any one of them. Another peine laid by the jury, that if the pinfold bee not sufficiently amended and repaired by the whole parish before the Feast of St. James next that everie one to forfeite severally to the lord of the mannor that maketh default. They present Thomas Lander, for makeinge of an encroachment on the commons, in iiij*d.* Present alsoe Henry Baddeley for forestalling a way into his fould of Thomas Nayler and William Tompson from the streete, in mercy iiij*d.* John Serjeant, Seneschal.

31st October, 1702. Estreat of Amerciaments (*i.e.*, a true copy and extract) and the fines forfeited and lost at the court baron of Wm. Vyse, Esqre., held for the mannor aforesaid the 31st day of October, A.D. 1702, before George Gattacre, Steward there. We present Sir John Egerton, Bart., for not appearing to doe his suit of court, 1s. ; Sir Bryan Broughton, for the like, 1s. ; Sir Charles Skrimsher, for the like, 1s. ; Sir Wm. Bowyers, for the like, 1s. ; John Chetwynd, Esqre., for the like, 1s. ; the heires of Robert Skrimsher, Esqre., 1s. ; Mathew Moreton, Esqre., his heyres, for the like, 1s. ;

Thomas Broughton, gent., deceased, his heyres, for the like, 1s. ; Thomas Green, gent., for the like, 1s. ; Thomas Asbary, for the like, 1s. ; John Fieldhous, for the like, 1s. ; Edward Knight, for the like, 6d. ; Robert Walter, for the like, 6d. ; Edward Cartwright, for the like, 4d. ; John Martin, sen., for the like, 6d. ; John Martin, jun., for the like, 6d. ; Francis . . . . Mice, for the like, 6d. ; John Peake, for the like, 6d. ; Wm. Tompson, for the like, 2d. ; Henry Bradbury, for the like, 2d. ; Peter Heafield (Highfield), for the like, 2d. ; Charles Hatchett, for the like, 2d.

A.D. 1702. QUEEN ANNE : 1ST YEAR.

We present and amerse James Badnall, and Gamaliel Crutchley, Esqre., for encroaching on the lord's waste, 2s. We amerse all other persons which incroached upon the lord's waste in 6d.   We present all persons which made defalt in repayreing Standon Pinfold betwixt and Candlemas Day next, each in 5s.   We present and amerce all persons that make defalt in repayreing the fence between Bower's Towne Meadowe and the Bent, each in 5s.   If the waye to the towne well, in Bowers, called the Lloyd Well[28] (Glide Well), is not sufficiently repayred with stiles and gates before Candlemas Day, everyone that makes default, in 3s. and 4d. to ye lord. 3s. 4d.

Mannor of Standon.—To the Bayliffe of the Mannor aforesaid. These are to authorise and require you to demand of and receive of the severall persons above mentioned the severall sumes affixed to their severall names or of such whose names are not menconed and make defalt, and return to me such as refuse to pay the same on demand, and hereof

---

[28] Glide or Gleide Well in field, in which is a footpath to Standon, called Standon Hills, and is in the holding now of Mrs. Hawkins. There are the following entries of meadows and fields connected with wells:— The Caldwell Meadow, the Holly Well Meadow, and the Well Yard in possession of Mr. James Cotton (size, 1a. 2r.), which is opposite Mr. Eardley's house.—(Note by Mr. W. Wright.)

fayle not. Given under my hand the said thirty-first day of October, Anno Dom. 1702. Georgium Gatacre, Seneschal.

An abstract of fines, &c., forfeited in . . . . at the court baron of Wm. Vyse, Esqre., 31 Oct., 1702.

Estreat of amerciament.

11 Oct., 1707. Standon Presentment.

Manor de Stawne, also Standon. The presentment of the jury att the court barron for the said mannor, the eleaventh day of Oct., 1707, as followeth. We present all persons that owe suit and service to this court and made default this day in every one. We present all free suitors that have made default in not appearing here to doe their suites of court in every one shilling a peece to ye lord of this mannor. We alsoe present all leaseholders and tennants six pence a peese. Wee likewise lay a paine upon all cottagers that have made default as aforesaid in not appearing in every tow pence a peese (two pence apiece).

We present all erectors of cottages and incroachers upon the lord's wast, viz., James Badnall and Gamaliel Crutchley, each of them tow shillings a peece, and all ye rest of ye cottagers, viz., William Meate, Peter Heafield, Richard Shaw, Widdow Landers, Ralph Linn, else Chesterton, in every six pence a peese. We present Charles Badnall for incroachinge on ye wast, two pence.

Memo^dum that John Heafield haith this day atested, that he hath formerly knowne a common and usuall foot way over ye backside of John Hardinge of Walford being ye usuall way towards Brown Bridge.[20]

By ye information of John Peake wee present and amercy John Marten, sen., for ridding a ditch and carring away ye land of ye aforesaid John Peake, in one shilling to ye lorde of

---

[20] Brown Bridge.—Bridge over stream in Walford for road from Standon to Eccleshall. This very likely is a footpath from Standon through the Nut Rough.

ye mannor. Edward Adderley, one of ye jury, present ye
aforesaid John Martin for takeinge ye water out of ye ditch
of ye aforesaid Edward Adderley, and doe amercye him in
one shilling to ye lord of ye mannor. We also present and
amercye ye aforesaid John Martin for incroaching on ye lord's
wast. And if he doe not sett ye ditch at ye head of Newle-
son (very likely New Leasow, Bowers) as of antient meere
betwixt and Christmas next five shillings to ye lord of ye
mannor.

We present and amercy all and every person which shall
lodge or harbour any vagabond or beggars, except for one
night as travaler upon journey, every one that makes default
forfits to ye lord of ye mannor five shillings for every night
as aforesaid. If ye antient way to ye Lodge Well (Glide
Well[80]) in Bowers be not suffitiently repared with stiles or
gates betwix and Xmas every one that makes default forfits
to ye lord of ye mannor three shillings and fourpence a peece :
William Levatt, Thos. Leeke, John Hardinge, John Badnall,
Edward Adderley, Thomas Lander, Robert Edwards, Walter
Willington, John Thorley, Wm. Heath, Thomas Key, Peter
Allman, Wm. Grinley, John Foord.

20TH OCTOBER, 1711, QUEEN ANNE. MANOR OF STANDON.

Verdict. Manor de Standon. The presentment of the
jury att the court barron, held for the said mannor, the
twentieth day of October, in the tenth year of the raigne of
Queen Anne, A.D. 1711.

We present all free suitors that have made default in not
appearing this day to do their suites of court in one shilling
a peice. We also present all lease-houlders and tennants in
six penie a peice.

We present Sir Charles (Skrimshere) his death since ye
last cort, as appears by formor jurys, for lands in High Offley,

---

[80] See note on Glide Well or Gleide Well, p. 116.

be reason thereof it appears that ye best beast at ye said Norberry Manor was due to ye lord of this mannor Ieased, for ye use aforesaid a fat ox of £12 7s. 6d., or otherwise ye best beast was due, and it was satisfied by ye Lady Skrimsher of Norbrey (Norbury) Mannor.

We present James Badnall and Gamaliel Crutchley for incroaching on the lord's wast sixpence a peice. We present Wm. Meat, Peter Heafield, Richard Shaw, Widd. Lander, and Ralph Linn, Else Chesterton, to ye lord of yis mannor in every sixpence a piece. We present all or any person which shall lodge or harbour any vagabonds or beggars, except as travelers on a journey for one night and away, forfets for every night one shilling to ye lord of this mannor.

Affeered by us William Levatt, Robert Edwards, William · Levatt, Tho. Brett, John Harding, John Smith, Robert Edwards, John Badnall, Robert Gregory, John Thorley, Thomas Lander, William Heath, Thomas Key, John Foord, William Grinley. John Harding, jur., Robert Edwards, jur., John Badnall, jur., John Thorley, jur., Thomas Key, jur., John Perkins, jur., Ed. Adderley, jur., John Foord, jur., John Turner, jur., John Wright, jur., Wm. Grinley, jur., Robert Gregory, jur., Walter Wittington, jur.

A.D. 1712, QUEEN ANNE, 12TH YEAR OF HER REIGN.
MANOR OF STANDON.

An extract of all the persons that made default in not appearing the last court day. Sir John Egerton, Bart.; the heires of Sir John Shrimsher, Knt.; Sir B. Broughton, Bart.; the heires of Sir Wm. Bowyer, Bart.; Walter Chetwynd, Esqre.; Thos. Greene, Gent.; Thomas Astbury, Gent.; John Skrimsher, Gent.; the heires of John Fieldhouse; Robert Walter, Edward Knight, John Kendricke, Widd. Cooper, Daniel Nevill, Charles Badnall, Francis Heamease, John Peake, Wm. Vyse, Thomas Roberts, John Marten, sen., Widd. Lander.

7TH NOVEMBER, 1712. MANOR OF STANDON.

Estreat of Presentments. Maner de Standon. An
extract of the fines and amerciaments forfeited and lost att
the court baron of Wm. Vyse, Esqre., held for the mannor
aforesaid the seventh day of November, A.D. 1712, before
Matthew Wright, steward there. We present all persons that
owe suite of cort to the mannor aforesaid, and have made
defalt in not appearing here this day, to doe their suites of
cort and doe amerce them in one shilling a peece. We
present all lease and rack tennants that have made defalt as
aforesaid in every sixpence a piece. We likewise present all
cottagers that have maid defalt in not appearing this day
in every two pence a piece. We present James Badnall,
Gamaliel Crutchley, Wid. Lander, Peter Heafield, Mary
Shaw, Wm. Meat, and Ralph Linn, Else Chesterton, erectors
of cottages and incroachers of the lord's wast, in every one
shilling a piece, to the lord of the mannor.

We present all or any person which shall lodge or harbour
any vagabonds, &c., &c., 1s.   John Harding, John Badnall,
Edward Adderley, John Thorley, John Foord, Robert Gregory,
Walter Whittington, Robert Edwards, William Grinley,
Thomas Key, John Perkin, John Turner, John Wright.

4TH NOVEMBER, 1713 A.D. MANOR OF STANDON.

Standon mannor. A particular of all ye free suitors and
also where ye lands of each one respectively doe ly as being
charged to appear at ye court Barron held for ye mannor
aforesaid the fourth of November, 1713.

Cheefe rents for each person within mentioned—2s. 6d.,
Sir John Egerton for lands in Onneley, Tenants Robert
Raven and George Willcox; 2s. 6d., John Skrimsher, gent.,
for lands in Onneley, Tenants Wm. Peake and Joseph
Scarrot ; 5s., Sir William Bowyers heires of lands in
Alston (Aston near Woore), Tenent John Kendrick ;
1s. 0d., Sir Brian Broughton for lands in Weston and

Bowers, Tenents Danl. Nevill, Tho Key, John Perkin, John Levit, in Bowers, Frauncis Heamies, John Martin; 2s. 0d., Acton Bauldwin, Esq., for lands in high Offley, tenant Elizabeth Rathbone (widd.); 6d., Walter Chetwynd, Esq., for lands in Ridge, Tenant Isabell Cooper, widd.; £1 s18 d4, Elizabeth Letby, for lands in Walford, Tenant John Harding; 8s. 3d., Thomas Green, gent., for lands in Charlton (Chorlton); 16s. 0d., Thomas Atbury for lands in Standon, Tenant Walter Whittington; 2s. 7d.——Byre, gent., for lands in Bowers, Tenant Mich. Levit; 9s., Robert Walter, gent., for lands in Bowers, Tenant Mich. Levitt; 12s. 9d., James Tompson for lands in Bowers; 18s. 0d., Wm. Wetwoods heires, for lands in Standon, Tenant James Bayley; 4s. 0d., Edward Knight, for lands in Mare (Maer). Fee farmers within ye mannor: 12s. 0d., John Harding for lands in Standon; £2 0s. 0d., John Badnall for lands in Walford; 6s. 0d., John Thorley for lands in Standon, 11s. 7d. for lands in Bowers; 2s. 4d., John Peake for lands in Bowers; 9s. 0d., Thomas Lander for lands in Bowers; 1s. 0d., George Watkin for lands in Bowers; 1s. 6d., Thomas Key for lands in Bowers. Note there is due to ye lord of this mannor upon every decease, release, change, alteration or alination of every free holder above mentioned one yeares cheefe for a releife. Onely Acton Bauldwin, Esq., paies best good for a herriot at decease, as appeares by antient Court Rolls. William Levatt, John Badnall, John Harding, John Thorley, John Smith, John Turner, William Heath, John Wright, Edward Adderley, John Foord, John Heafield, Wm. Grinley, Robert Edwards.

4TH NOVEMBER, A.D. 1718. MANNOR OF STANDON.

The presentment of the jury at ye Court Barron and Court of Survey for the mannor aforesaid, held ye 4th of November, A.D. 1718, and adjourned to the 4th day of January next ensueing, Blest Colclough, Esq. (gent.), steward. Wee present all persons that owe suites of court to ye mannor aforesaid, and have maid defalt as aforesaid in every sixpence a piece.

Likewise we present all cottagers that have maid default in not appearing this day in every 4d. a piece.

We present James Badnall, Gamaliel Crutchley, Peter Heafield, Mary Shaw, Wm. Meate, and Ralph Linn, Else Chesterton, for erecting of cottages and incroaching upon ye lord's wast, and doe amerce them in one shilling apiece to ye lord of ye mannor. We present Frauncis Heamile (or Heamise) and others who stand in contempt of this court, and doe amerce them in tenn shillings a piece.

We lay a paine, all persons which shall lodge or harbour any vagabond, &c., &c., &c., 1s. The boundrys of this mannor in generall are the antient water courses from ye lower end of ye broad meadows (I think in Walford), upwards butting upon Mees, Coates, and Swinerton lands (Cotes and Swynnerton) to ye upper end of Bower's Toun Meadow, one plat of land in ye possession of Wm. Heath, called by ye name of ye Coningeyhook (Coneygree Hook near Mill). Adjoining to Coates Meadowes, about ½ of an acre of land upon Coates March (marsh) on this side ye ould water-corse ajoining to . . . . . . Meadow, beyond the foard as it now runeth, is a plat of common abt two acres, beloings to ye mannor, from Bower's Towne Meadow. A little brook deviding ye said mannor and Charlton (Chapel Chorlton), to ye upper end of a piece called ye Dony Meadow (Deany Meadow, Weston), now in ye possession of Mr. Daniell Nevill; there we bound upon lands of Mr. Maulesfield, Mr. Foden, and Mr. Fowler.

From the lower end of John Levitt ground a little brook, deviding betwixt Podmore, Chatcuell, Aspley (above Walford), and Slindon lands down to ye aforesaid broad meadow, now in possison of Mr. Wm. Levat, of Walford, a meadow called ye Doales, and also ye broad meadow aforesaid, boath lying beyond ye water adjoining lands of John Whittington and ye Claybuts, or Laybuts, Clover Meadow. (We have in Walford the Clover Leasow and the Butty Meadow.) We present Robert Ashley and Thos. Levit for taking water

out of ye ould course for severall years, and also for diging
and making a ditch in a piece of land called by ye name of
ye Sare Meadow, now in ye possession of John Smith of
Shortwood, and amerce them and lay a paine of them in 20s.
if they do not suffitiently scowre and open the said water
course before ye fifteenth day of May next ensueinge the
date hereof to the lord of this mannor. (I cannot find any
name similar to this in the survey of A.D. 1818.) The auntient
(ancient) course of the water runneth through two plats of
land belonging to ye Layfield (Leyfield, Standon Hall)
Meadow, now in ye possession of Robert Edwards, the water
running in this side ajoining to lands of Ma⁴ Ann Persall,
neare to an acre. We present a privilidge and right of comon
to Coats and Swinerton Commons to depasture with any sort
of cattles belonging to ye said mannor.

A paine laid upon ye Hinbridge brooke, and that every
person within his respective liberty doe cut up and ridge ye
antient water corse, befoure ye Feast of St. James, upon
paine of 5s. forfit ye lord of this mannor.

William Lovatt, John Badnall, John Harding, John
Smith, John Thorley, John Turner, Edward Adderley,
Wm. Heath, John Foord, John Wright, John Heafield,
William Grinley, Robert Edwards (jurors).

William Heath and Edward Adderley affeerers, 4th
November, A.D. 1718. Manor of Standon, Stawne, also
Standon. Court Baron and survey for Thomas Gaywood and
Obediah Adams (Generosi), et William Vyse (Armiger),
held at Boures, &c., A.D. 1712 (in last year but one of Queen
Anne's reign), before Blest Colclough, generosus, Seneschal.

The same names as above, William Lovatt, &c., &c.,
appear as jurors.

11TH MARCH, 1718. STANDON. COURT BARON AND SURVEY.

Thomas Gaywood and Obediah Adams, generosi, as guardians
of Willm. Vyse (Armiger) infant, held at Bowers in the 4th
year of George the 1st, 1718, before Blest Colclough

(generosus), seneschal. Essoins: Wm. Lovatt, Robert
Edwardes. Homage: Wıllm. Heath, Joseph Harding,
William Hardinge, John Turner, Walter Whittington, John
Thorley, John Perkin, Edward Adderley, John Ford, John
Wright, John Heighfield, jurors. We present all persons
that owe suit of court to ye mannor aforesaid, and have made
default in not appearing here this day to do their suit of
court, and do amerce them in one shilling a piece. We
present all lease and rack tennants that have made default
as aforesaid in every sixpence a piece. Likewise we presant
all cottagers yt have made default in not apearing this day in
every 4 pence a piece.

We present James Badnall, Gamaliel Crutchley, Peter
Heafield, Mary Shaw, Wm. Meat, and Ralph Linn, Else
Chesterton, for erecting cottages and incroaching upon the
lord's wast, and do amerce them in one shilling a piece, to
the lord of this mannor.

We lay a paine upon Francis Heamis and others who
stand in contempt of this court, and do amerce them in 15
shillings a piece. This paine laid the last court being now
forfeit.

We present a relief due to the lord of this mannor at the
death of Robert Walter, for lands in Bowers, 9s. 0d. At the
death of Thomas Roberts, a relief due to the lord of this
mannor, 11s. 7d. We present at the death of Mr. Thomas
Astbury, due to the lord of this mannor for lands in Standon,
16s. 0d. We present at the death of John Harding, a releef
due for land in Standon, 12s. 0d. At the death of Edward
Knight, for land in Mare (Maer), to this lord of this mannor,
4s. 0d. We present John Wright for an alienation for lands
in Walford, bought of John Badnall, £2 00s. 00d. We
present Francis Stedman for alination for lands in Standon,
bought of Wm. Wetwood, 18s. 00d. We present an herriot,
due at the death of Madam Baldwin, for lands in High Offley.
All the abovesaid being forfeit since the last court to the lord
of this mannor.

We lay a pain upon all persons harbouring vagabonds, &c., 1s.

We lay a pain upon W. Mellar for stopping a road from Walford leading to Brown's Bridge on the complaint of Joseph Harding and if not opened betwixt and Michaelmas next to forfeit to the lord of this mannor one pound ten shillings.

We lay a pain if Benjamin Walford, or Benjamin of Walford, does not sett a stile in to Wm. Heath's by Michˢ⁻ next, and . . . . ten shillings. We lay a pain upon the Pinfold of Standon yt ye part thereof belonging to Bowers if not repaird betwixt an Easter Tuesday that the persons whoe ought to repaire the same shall forfeit to the lord of this mannor ten shillings. We alsoe find the reliefe due upon Robert Walter's death. Thomas Roberts, Thomas Astburys, John Wright, alienacion, all paid.

Wm. Lovatt, Rob. Edwards, John Thorley, William Heath, Joseph Harding, John Perkin, John Foord, John Heighfield, × his mark; Edward Adderley; Walter Whittington, × his mark; John Turner, Willm. Harding, John Wright.

2nd Nov., Manor of Staundon.

Court Baron, held by Obediah Adams and Willm. Gaywood, generosi. Trustees of Willm. Vyse (Armiger), infant before Blest Colclough, generosus, seneschal.

6TH YEAR OF GEORGE I., 1720.

Jurors for the lord of the manor.—William Lovatt, gen., John Wright, Walter Whittington, Wm. Heath, John Turner, John Ogeley, John Foard, Willm. Adams, Edward Adderley, John Perkin, Wm. Grindley, John Heighfield, Rob. Edwards.

We amerce all free suitors that have made default in not appearing here to doe there suite of court in every one.

We also amerce all lease houlders and tenants in one shilling a peece for not appearing (except persons after menconed). We also amerce James Badnall and Gamaliel

Crutchley, each of them twelve pence a piece for incroaching upon the comon.

We likewise amerce all cottagers that have made default in not appearing every one four pence. All the rest of the cottagers, viz., Wm. Meat, Peter Highfield, Mary Shaw, Charles Badnall, Ralph Chesterton, in six pence apeece for incroaching upon the lord's comon. We amerce all gentlemen and gentlewomen yt have not appeared this day in court 2s. 6d. apeece.

We amerce John Peake and Francis Heamis, James Martin five shillings a piece for standing in contempt.

We amerce Francis Steadman, for diging clods upon the lord's wast, two shillings and sixpence. We present the death of Tho. Key, whereby there accrues to the lord of the mannor a relief of 11s. 6d. We amerce Wm. Mellard, for stopping a road[81] which leads from Walford to Eagleshall (Eccleshall), to the sume it was presented to the last court.

We lay a pain of all persons who stop the road to Glide Well (Lodge or Lloyd Well), and if not repaird with sufficient styles betwixt and Lady Day next in 2s. apiece.

Wm. Lovatt, Robert Edwards, Walter Whittington, John Perkin, John Ogle, John Wright, Wm. Adams, Wm. Grindley, Edward Adderley, Wm. Heath, John Foord, John Highfield, John Turner. Afferors: Wllm. Heath, Robert Edwards.

7TH OCT., 1725. STAUN VERDICT. MANNOR OF STANDON.

Court baron of William Vyse, infant (Armiger). Lambrooke Adams, gen., guardian in the 11th year of George I., King of Great Brittain, France, &c., &c., before — Blest Colclough, gen., seneschal. Jurors: John Turner, Richard Roberts, Walter Whittington, John Perkin, John Wright, Edward Adderley, Wm. Heath, John Smith, Willm. Adams,

---

[81] This evidently refers to a highway, not a footpath or road, and is no doubt the same as the present road to Eccleshall from Walford.

John Ford, Wm. Grindley, John Walton, John Reade. We amerce all free suitors that have made default in not appearing here this day to do there suite of court in everyone 1s. 0d.

We amerce all lease houlders for making a default in not appearing att this court in every one 1s. 0d.

We amerce all tennants at will for not appearing here this day each 6d.

We amerce all cottagers for encroaching upon the lord's common, viz., James Badnall, Gamaliel Crutchley, William Meat, Peter Hiefield, Mary Shaw, Widdow Badnall, Ralph Chesterton, Tho. Badnall, in every one 4d. We amerce all gentlemen and gentlewomen that have not appeared this day in court, everyone 5s.

We amerce Francis Heamys, and all persons that stand in contempt of this court, every one 10s. 0d. We amerce John Peake for refusynge to serve upon the jury when impaneled, altho hee appeared att court, 5s. 0d.

We present the death of Tho. Plant, and that there happened to the lord for a relief for his land in Standon £1 16s. We present John Thoreley, for a relief for an alienation of his land in Staun upon his sonne to the lord of this mannor, 12s. 0d. We lay a pain of any one that lodges any traviling people above one night and away in 2s. 6d.

We present William Harding for encroaching upon the comon in Standon Street over against John Shelleys.

We lay a pain of any one that breaks the sile (soil) upon the common without leave of the lord of the mannor, 6d.

We amerce Mr. Jervis, Edward Adderley, William Harding, Willm. Grindeley, Will. Addams, Richard Roberts, Robert Gregory, for a sile (soil) breech, every one 1d. Afferors: Walter Whittington, John Smith, John Turner, Edward Adderley, Walter Whittington his mark, William Heath, John Perkin, William Grinley, John Wright, the mark of Willm. Addams, Richard Roberts, John Reade his mark, John Waltton his mark, John Ford, John Smith.

7TH OCTOBER, 1725. STANDON, SUIT ROLL.

11th year of George I. Free suiters: Sir John Egerton, John Skymsher, gent., the heires of Sir W. Bowers (Bowyer), Sir Brian Broughton, Thos. Boothby Skymsher, Esqre., Walter Chetwynd, Esqre., Mr. Selby, Thos. Greene, John Astbury, John Wright, Wm. Walter, James Tompson, Francis Steedman, Widdow Knight, Mr. Jervis. Fee Farmers: William Harding, Daniell Nevill, John Thorley, Richard Roberts, John Peake, Thomas Lander, Wm. Watkins, Eliz. Key (Wid.), Henry Buckley; *Walford*—Wm. Lovatt. Joseph Harding, Wm. Melior, Wm. Bedson; *Staune*—John Shelley, Widdow Wetwood, Walter Whittington, Robert Edwards, Wm. Tompson, Wm. Grindley, Wm. Heath, John Turner, John Smith, Robert Gregory, Thomas Wharton, John Read; *Bowers*—Wm. Vyse, Wm. Adams, John Walton, obiit (dead), John Levitt, exit (left), John Ogeley, Mathias Gregory, John Ford, James Martin (exit), John Martin, jun., Wm. Martin (exit), John Martin, sen., Willm. Freakley, Mathias Gregory, John Highfield, Fra. Taylor (in ye roll before), Henry Buckley, Geo. Taylor, Edward Adderley, John Highfield, of Bowers Bent; *Weston*—John Perkin, Stephen Forest. *Cottages:* Wm. Meate, Mary Shaw, Tho. Blakeman, James Badnall, Gamaliel Crutchley, Widdow Badnall, Tho. Badnall, Peter Highfield, Ralph Chesterton, mort (dead), Charles Bagnall; *Ridge*—Widdow Cooper, John Kendrick, Mr. Ralph Cleaton, Robert Rain.

21ST OCTOBER, 1731. STANDON SUITE ROLL.

Standon Court Papers. Free suiters: Sir Edward Egerton, Bart., John Skymsher, gen., the heires of Sir Wm. Bowyer, Sir Bryan Broughton, Bart., Tho. Boothby Skrymsher, Esqre., Walter, Viscount Chetwynd, the heires of Mr. Selby, deceased, Edward Green, Widdow Astbury, now Thos. Astbury, Wright (widdow), Wm. Walter, now Charles Swann, James Tompson, now John Farmer, John Steedman, Wid. Knight, Widd. Martin.

Free Farmers: Tho. Martin, Wm. Harding, Nevill, widdow, John Thorley, Richard Roberts, Mary Peake, wid., John Lander.

Walford: John Lindon (Lindop?), John Harding, Thos. Peck. *Staun:* John Shelley, Wm. Hall, Wm. Edwards, Wm. Grindley (dead), Griff Peat, Thos. Turner, Tho. Perkin, Mr. Smith (gone), Wm. Turner, Robt. Gregory, Rob. Richer, John Cartwright (gone), Wid. Read, Wm. Bedson, Joshua Stockley. *Bowers:* Peter Read, Wm. Vyse, W. Adams (void), Ed. Adderley, Mathias Gregory, Tho. Ford, Widd. Martin married Jo. Selby, Geog. Pendlinton (gone), Walter Martin (deceased, now void), Henry Hodgkin (gone), Jo. Shelley, John Gregory, now John Lander, John Highfield, in Wm. Vyse's holding, Fra. Taylor, in Wm. Vyse's possession, Geo. Taylor, Robt. Gregory, jun., John Grindley, John Highfield, of ye Bent, Thos. Shelly (gone).

Weston: Wm. Key, Tho. Wright, Tho. Forest, now John Forest. *Cottages:* Wm. Meat, Edw. Berks, Mary Shaw, Tho. Blakeman (gone), Crutchley, widd, W. Badnall, Wid. Adams, now Thos., Mark Highfield (dead), Ralph Chesterton, in Mathias Gregory's holding.

Rudge: Wid. Cooper now Wm. Cooper, John Plant, John Kendrick, now Isaac Royd, Mr. Ralph Cleyton (?), Robert Reine, Mary Barnitt, Tho. Thompson, Joseph Turner, Tho. Lander.

21st October, 1781. Standon.

Verdict, with schedule of the cheife rents of that mannor.

Standon Mannor.—A perticuler of all ye free suiters, and also where ye lands of each one respectively doe ly as being charged to appeare at ye Court Barran held for ye mannor aforesade, the 21st October, 1781. Chief rents presented by each:—The heir of Sir John Egerton, for lands in

I

Onneley, 2s. 6d.; tennants, Robert Raven and John Perk.
John Skrimsher, for lands in Onneley, 2s. 6d.; tennants, Will.
Peake and John Poynton.   Sir Will. Bowyer's heirs, for
lands in Aston, 5s.; tennent, Thos. Eardley.   Sir Bryan
Broughton, for lands in Weston Bowers, 1s. 5d.; tennants,
Tho. Nevill and Wm. Key, Gaustylee (Gorsey Bank is
above Weston).   Tho. Forrest, Bowers; Widdow Keen, and
Walter Martin.   Tho. Boothby Skrimsher, Esqre., for
lands in High Offley; tenant, Wm. Littleton, 2s.   Widdow
Chetwynd, for lands in Rudge; tennent, Willm. Cooper, 6d.
The heirs of Elizabeth Selby, for lands in Walford, 18s. 4d.;
tennant, John Harding.   The heirs of Thomas Green, gent.,
for lands in Charlton (Chorlton), 8s. 3d. John Astbury, gent.,
for lands in Standon, 16s.; tennant, Wm. Hall.   Widdow
Wrighte, for lands in Bowers, 2s. 7d.; tennants, George
Taylor and Tho. Shelley.   John Walters, gent., for land in
Bowers; tennant, Edward Adderley, 9s. ½d.

James Tomson, for lands in Bowers, 12s. 9d.

John Steedman, for land in Standon; tennant, Will.
Bedson.   Widdow Knight, for land in Mare (Maer).

Farmers within the mannor: Will Harding for land in
Standon; Tho. Nevill for land in Walford, tenant, John
Harding; John Thorley for land in Standon; Richard
Roberts for land in Bowers; Widdow Peake for land in
Bowers; John Lander for land in Bowers; James Tomson
for that as was Watkins land in Bowers, tenant Tho.
Tomson.

Note.—There is due to the lord of this mannor decease,
release, change, or alteration or allination of every free holder
above mentioned, one yeare's cheefe for a releife.   Onely,
Tho. Boothby Skrimsher, Esq., paies best good for a herriott
at decease, as appears by antient Court Rolls.   Thomas
Nevill, John Thorley, Thomas Turner, William Smith,
Griffith Peat, William Holl, Wm. Key . . . .
Gregory Edward Adderley, William Vyse his mark; John
Shelly, his mark; W. Benson his mark, Richard Robarts.

Mannor de Stawn, also Standon.—Court Baron of Willm. Vyse, Armiger, held 21st day of October, in A.D. 1731, 5th yr of George II., King of Great Brittain, &c., before Blest Colclough, generosus, seneschal.

Homagers: Thomas Nevitt, John Thorley, Thos. Turner, Willm. Smith, Griffith Peate, John Shelley, Willm. Key, Robert Gregory, Edward Adderley, Willm. Vyse, Ricus (Richard) Roberts, Willm. Bedson, Willm. Hall. We present all freeholders that have not appeared this day sixpence a piece; rack tennants fourpence a piece; cottagers, twopence a piece.

We present Walford Towne Well five shillings if not cleand[32] in six months from this court, payable to ye lord of this mannor. We present Stawne Town, Causey (Causeway),[33] everyone ten shillings, whose part is not mended well in a month's time, payable to ye lord of this mannor.

Adjourned to ye 27th December. We lay a pain upon all persons which shall lodge or harbour any vagabond, &c., &c., 1s.

We present a relief due to ye lord of this mannor upon the death of Thos. Lander for lands in Bowers, 9s. 0½d. We present a relief due to the lord of this mannor upon ye decease of John Peake, for lands in Bowers, 2s. 4d. We present a relief due to the lord of this mannor upon ye decease of Thos. Peake for said lands in Bowers, 00. 02s. 4d. We present a relief due to ye lord of this mannor upon ye death of John Wright for lands in Bowers 00. 02s. 7d.

The antient water courses from the lower end of the Broad Meadow towards butting upon Meese, Coates, and Swinnerton, lands to the upper end of Bowers Toune Meadow; one platt of land called the Coney Grey Hook, in possession of Griffith

---

[32] I cannot exactly specify this well. There are two or three wells at Walford.

[33] Causey is the proper spelling rather than Causeway (a path). Teutonic, Kautsije; old French, Caucé and Calsae; Lat., Calceatum: A way raised or paved. "The other way Satan went down the causey to Hell Gate."—*Milton, "Paradise Lost."*

Peake adjoining to Coates Meadow, abt. ¾ of an acre of land
upon Coates Marsh on this side, the old watercourse adjoining
to William Rowlege Meadow beyond the Ford, as it now
runneth, is a platt of comon abt. two acre belonging to this
mannor from Bowers Toun Meadow, a little brook deviding
the said mannor, and Charlton (Chorlton) to the upper end
of a piece of land called the Deny Meadow, up ye New
Weller Hedge, by ye water course . . . . . . now in
possession of Mr. Thos. Nevill and Richd. Grinley as devided.
There we bound upon lands of Mr. Macclesfield, Mr. Foden,
and Mr. Fowler's heirs.   From the lower end of, lately held
by John Levitt, a little brook deviding betwixt Podmore and
Chatcull, takeing in two platts of land belonging to the
Layfield Meadow, now in possession of William Edward.
The water running on this side adjoining to lands of the
Right Honble. the Lord Viscount Glenorchie, near ¼ of an
acre.   Down the brook to the timber bridge, from thence
along the road to the Rudge, then through Rob Shelley's
fold, in Chatcull, from thence following the roads to Bromley
Mill ; from thence up the Mill Lane to the gate at the topp
of ye lane, through a gapp near to ye said gate on the right
hand, betwixt two roes (rows) of young oak trees, formerly a
roade ; then into ye roade over ye end of ye meadow betwixt
the said oakes.   Then along the roade through Bromley
Fold, following the roade to Spittleford Brooke on the left
hand to the Dromble.   Then up ye Dromble on ye right
hand, bounding upon ye land of Sir Bryan, Broughton, Barrt,
up the hedge side betwixt the woods, up the woodside joining
to Broughton Britch, crossing ye lane to Hook Gate up to
the well, following the watercourse at the bottom of Ashley
Heath, still following the watercourse to the nearer corner of
Bromley Bent, up the hedge side bounding upon Bromley
Bent to Spittleford brook, from thence back again to the
timber bridge, following the brook to Browns Bridge, from
thence following ye brook to the upper end of the Doles.
Down ye outside of the Doles bounding upon Joseph

Steedman's land into ye Broad Meadow, down ye outside
bounding upon Beech Meadow, over the neither end of the
Broade Meadow bounding upon ye Lee Butts, belonging to
Joseph Hawley, to the river.

We find the lord of this mannor to be entitled to ye
fishing, on each side of ye water, from ye stepping stone down
to ye mill; and that he is entitled to ye fishery, on ye nearer
side said river, down to ye lower end of Broade Meadow, and
likewise on ye nearer side each water within his boundaries,
and entitled to all waifs and estrays within this said
mannor.

We lay a pain of 10s. on Anne Heamies if she does turne
ye water into the usuall course down ye Back Lane betwixt
and Candlemas next, payable to ye lord of this mannor.

Thomas Nevill, John Thorley, Thomas Turner, William
Smith, Griffith Peat, John Shelley (× his mark), Wm. Key,
Rob. Gregory, Edward Adderley, Wm. Vyse (× his mark),
Wm. Bedson (× his mark), Richard Robearts, William Holl.
Afferors : William Vyse, Will. Bedson.

We do hereby affere the severall presentments according ·
as they stand charged on or over each person's name, and as
they now stand we think to be just, Wm. Vyse (× his mark),
Wm. Bedson (× his mark).

21st October, 1734. Mannor of Standon.

Verdict. The Mannor of Stawn, otherwise Standon, in
the county of Stafford. The court baron of the Reverend
William Vyse, clerk, held in and for the mannor aforesaid
21st of Oct. In 8th of our Sovereign Lord George the
Second, &c., &c., in the year, A.D. 1784, before Blest Colclough,
gent., steward.

Homage.—John Lindop, Tho. Neville, Tho. Turner,
Wm. Turner, John Thorley, Wm. Edwards, John Shelley,
Wm. Key, Edward Adderley, Griffith Peat, Richard Robberts,
Wm. Hall, and Wm. Vyse.

We present all free holders that have not appeared this day 6 pence a peece; rack tennants, 4 pence a peece; cottages, 2 pence a peece.

We present a relict due to the lord of this mannor of John Asbury, deceased, 16 shillings. We present the Stocking Bridge betwixt and Meece, 2 shillings and sixpence, if not repaird in one month's time.

We present for the time to come any one that carys (carries) away sand out of the new lane belowe Edward Berks to damage the rode or hedge paying 2 shillings and sixpence for every load.

We present the Long Croft Lane belonging to Wm. Harding paying 2 shillings and 6 pence, if not repaird in a fortnight's time.   John Lindop, Thomas Nevill, Wm. Edwards, W. Turner, Wm. Key, Edward Adderley, John Thorley, Griffith Peat, Richard Robarts, Thomas Turner, Wm. Hall, Robert Gregory, John Shelley. Afferors: Tho. Nevill, John Thorley.

We do hereby affere the severall presentments according as they stand charged on or over each person's name, and as they now stand, we think to be just.—Thomas Nevill, John Thorley.

24TH OCTOBER, 1739, 12TH YEAR OF GEORGE II.

The court baron of the Reverend William Vyse, clerk, held for the mannor of Staun, otherwise Standon, before Blest Colclough, gent., steward. Homagers: John Thorley, W. Turner, Wm. Edwards, Tho. Wright, John Holland, Tho. Turner, Wm. Key, Edward Adderley, John Lander, Thomas Ford, John Shelley, Richard Roberts, Wm. Hall, all sworn.

We amerce all the freeholders that have not apaird (appeared) this day . . . . rack tennants . . . . for the cottiches (cottages).

We present a relief due to the lord of this manner from John Thorley for a purchase of Richard Roberts' estate within this mannor.

We present that George Tomson, a freeholder within this mannor, died since the last court, that upon his death there happened a relief to the lord, and that John Farmer is now in possession for seven yeares, that from the end of that term the said estate is limited to . . . . . the sister of George, for her life, and after his decease to Thomas Tompson, his brother.

We present the death of Lucy Chetwynd, widdow, she died seized of a messuage or tenement in Rudge, within this mannor, in the possession of Wm. Cooper, that there happened to the lord 1s., being a double cheif as a releife ; and that the Right Honble John Lord Viscount Chetwynd is her heir.

Wee lay upon Marmaduke Flide (Floyd) if he does not mend his fould (fold) in a month's time, stand sufishantly (sufficiently), wee lay a pain of 10s. if not done by the 80th of Novemb.

Wee lay upon Jos. Stokley, if he dos not cut his hedg and scour his drain adioning (adjoining) to Mr. Lindop, and likewise the river from Standon Mill to the bottom of Broadmeade. If Jos. Stokley, John Harding, of Walford, Griffe Peat, John Lindop, if not done by the latter end of May next, We lay a pain upon Jos. Stokley, for his part one pound fiftine shillings, £1 15s. We lay upon John Harding, for his part, one pound fiftine shillings, £1 15s. We lay upon Grif Peat, for his part, ten shillings, 10s. We lay upon Mr. Lindop, for his part, ten shilling, 10s. We lay upon John Harding, if he dos not sufishantly bruch (brush) his hidge and scour his ditch ajoyning to Grif Peat, and likewise to Jos. Stockley, and the drain acros the meddow to the river, one pound, £1.

We lay a pain upon Grif. Peat and John Harding for the brig (bridge) ajoning to the Broad meadow fiéld, if not done in a fortnight, five shillings, 5s. each. We lay a pain upon John Harding, of Walford, for the road acros the meadow and the brig on the far side, if not done between the first of Dec., ten shillings, 10s.

We lay a pain upon the inhabitants of Walford for the fut (foot) road at eich (each) end of Brons Brig (Brown's Bridge), if not suffishantly done by Christmas, 10s. We lay a pain upon Mrs. Nevill if she does not suffishantly cut her hedge and scour her ditch ajoning to the Brons Brig Lane betwin and Christmas, 15s.

We lay a pain upon William Harding, and W. Turner, and John Thorley, if they do not cut their hedges and scour their ditches in the lane ajoning to Harding's Long Croft. If they are not betwen and Kandlemas next, Wm. Harding 15s., Willm. Turner 5s., John Thorley 2s. 6d.

We lay a pain upon Wm. Bedson for the Church Roade betwen the fold gate and the yerd. If he does not suffishantly mend it betwen and the 24 of Nov., 5s., and for the hedg upon the Dodggrave[34] and the Crabtree Croft, ajoining to the Rysich Lane. If the be not done betwen and Candlemas, 5s.

We lay a pain upon Wm. Harding if he dos not open his gutters in the New Piece Meadow, between & Candlemas next, 5s. Wee lay a pain upon Wm. Vise, if he dos·not brush his hedg and scour his ditch on the bottom of the Big Rysich and the Coblers Lanes (road to Weston), if not done betwen and Candlemas, 10s. We lay a pain upon John Coton, if he does not brush his hedg and scour his ditch suffishantly, betwen and the 1st of Dec. next, 5s. We lay a pain upon Edward Adderley, if he dos not cut his hedges and scour his ditches and mend his road in Chala (Chorlton?) Brig Lane, if not done in a month's time, 10s. We lay a pain upon Thos. Marten, if he dos not cut his hedge in the Rowldfield (I think Role Field in Bowers) Lane, in a month's time, 2s. 6d. We lay a pain upon Mr. Forde, if he dos not mend his roade in the Rowldfield Lane, in a month's time, 5s. (Role Field.) We lay a pain upon John Reade, if he

---

[34] N.B.—Dodggrave is the same as Dodsgrave mentioned in the Survey of 1818; so also are Crabtree and New Piece Meadow, mentioned in that Survey. Rysich is probably Rousage. All are in the township of Standon.

dos not get his soil out of the Wayhill Lane in a fortnight's time 5s. (I think in Bowers.) We lay a pain upon Widdow Wright, if she does not mend her roade and hang her gate betwen John Stockley, in a month's time, 10s., and for the twon (town) well, 5s. We lay a pain upon every person that belongs to the hedges in . . . . . back . . . . . in Bowers, of 5s. a piece, if not done betwixt and Candlemas next.

John Thorley, Willm. Turner, Wm. Edwards, Thomas Turner, Wm. Key, William Hall, John Lander, Richard Robarts, Thos. Ford, Edward Adderley, the mark of John Shelley, John Holland, Tho. Wright, Afferors, John Thorley, Wm. Key, sworn.

We do affere the severall persons amerced, as they are severally amerced of the jurors adjudging the same, reasonable. John Thorley, Wm. Key.

5TH OCT., 1750. STANDON.

Verdict. Mannour of Standon. The Court Baron of the Revd. William Vyse, clerk, lord of the said mannor, held at house of William Vyse, carpenter, at Bowers, within the said mannor, the 5th day of Oct., 1750, before Edmund Antrobus, gentleman, steward, 28rd year of George II.

Homagers : Thos. Wright, Wm. Turner, John Thorley, William Key, Joshua Stockley, John Harding, John Wright, Thos. Martin, Edward Wright, Willm. Hall, John Cotton, William Bedson, John Lander.

We amerce all freeholders that have not appeared this day, 6d. each ; Rack tennants, 4d. each ; Cottagers, 2d. each.

We present a releiff, due from Charles Holland, Esqre., to the lord of this mannor upon his purchase of the estate at Walford, formerly Mr. Selby's, being one year's chief-rent.

We present a relief due from Mr. Astbury to the lord of the mannor on the death of Mr. Thos. Astbury of Blakelow.

We present a relief due from John Harding, of Standon, to the lord of the mannor, for an alienation from Wm. Harding.

We present a relief due from Sir Bryan Broughton Delves, infant, to the lord of the mannor, on the death of the late Sir Bryan Broughton Delves.

We lay a pain of 15s. each upon Joshua Stockley, Thos. Higginson, and Mr. Lindop, if they do not scour the river from Standon Mill to the bottom of the Broad Meadow, between and midsummer next.

We lay a pain of 10s. each upon William Turner and John Harding if they don't brush the hedges and scour the ditches in the lane leading from Standon to Walford between and Candlemas next.

We lay a pain of 10s. upon Edward Adderley if he does not mend the slack in the lane leading to Char . . . (Chorlton ?) Bridge, between and Candlemas next.

We lay a pain of 10s. upon Wm. Vise, of Bowers, if he does not mend the lanes known by the name of C . . . lanes, between and midsummer next.

We lay a pain upon all persons that dig for turf or peats between Cliffs and Meese liberty of 15s. each.

We lay a pain of 5s. on John Wright if he does not throwe out the Town Well between and May Day next, and William Key and John Lander have agreed to guard it. Thos. Wright, William Turner, John Thorley, Wm. Key, Joshua Stockley, John Harding, John Lander, John Wright, Edward Wright, the mark of Tho. Martin, John Cotton, and Wm. Betson.—John Thorley, William Key, affearers sworn. We affere the several presentments as they are now marked and figured, each person's name. John Thorley, Wm. Key.

Nov. 28, 1753. Memorandum. That the Rev. William Vyse, clerk, Lord of the Mannor of Standon, doth acknowledge That the messuage, lands and premises of Charles Vellard, Esqre., lying at Walford within the said mannor,

and which are charged with an yearly rent charge[85] of
33s. 4d. are not holden or tenable of or to the said mannor
by any rent or payment, suit, custom, or service whatsoever,
but are totally free and clear from any such tenure, payment,
suit, custom or service.—E. Antrobus, Steward.

IN A.D. 1818: 48TH YEAR OF GEORGE IV.

A survey of the Parish of Standon gives us the names of
the fields in the parish.   I publish these names as giving us
the nearest approach to the names of fields in more ancient
times.   Many of the fields and boundaries have been altered,
but the alteration is not so general as to make a very great
difference in the names.   In the Rudge we get these names.
Ottersley, Rough in Ottersley, Meadow, Little Hay Field,
Rough in Little Hay Field, Rough Meadow, Bend Dale,
Sandy Field, Rough Coombs, Little Coombs, Oat Leasow,
Coppice Leasow, Coppice, Bates' Leasow, Marlpit Leasow,
Upper Salter's Ley, Calves' Croft, Lower Salter's Ley, Nether
Field, New Meadow, Barn Meadow, Lower Stocker Field,
Upper Stocker Field, Common piece, Old Yard Croft, Way
Leasow, Gorsty Bank and Broomy Croft, Rough Meadow and
Little Hay Meadow, Little Hay Rough, Little Hay, Well
Leasow, Lower Rudge Brook Meadow, Meadow piece, Keys'
Leasow, Long Leasow, Far Cote Leasow, Marl Ruck Bank,
Gig Bridge, Near Cote Leasow, House Pieces or Way Leasow,
Barn Close, Well Piece, Hill Piece, Near Moss, Hill by the
Barn, Heath Piece, Far Moss, Moss Bank, Rough in Moss
Bank, Upper Rudge, Brook Meadow, Coppice Leasow next
Road, Far Coppice Leasow, Part of Cow Pasture and Part of
Little Meadow, Upper Dale Meadow, Lower Dale Meadow,
Part of Whitening Yard.

---

[85] The chief rents now paid to the lord of the manor are paid by
the Earl of Wilton from Onnely, by Mr. H. Davenport from Maer,
from Aston, near Woore, and by Mr. Thompson and Rev. E. Salt from
Standon, the latter paying on land bought from the Highfield family.

At Shortwood we have after mention of House, Home Croft, Great Shortwood in two parts, with Road adjoining, Near Shortwood, Upper Wicket Leasow, Lower Wicket Leasow, Brickkiln Leasow with Intakes.   Nether Shortwood, Meadow Rickyard, &c., Clover Close and Road adjoining, Upper Four Acres, Far Four Acres, Lower Four Acres and road, Banky Wood, the Keely in two parts, Rough in two parts, Keely Meadow, Banky Linacre, Middle Linacre, Middle Linacre Barn, Stackyard, and Garden, Big Linacre, Left-hand Linacre, Little Linacre, Near Nunnery Wood and road, Far Nunnery Wood, Middle Shortwood in two parts, Far Short-wood, Over Linacre Meadow, Nether Linacre Meadow in two parts, Allotment in Bent Bowers.   In Weston, after mention of Houses—Hall Leasow, Near Stockings, Far Stockings, Big Shutts, Little Shutts, Thistley Field, Marlpit Field, Way Leasow, Pit Stockings, Holly Meadow and Ashes Croft in one, Rough Leasow, Upper Clay Alders, Upper Lunts, Middle Lunts, Lower Lunts, Lower Clay Alders, Hall Lane and Patch, Big Chapel Field, Little Chapel Field, Maer Field, Deany Meadow, The Rails, Hall Meadow, Clay Alders Wood, Near Bank, Peartree Bank, Pease Croft, Way Leasow, Near Cote Leasow, Far Cote Leasow, Wood piece, Cawdy Crofts, Cote Meadow, Great Way Leasow, Near Rousage, Middle Rousage, Little and Far Rousage, Lower Rousage, Piece, Bridge Field Meadow, Near Birch Field, Middle Birch Field, Far Birch Field, Butty Meadow, Little Broad Croft, Birch Field, Croft and Big Broad Croft, Upper Croft, Lower Cote Ground, Upper Cote Ground Meadow, Cote Ground Meadow, a moiety of Gorsty Leys Lands in six pieces ; also a moiety of Gorsty Leys Lands, the whole in six pieces ; Little Birch, Birch Meadow.

Standon, beginning with Standon Hall, and with different houses : Near Widow's Croft, Home Meadow, Widow's Croft, Standon Flatts, Leese Leasow, Far Ley Field, Ley Field Meadow, Great Ley Field, Toley Moor, Little Toley, Toley Meadow, Great Toley, Great Burness, Little Burness, Little

Paddock, Paddock, Green Yard, Near Blake Yard, Far Blake
Yard, Upper Rousage, Lower Rousage, Long Rousage,
Near Rousage, Oldery Leasow, Upper Intake, Lower Intake,
Home Croft, Marlpit Croft, Pinfold Croft, Bowers Field,
Broom Croft, Three Tappilocks, Lower Standon, Hall
Orchard, Cote Croft, Long Field, Long Meadow, Upper New
Piece, Long New Piece, New Piece Meadow, Standon Water
Corn Mill, Mill Pond, River, Mill Yard, Caldwell Meadow,
Pool Well, Dales, Mill Meadow, Coneygree Hook, Whitening
Meadow.

Part of Allotment on Standon Common, Houses and
Gardens, &c., &c.—Crabtree Croft, Ten Lands, Tappilock and
Smithy Croft, New Piece, Aldery Meadow, Swaithes Croft.

Plantations in Standon.—Hall Lane, Coppice in Ashton's
Croft, part of Big Burness and part of Little Burness at
Standon Hall, Coppice in Rough Readings at Walford,
Coppice in Lower Far Cutups at Walford, Coppice in Banky
Coneygree at Walford ; Willow Beds at Standon Mill, with
land on the opposite side of the river there ; Alder beds and
land on each side the river at the Bent.

Home Meadow, Batch Croft, Cow Croft, Hall Leasow,
Wheat Croft, Wheat Meadow, Dod's Grave, east part of New
Leasow, west part of New Leasow, Middle Intake, Far
Intake, Triangular Field, Near Intake, Bowers Field ; Rose
Yard, with additions from road ; Lane Croft, Well Yard, New
Piece, Timbridge Bank and Meadow, Slank Leasow, Black
Butts, Black Butts Meadow, New Piece, Lower New Piece,
Lower Piece Meadow, Little Meadow, Lower Ox Croft, Little
Ox Croft, Near Ox Croft, Well Meadow, Far Meadow, part of
Long Croft, Upper and Lower Flatt, Lower Flatt, Upper Flatt,
Little Flatt, Peartree Leasow, Fish Pond, Pool Croft, Church
and Church Yard, Batch Yard, Batch Croft, Brown's Field
and Plantation ; Long Croft, with road ; Gorsey Field,
Tansley Batch Croft ; Hall Leasow, with plantation adjoin-
ing ; Croft, with enclosure from road ; New Piece ; Batch
Crofts, in two parts ; Little Slank Meadow, Sprink. Walford,

with Houses; Rough Readings, Far Broom Field, New Broom
Field, Upper Readings, Lower Readings, and Plantation,
Slang, Well Yard, Horse Pasture, Horse Pasture Meadow,
Banner Yard, Near Cutups, Far Cutups, with Gravel Pit and
road.

Lower Far Cutups, Cuckoo's Nest (with two Cottages),
Long Coneygree, Lower Coneygree, and Plantation, Banky
Coneygree, Stocking Meadow, Near Broad Meadow, Far
Broad Meadow, House Close, Well Meadow, Rushy Croft,
Bridge Field, Lodge House Garden, Rough and Plantation,
Custard Croft, Lower Rushy Field, Brook Meadow, part of
an allotment on the Bent, Walford Yards, Sweithole, Brook
Croft, Walford Bank, with roads, Little Walford Bank, with
roads, Banky Leasow, Stonepit Leasow, Little Old Field,
Coppice, piece below the Coppice, Upper Moor, Middle Moor,
Lower Moor, Moor Flatt, Big Old Field, Marlpit Leasow,
Brown Bridge Field, Springy Leasow, Broad Meadow Field,
west part of Butty Meadow, part of allotment on the Bent
(Bowers), Folley Barn and Over Field, Clover Leasow, Far
Field, Butty Meadow, part of allotment on Standon Common.
Bowers, with houses, Lane Croft, near Bent Field, Far Bent
Field, Dole in Town Meadow, near Standon Hill, Middle
Standon Hill, Little Standon Hill, Upper Over Field, Lower
Over Field, Beech Hill, and Beech Hill Meadow, Plumbton
Park, Seven Ridges, near Black Meadow, Far Black Meadow,
Allen's Birch, allotment on the Bent (Bowers), Rough Yard,
Stean's Croft, Lane Croft, Nether Birch, Near Birch, Upper
Lower Field and Meadow, Lower Field, with Meadow Patch,
Lower Field and Meadow, Caldwell Meadow, Hop Yard,
Little Lower Field, Upper Lower Field, Lower Field and
Meadow, Hollywell, or Brown Bridge Meadow, Allen's Birch
Meadow, Cart Gapps, Harrow Head, Little Birch, Great Birch,
The Patch, Allen's Birch, Hempbutt, Caldwell Meadow, Near
Lower Field, Far Lower Field, Upper Field, Upper Field in
two parts, Backlane Croft, Harrow Head, Broom Croft,
Charlton (Chorleton) Bridge Meadow, Caldwell Meadow, part

of Town Meadow, Hempbutt, near Lower Field, in two parts,
part of Cross Flatt, Role Field, Lower Field, part of Cross
Flatt, allotment on the Bent, The Patch, Well Yard (in
Bowers), Wall Hill, Hempbutt, Blasehill, Near Leasow, Red
Hill, Big Meadow, Town Meadow, Calves' Croft, Lane Croft,
Upper Intake, Lower Intake, Near Birches, Far Birches and
road, Rough Meadow, allotment on the Bent, Backlane Croft,
Caldwell Meadow, Hempbutt, Upper Intake, Lower Intake,
Intake Meadow, Near Leasow, Upper Field, Beech Hill, Red
Hill, Broad Croft, Charlton (Chorleton) Bridge Meadow,
allotment on the Bent (Bowers), New Field, New Field
Meadow, Lane Croft, in two parts, Lower Intake, Upper
Intake, Wet Reans, Standon Hill, Lane Croft, Bent Field,
part of Town Meadow, allotment on the Bent, Clay Lake,
Lower Birch, Middle Birch, Upper Birch, Backlane Croft,
Little Town Meadow, Dole in Big Town Meadow, allot-
ment on the Bent, adjoining river, Upper Meadow,
Near Croft, Middle Croft, Far Croft, Big Clay Croft,
Little Clay Croft, Near Clay Croft, allotment on the
Bent, Near Leasow in three parts with road, parcel in
Town Meadow, Rough Yard, Root Yard, Beech Hill, Beech
Hill Meadow, Backlane Croft, Upper Field, Upper Birch,
Lane Croft, Lower Birch, Beech Hill, Upper Field, Charlton
(Chorleton) Bridge Meadow, Two Butts and road, Hempbutt,
Yard, Red Hill, Cart Gapps, part of allotment on the Bent,
Dole in Town Meadow, Dole in Beech Hill Meadow, part of
allotment on the Bent, Landers Birch, Upper and Lower
Beech Hills in one, Clay Lake, Black Butts, part of allotment
on the Bent.

Many of the names of these fields are sufficiently clear by
their own meaning, others are obscure, but one name—the
Leasow—deserves some attention. Leasow is a Saxon word,
meaning pasture, and is a very old word in our language.[86]

[86] " He schal go yn, and shall go out ; and he shall finde lesewis."—
Wicliffe, St. John x, 9. " They arrived in a close of Mr. Whitgreave's
called the Pit Leasowe."—" Boscobel," 1651 ; reprint, 1822, p. 65.

The same word is found in the Norman-French Leswes (a pasture ground).

But as the name Leasow appears in different parts of Standon, where also a habitation or cultivation from the Norman Conquest existed, we trace, no doubt, the Leasow, meadow or field, to the earliest times when Standon land received its first cultivation.

Much of the information given in this chapter may seem disconnected through a consecutive list of Court Rolls not being forthcoming, but what is given gives an insight into a period stretching from A.D. 1838 down to our more modern times.

CHAPTER V.

THE CHURCH OF STANDON.

N account of the antiquity of Standon as a parish, we are enabled to trace some way back the existence of a Church, and also a succession of rectors who have served in different ages as ministers in that church.

The legend common in many villages exists here, that angels from a hill above in a night brought down the stones, with which in an ancient time the church was built. The approximate date, however, which we can arrive at of the existence of a church is in the Domesday Book, in the words, "In Stantone ibi pbr, &c.," (p. 19), "there is a priest;" or, more significantly taken, it means in Standon there was a church at the time of the Norman Conquest. This church would have been of stone, not wood, as in that latter case it would hardly have been included in the Survey (Domesday).

But it being evident that a church at Standon existed in the Norman Conquest age, or rather the Domesday age, A.D. 1086, then there is the greater likelihood the church

was not only Norman but Saxon; and that the early
Christian worship had been conducted and carried on in
Standon some generations before the Norman time.

We can date, then, the existence of a church by
document from A.D. 1086; may we not trace back to an
earlier date than that for the foundation of our Standon
Church? . To do so we cannot fall back upon any formal
deed; we have none existing before A.D. 1086. But we have
the very stones, the forms in engraving, which seem to carry
us to earlier times than the Conquest. As an authority for
this I quote from a writer of much authority. He says:—
[1]"On that part of our architectural history which follows
the departure of the Romans from Britain, and which precedes
the Norman Conquest, there is of course obscurity; but
while in the days of Horace Walpole, &c., there appears to
have been much too easy an admission of Saxon dates on
mere appearance of the semi-circular arch, I think there has
been of late perhaps too great a leaning the other way.
And because we cannot directly prove that certain edifices
are Saxon by documentary evidence, we have been induced,
too easily perhaps, to consider that no Saxon buildings did
exist, and have not given ourselves the trouble sufficiently to
examine our earlier Norman works to see if there were not
some of them entitled to be considered as erected before the
Conquest.

"I confess I have myself been heretofore of this class of
doubters as to Saxon dates, but having in various parts found
buildings which are not Norman and which, from their
peculiar construction, cannot well be considered either as
modern, or as of any intermediate style, I think they must be
anterior and, therefore, entitled to be called Saxon.

"I was much impressed by a conversation I had, before
a visit to France, with an aged and worthy dean, who was

---

[1] Letter of T. Rickman, Esq., &c., "Archæologia," Vol. XXV., p. 166.

speaking on the subject of Saxon edifices with a full belief
that they were numerous. He asked me if I had investigated
those churches which existed in places where Domesday
Book states that a church existed in King Edward's days
(*i.e.*, King Edward the Confessor), and I was obliged to confess
I had not paid the systematic attention to this point I ought
to have done."

We are thus thrown on architectural work to bring out
the probability of our Standon Church being Saxon. Near
Standon stood the ancient monastery of Stone, that is to say
about six miles off. Eccleshall, which by name points to an
early church (I take that derivation rather than that of
Eagleshall), at a distance of but four miles, gives evidence to
Christian teaching of an ancient date; and though Standon
seems never to have come in any way parochially under these
two extensive church districts, yet, having inhabitants before
the Norman Conquest—namely, Godwin and Siward—we
look to the most ancient part of Standon Church to tell us
something.

Outside, on the west side of the square tower, we find the
most ancient stone work, work evidently of a date cotemporary
with early Norman work, most likely Saxon. The stones,
with a wide breadth of mortar, are of such a size as to be
taken up, with some lifting, not more than one stone being
able to be lifted at a time on account of its size. Again, the
same kind of work is seen outside in the wall that divides
the body of the church from the chancel, but very little of
this work at that eastern point of the church has been
preserved.

The change from this deep setting to the finer lining did
not come till later. "Malmesbury"[2] says, speaking of Roger
of Salisbury, Bishop:—" He was a prelate of great mind, and
spared no expense towards completing his designs, especially

[2] Malmesbury, Sharpe's Edit., p. 504.

in buildings which may be seen in other places, but more particularly at Salisbury and at Malmesbury. For there he erected extensive edifices at vast cost and with surpassing beauty, the course of stone being so correctly laid that the joint deceives the eye, and leads it to imagine that the whole wall is composed of a single block.—A.D. 1119, Henry the 1st." We see here the vast difference between the early Norman work and the later style. Outside in the churchyard the base of a cross, without its shaft, in the simplest work, rough and with no defined chiselling, standing on a mound, seems to recall the primitive Christian worship in Saxon days. This base of a cross may be of a later date than I suppose, but, if later or earlier, it recalls the custom mentioned by Dr. Stubbs, the Bishop of Chester, &c., &c., who says:—" There were as yet very few churches; crosses were set up in villages and on the estates of Christian nobles, at the foot of which the missionaries preached, said mass, and baptised."[3] This reference here relates to the eighth century.

A cross, or the remains of a cross, are found in many churchyards in Staffordshire. In Eccleshall, Blithfield, Ellenhall (which has lately been beautifully restored) Churchyards; also a cross is mentioned in certain deeds as existing at Maer.

The base of the cross in Standon Churchyard may have been once used for either a wood or stone shaft, having a deep square for the setting. The trees in a place or its surrounding point to antiquity. In the churchyard at Standon there are some full-butted yews, and near the fish-pond, opposite the church, there is one of a large butt. King Edward the 1st[4] caused yews to be planted in churchyards, A.D. 1272 to 1307. Within the church the chief features that point to antiquity are an old arch and a stone (child's) coffin,

[3] "Constitu. Hist. of England," Stubbs, Vol. I., p. 225.

[4] See Miss Yonge, "Herb of the Field."

and some stone work broken in the form and shape of the shaft of a cross, the stone work of this latter being very curiously tooled. Conjecture, or the skill of an antiquarian might point to the exact date.[5] The stone coffin, although not marking an age, brings us to various periods. The stone coffin has been found in Roman burial places in England.

In the account given in "Archæologia"[6] a stone coffin was found in the parish of St. Michael, adjoining St. Alban's. This coffin was lying at a considerable depth, and was in the form of a great oblong trough, perfectly plain and unornamented, without any circular enclosure for the head, which seems, when so made, to give a later date to stone coffins. It was supposed that this place was a burial ground of the Romans. Within this year[7] a stone coffin has been found with the remains, it is thought, of Thomas à Becket, at Canterbury. The stone coffin found here at Standon has a clearly defined line for the body and head. It was built into the wall of the church and found at the time of the restoration of the church in A.D. 1846. This coffin may, however, be of an earlier date than the Norman time.

The most important feature in the church is the Saxon arch (I say Saxon advisedly, rather than Norman).

It stands in the north-west portion of the church, and is a very fine piece of work, with no ornamentation. It has what may be termed a cushion capital, and may be "Romanesque" in its piers. The transome, in stone, however, looks as if made more to support the arch than to be of use for the door. I conjecture that this arch is of earlier work or earlier date than the Norman conquest. In the

---

[5] Camden, Vol. II., 829, 830, mentions a pillar or carved monument on Mostyn Mountain; and Dr. Plot, in his History of Staffordshire, gives one or two such monuments, and considers them to be erected by the Danes. A small portion of the work at Standon is not unsimilar to the engraving in Camden.

[6] "Archæologia," Vol. XVII., p. 336, year 1813.

[7] February, 1888.

description of Conisborough Castle, by Edward King,[8] &c.,
&c., he says, speaking of the grand entrance, " At the top of
this ascent is a great doorway, very low, however, in
comparison of those of Norman towers, and of singular
construction, for although there is a stone arch turned over
it, in imitation probably of those which had been seen in
Roman buildings, and yet this arch does not seem to be
understood, for underneath is a beam (transome) as if to
support the arch. This arch gives us, however, a date, as it
is in all probability a copy of Roman architecture, but when
enough knowledge had not been sufficiently used to entirely
comprehend them."

This bears very closely on the arch in Standon Church
by its form of architecture. I reckon its date some considerable time before the Norman Conquest. Architecturally
speaking, then, I think there is a proof of the existence of a
church before the Conquest, which is in accordance with what
has been said that a church being mentioned in Doomsday,
it is even yet of an earlier date than that time.

The earliest monument we have in the church is a small
stone in the floor in the body of the church, just before the
chancel gates, which has a brass cross, very old, and is
shaped, as a herald would say, like a cross fleury, " fleur de
lis," or " cross patonce." At the bottom, in old abbreviated
letters, is "Radulphus." This brass may have been on some
former monument or coffin, and thus placed on stone. This
brass is alluded to in the cover of the parish register book,
dating from 1558 A.D. I believe this brass is in memory of
either Radulphus de Staundon, living, as mentioned, A.D.
1100 to 1185, or else Radulphus or Robertus de Staundon,
grandson of Brien de Staundon, who is dead, before A.D. 1181,
or else Ralph-Harewell, Rector of Standon, in A.D. 1407 ; but
of these three I think it is the first Radulphus de Staundon.

---

[8] " Archæologia," Vol. VI. This article is quoted by Hallam in
his " Middle Ages," Vol. III. : Architecture.

The font in the church is old, and of Norman work. There is the remains of an old door, evidently leading to the rood loft, of which there is nothing left; but the door is placed on the south side by the entrance to the chancel, some height from the ground. All these structural records point to the days which many of us would like to see, if only but for one short glimpse.

The church tower is of Norman structure, but has been altered in later times, and thus shows out distinctly the early work at its base. The towers of churches evidently were the most fortified places in the parishes of old, and were often in the time of civil war and marauding parties the resort of those who were in danger of being attacked; and no doubt the well-built walls were used as a means of defence as well as a shelter. Standon Church, with its substantial stone work, would be no exception to this rule. But the Church of Standon would be a place of safety in another sense. It is numbered amongst those many religious buildings, whether churches or abbeys, which had within their walls sanctuaries. A work on sanctuaries has just been published.[9] It is necessary to explain shortly the meaning of sanctuary. The sanctuary was the place of safety, like of old the cities of refuge in Israelitish history. If anyone, for an offence, fled to the sanctuary of abbey, or church, or sacred place, he might either give himself up, or else leave the kingdom, a certain time being allowed him to reach the frontier. He was not allowed to stay more than one night in any place, and so quickly pass. He gave up his chattels[10] and lands; often they were thus a benefit to the religious house or church. In Mr. Mazzinghi's interesting book, lately published, we have mention of Standon church being used as a sanctuary. In Assize Roll, 56 Henry III., A.D. 1272,

[9] "Sanctuaries." T. J. de Mazzinghi, M.A., &c., &c.

[10] See "His. Coll. Staff.," Arc. Soc., Vol. iii., p 23.

" Richard, the miller, put himself in the church of Staundon, and confessed himself a robber, and abjured the realm before the coroner. He had no chattels. The village of Staundon did not arrest him, and is therefore in mercy."

In Sir W. Scott's novel, "Fair Maid of Perth," there is the following account of sanctuaries: " Nay, they were not satisfied when our porter and watch told them that those they pursued had taken refuge in the Galilee of the church." The note says: " The Galilee of a Catholic Cathedral is a small side chapel, to which excommunicated persons have access, though they must not enter the body of the church."

Mr. Surtees suggests that the name of the place thus appropriated to the consolation of miserable penitents, was derived from the text, " Ite nunciate fratribus meis ut eant in Galileam : ibi me videbunt."—Matt. xxviii. " History of Durham," Vol. I., p. 56.

Leaving the other important monuments in our church for further mention in this chapter, I now proceed to give what is known in early deed and record of Standon church. According to ancient deeds, the first mention of a parson at Staundon is at the end of King Henry III.'s reign (although the existence of a church is known before), in A.D. 1272, when Parson Thomas, of the Church of Staundon, is mentioned in connection with some land in Mere, and also one fourth of the advowson of the Church of Mere. This Thomas, parson of Staundon, seems to be Thomas de Mere.

A deed exists, without date, but which I think belongs to the time of Edward I., A.D. 1272, &c., &c., in which it is stated, " That Robert de Estaundon (Standon) grants and confirms to God and the Church of St. Mary,[11] Estaundon (Standon), four shillings worth of annual rent issuing out of one messuage, one curtilage (garden), and one croft in Standon, which he purchased of Thomas de la Fountayne, and

---

[11] The change of a name of a church is not unusual at this time: any desecration would cause reconsecration and rededication

burthened with finding wax lights to burn before the altar of the said church. Witnessed by Vivien, son of Gerveyse ; Adam de Boures (Bowers); Richard, clerk of the said Robert; Robert de la Lowe, and others." I fix this deed by the names of Robert de Staundon and Robert de la Lowe.

Another deed exists, without date, which I put down to the end of King Henry III.'s reign, probably A.D. 1269, and from that date into King Edward I.'s reign, A.D. 1272, &c., &c., by which charter, Robert, son of Robert de Sweneshesd (Swineshead), grants and confirms to the lord, Robert de Staundon, seven acres of land, with appurtenances, in Bures (Bowers), which Adam, brother of the said Robert de Sweneshesd, holds of him, rendering annually therefore three half pence for all services and secular demands. Witnessed by the Lord Robert de Bromley ; Master Thomas, Rector of the Church of Standon ; Reginald de Charnes, Thomas de Witindon, Adam de Boures, Warine de Rossale, and others.

In 18th year of Edward II., A.D. 1325, a charter exists, by which William de Weston, chaplain,[12] confirms and grants to Adam, son of Thomas, the Shepherd of Chelton. (I think this is Cherleton, Chorlton), &c., &c.

In 14th year of Edward II., A.D. 1321, John de Brikehull, rector, a deed exists by which Roger, son and heir of Nicholas Boures, releases and quits claim, &c., to land in Bowers, two acres and two selions,[13] &c., &c. The deed goes on to say : "One selion lies between the land of the lord of Standon and the land of the Rector of the Church of Standon."

The following is a list of the Rectors of Standon, commencing from the early date of A.D. 1301 :—

---

[12] I do not think this is William de Pulteneye, Rector of Standon, but a chaplain to the house of Weston, which evidently was of some consequence. In the former chapter on the Court Rolls the mention of chaplain occurs.

[13] Selion : French word, meaning a furrow—that is, as far as the plough would go without turning.

Date of Institu.	Name.	Cause of Vacancy.	Name of Patron.
1801—April 21.	Brikehull, John de.		Robert de Standon Miles.
1822—Dec. 21.	Pulteneye, W. de.	Resignation of J. de Brikehull.	Rud. de Stafford Miles, afterwards Earl of Stafford.
1884—Jan.	Shulton, Oliver de.	Resignation of W. de Pulteneye.	
1888—Mar. 18.	Melbourne, Henry de.	Exchange of Oliver de Shulton.	Herman[14] de Standon.
1840—Dec. 18.	Brompton, Ric. de.	Exchange of H. de Melbourne.	
1869—Sept. 15.	Andrewe, Robert.	Death of R. de Brompton.	John Nowen.
1402—Sept. 15.	Hallum, John.	Death of Robert Andrewe.	John Shotesbroke and Geoffrey Boydelf.
1407—May 14.	Harewell, Rulph.		John Shotesbroke and Geoffrey Boydelf.
1408—Aug. 10.	Eiton, Robert.	Exchange.	Same patrons.
1411—Aug. 6.	Boydell, Henry.	Death of Robert de Eiton.	Same patrons.
	Wollaston, John.		
1485—July 18.	Lutte, John.	Resignation of John Wollaston.	John, Bishop of Bath and Wells, and Sir Rob. Shotesbroke and William Lee, Esqre.

14 A "Phiman de Standon" appears about this time in a deed preserved.

LIST OF RECTORS OF STANDON (*continued*).

Date of Institu.	Name.	Cause of Vacancy.	Name of Patron.
1486—Sept. 1.	Groute, John.		Sir Rob. Shotesbroke and William Lee, Esqre.
1488—Mar. 27.	Dawson, William.	Resignation of John Groute.	Patrons, the same.
1442—Sept. 2.	Piamour, Hugh.	Resignation of W. Dawson.	John or Thos. Rogers and Elizabeth, his wife. (She was a daughter of John Shotesbroke.)
1451 to 1452.	Wode, Richard de. or Wade.	Death of Hugh Piamour.	
	Hyde, Nicholas.		
1526—Sept. 20.	Bacon, William.	Death of Nicholas Hyde.	Sir William Essex, in right of his wife
1570—Dec. —	Aston, Robert. (He married Mary, daughter of Roger and Mary Broughton.)		Simon Harcourt. (Simon Harcourt of Ranton.)
	Nevell, Edward.		Andrew Vyse.
1672—July 20.	Alsager, Samuel.	Death of Edward Nevell.	Humfrey Vyse, Esqre.

About the end of the seventeenth or early in the eighteenth century the church was restored (see further account).

| 1708—May 10. | Asteley, Walter. | Death of Samuel Alsager. | William Vyse, Esqre. |

LIST OF RECTORS OF STANDON (continued).

Date of Institu.	Name.	Cause of Vacancy.	Name of Patron.
1712—June 28.	Vyse, Andrew.	Resignation of Walter Asteley.	Felicia Wright, widow. née Felicia Vyse.
1720—July 28.	William Jervis.	Death of Andrew Vyse.	
1729—Dec. 12.	William Jorden.	Death of William Jervis.	
1738—Oct. 18.	William Vyse.	Resignation of William Jorden	William Vyse.
1768—Aug. 25.	Falconer, James.	Cession of William Vyse.	William Vyse.
1765—Sept. 11.	Walker, William.	Resignation of James Falconer	Ven. Archdeacon Vyse.[15]
1774—April 14.	Walker, Thomas.	Resignation of William Walker	William Walker, Clerk in Holy Orders.
1799—Aug. 7.	Moseley, John Peploe.	Death of Thomas Walker.	Jane Walker.
1812—Oct.	Thomas Walker.	Resignation of John P. Moseley.	Thomas Walker.
1845—June 24.	Salt, Joseph.	Death of Thomas Walker.	John Stevenson Salt.
1862—Sept. —	Madan, Spencer.	Death of Joseph Salt.[16]	Trustees of the Rev. J. Salt.

[15] Ven. Archdeacon Vyse was brother to Mary, wife to Dr. Madan, Bishop of Peterborough, great-grandfather to Spencer Madan, Rector of Standon. The Bishop's first wife was Lady Charlotte Cornwallis, daughter of Earl Cornwallis, whence S. Madan descent. Spencer Madan married the eldest daughter of the Rev. J. Salt, of Standon.

[16] Since the Rev. J. Salt, M.A.'s death, the Rev. Spencer Madan, M.A. (obiit 1869), and the Rev. Charles Steward have been rectors. The Rev. J. Till, curate at Standon, 1845, since that date has been and now is Vicar of Gnosall (1888). The Trustees of the late Rev. J. Salt are the present patrons of the living.

In one of the former deeds we have mention, in connection with Standon, of Master (Magister) Thomas, Rector of Standon. (I place the deed at the end of Henry III.'s reign.) The term Magister here may have some significance, and gives, no doubt, distinction. For an explanation of this, I allude to a note on "Dominus, Sir, and Magister" (Master), by G. Moberley, M.A., &c., &c., in his life of William of Wykeham. He says, speaking of William of Wykeham:— "That the addition of Dominus, or Sir, was not nearly so honourable as that of Magister, or Master." Also he (Mr. Moberley) quotes from Fuller's "Church History,"—"Such priests as have the addition of Sir before their Christian names were men not graduated in the University, being in orders, but not in degrees, whilst others entitled masters had commenced in the arts."

John de Brickhull, or Brikehull, is mentioned in the register of Roger de Norbury, Bishop of Lichfield, from A.D. 1322 to 1358. The next rector of Standon who commands our attention is Nicholaus Hyde. He is mentioned as being rector at Standon in the list mentioned above; and has a monument erected to his memory, in alabaster, in the chancel, on the north side. The monument is arched over, and the effigy cut into by the stone work that divides the two recesses. This might have been, at first sight, only a skilful way of hiding the broken effigy; but as the label, with date, &c., runs at right angles with the other portion of the label, it is evidently a faithful representation, on Sir G. Scott's part, of what previously existed. The effigy is of a priest in his robes, and marked with the tonsure. The label at the bottom of the monument is as follows:— "Hic jacet: Nicholaus Hyde, quondam Rector hujus ecclæ, qui quide obiit die Aprilis, Anno d̅m̅ cujus anæ (animæ) propitiet Deus. Amen." Which may be shortly translated:—"Here lies Nicholaus Hyde, formerly Rector of this Church, who indeed died in April, in the year of our Lord——(obliterated 1526). On whose soul may God show favour. Amen."

I am indebted to the late Mrs. Henley Jervis for some account of Nicholaus Hyde. She says, " I found the will of Sir John Hyde, vicar of Sonning, then a peculiar of the Dean of Salisbury, A.D. 1501. He must have been a man of distinction and substance, bequeathing about £276 worth of vestments alone to Sonnynge, &c., &c. To his cousin Nicolas Hyde, 5s. and the residuary legateeship. There is a family of Hyde, of South Denchworth, co. Berks, but I find no Nicolases, whereas Hyde of Norbury, in Cheshire, has that name in several generations. The famous Lord Clarendon was of the Norbury family."

William Bacon for a time held the living of Standon as patron, having purchased the advowson, for a deed exists at W. Salt Library in which, in A.D. 1564, an indenture is made between Thos. Essex, of Chilrey, in co. of Berks, lord of the manor of Standon, and Wm. Bacon (clerk), of Standon, for the sale to W. Bacon, for a valuable consideration, the advowson of the rectory of Standon. In A.D. 1565, however, the same W. Bacon sells the advowson and patronage to Simon Harecourt (Harcourt), of Ranton, and he appears as patron on list mentioned above.

On the north side of the chancel, in alabaster and marble, there is a mural monument to the Rev. S. Alsager, rector, with these words, " Hic situs est Samuel Alsager, hujus ecclesiæ rector, filius natu secundus Radulphi Alsager (gen.), de Alsager, in Agro Cestriensi, qui in hac ecclesia prædicavit xxxvi annos. Et cursum absolvit Decembris xv., A.D. mdccvii. Ætat suæ lxii." He was son of Ralph Alsager, of Alsager, in the county of Chester, and rector for 86 years. He died, aged 62, in A.D. 1707. The arms of the Alsager family are on the monument, " or on a chief three lioncels (hunting) rampant," a gold field.

Although not buried at Standon, but at Cheswardine, William Jervis, rector, is mentioned (see the registers) as being, " The friend of mankind, whose study was to do good in his lifetime, and his death lamented by most that knew him." He died A.D. 1729, and was of the family of Jervis (Lord St. Vincent), owners of Chatcull, Meaford, Darlaston, Aston, &c., &c.

Members of the family of Walker, rectors of Standon, have a monument in the churchyard, so also the Rev. Mr. Lamonby, curate. In the church, within the last few years (1888), a stained glass window has been placed to the memory of the Rev. J. Salt and Rev. S. Madan, former rectors, by their relations, the subject being All Saints—the dedicatory name of the church.

The other monuments in the church, which remain at the present day, I take in their order according to date, beginning with a monument of the Elizabethan period, which is an altar tomb, of alabaster, to Francis Rose, Roos, or Ros; on it is this inscription, "Here lyeth the bodyes of ffrances Rose, esquier, lord of Laxton, in ye countie of Nottingham and Weston,[17] and Elizabeth his wyffe, on of ye daughters of Thomas Skrimshier, Esquier, which Elizabeth deceased the xxviii. daye of deceber, Anno . . . . . . lxi. (The date of her burial in the parish register is 29 Dec. A.D. 1561, 8 yr Queen Elizabeth). And the sayde france . . . . . departed ye daye of . . . . . . Anno dni M.D. . . . . . on whose solles God have merci."

The date for the husband's death has been left blank, and never filled in; however, in the parish register we have "1576, ffrancis Roos, Esq., buryed ye 18th day of ffebruary." On the monument there is a dog at the feet of the man, and ten children represented. At each corner of the rim for the inscription is a cross pattee or formy, that is to say, a cross with broad ends. The coat of arms on the monument is obliterated, but is supposed to be 1st, Roos, the others obliterated. The arms of Lord de Ros, the same family, are

[17] Weston in Standon.

a saltire and three water bougets[18]—taking saltire to mean
St. Andrew cross. We find on the arms at Standon also
there is a cross, but not of the shape of St. Andrew cross.
Peter Roos, of Swyneshead,[19] son of Francis Roos, I presume,
has on his coat three water bougets. This Francis Roos had
considerable possessions ; he has already been mentioned in
Chap. III. (Chetwynd MSS.). I believe, through his heirs a
good deal of landed property passed to the Broughton family,
also a portion of Weston, in this parish. The other portion of
Weston belonged to the Chetwynds ; this may account for the
two halls standing at Weston. The property of Weston is
now consolidated, and is held by F. C. Twemlow, Esq.

It seems that the second wife of Peter Roos, son of Francis
Roos, was brought to great poverty, as is mentioned in Chap.
III., Peter having married first Agnes, d. of Sir J. Harvey.[20]
The marriages of F. Roos's daughters appear to have been :—
Mary to Thos. Broughton, Ursula to Wm. de Macclesfeld de
Meare,[21] in Staffs. ; Anne to John Badduley, of Ellerton
Grange, Staffs. (The other daughters married into the
Fairfax and Stapleton families). A Thomas Roose marries
Anne Mainwaring, of Whitmore. This monument to Francis
Roos has evidently been coloured, the remains of red is still
seen in the lines of letters. It seems probable that Francis
Roos had purchased considerable property from the lands of
Ranton Abbey, near Ellenhall. (See Chap. III.).

The next monument which is in order of date is to Roger
Broughton and his wife Maria (Mary), and is also an altar

---

[18] A water bouget was one of the most ancient signs in heraldry,
being a water bottle (bouget) used by soldiers in camp. Lord de Ros,
premier baron, has three bougets on his shield.

[19] Swyneshead, in Chapel-Chorlton parish.

[20] Whose daughter married Sir Griffin Markham, an ancestor of the
late Mrs. Henley Jervis, to whom I am again indebted for this
information.

[21] There is an indenture of this marriage 15 yr of Q. Elizabeth,
1573.

tomb, though not well preserved. The inscription is as follows:—" Hic et intra eccleiâ jacet Rogerus Broughton de Chorlton (Chapel Chorlton), gen.; et Maria, uxor ejus . ·. . . . . Octo Fillii et quinq . . . . . . gnatæ eorum. Tho. Sextus fillius de Bowers, gen., hoc posuit, Ano ætatis 62 Anno 1617." Briefly translated, it is:—" To Roger Broughton, of Chorlton, and Mary, his wife." There seem to have been eight sons, and also grandchildren. Thos., the sixth son, placed the monument in Standon Church.

This same Roger Broughton was buried in Standon Church, the 31st of Jan., A.D. 1570, and his wife the 2nd of Feb., A.D. 1583. And in the year A.D. 1622, the 8th of November, Thomas Broughton is buried at Standon.

I think it not at all unlikely that this Roger Broughton was a son of Richard Broughton, of Broughton, and Catharine, d. of John Aston (Armiger, county of Chester), and that this Roger married . . . . Mary (?), d. of . . . . Holcott, of Holcott, in Berks, and had issue beside Thomas, also George, as an entry (see Chapter VI.) in the Register speaks of Thomas Broughton, born A.D. 1579, son of George (gen.), and Margaret, whose descendant, George, records his pedigree in London, A.D. 1684. However, it is evident that Thomas Broughton, who marries Mary, daughter of Frances Roos, of Weston, Standon, &c., ... is the forefather of the Broughtons of Broughton (see Chapter III.), Sir Bryan Broughton, Bart., from whence the line of baronets descends; also of Peter Broughton, of Lowdham, Nott, whence are descended the late T. Broughton, Esqre., of Tunstall, and J. L. Broughton, Esqre, of Almington, Staffs. The Broughtons had possessed Broughton and other lands many generations before the date of the monument in Standon Church. The pedigree of their family would be an interesting study in connection with Eccleshall and the adjoining parishes.

A considerable light is thrown on the branches of this family in the Standon Register Book, as is given in Chapter VI.

The family of Vyse, as is right from their possessions and antiquity, also in their connection with Standon, have two early monuments in the Church of Standon, but not earlier than A.D. 1634, whereas the family of Vyses dates much further back.[22]

The monuments in the church on the south wall consist of an ancient brass, framed in oak (A.D. 1847), which has the following inscription : " Here lyeth the body of Andrew Vyse, of Standon, Esqre., who married Elizabeth Gattacre, of Gattacre (Salop), Esq. And had by her X. children. And he was buried the 14 of June, 1634." " Here lyeth the body of Elizabeth Vyse, wife to Humphrey Vyse of Walford, who left behind her 4 sonnes and 3 daughters, who deserved everlasting memorie, and was buried the 6 of August, 1634."

Another monument is mentioned by Hatfield, but which does not still remain in the church—it was on a stone partly between the pew of the Vyses—and had on it this inscription, " Here lyeth the body of Felicia Vyse, who dyed July ye 17, 1691."

The Vyses became possessors of the manour house of Standon and other lands in the 6th year of Queen Elizabeth, A.D. 1564 (but it was not till the 12th year of James 1st, A.D. 1615, that Sir W. Essex sold the manour rights[23]), the first possessor of that name being Humphrey Vyse. In the 4th year of King James, A.D. 1607, Andrew Vyse was possessed of the advowson of Standon. The Vyses, who held freehold in Walford before the time that they became the lords of the manour, trace back in line to John Vise; then Roger; William

---

[22] Walford Hall, where Mr. E. Swift now resides, was the ancient house of the Vyses. We read of the Vyses living at Walford in the Chetwynd MSS. In 1790 this house at Walford was a black and white house, with dormer windows.

[23] Chapter III.

Vise of Staune ; then William ; then another William ; then John, John who married Margery Broughton ; then Humphrey mentioned above. Their after pedigree in connection with Standon is given in full in Chapter VI. They married into important families. The marriages of the daughters of the house of Vyse give additional interest to the church registers, which are given further on.

Humphrey Vise married Isabell Fitton. There is a splendid brass to a member of that family (Fitton) in Sonning Church, Oxford. (H. Vyse bought the manour house of Standon.) Ciceley Vyse, d. of Humphrey[24] and Isabell, marries John Jervis, A.D. 1565. This John Jervis is of the family of Chatcull and Meaford, and whose ancestors, in times back, are witnesses to many important deeds and charters. As Standon adjoins Chatcull, the church register is able to give the names of many members of that ancient family.

One of the burying places of the Chetwynds, who are connected with Standon, seems to have been at the church of Ashley, in Gerard's chapel, for there is a brass on the chancel floor which gives the name of " Johannis Chetwind filii Johannis Chetwynd de Rudge, obiit Nov., 1674." This is accounted for by the Rudge being so near Ashley. (He, John, married Susanna Broughton de Whittington.) Their son, John Chetwynd, seems to have bought Maer from Ralph Macclesfield, A.D. 1693, although there is some obscurity about this. This John Chetwynd was father to the first Viscount Chetwynd (Walter of Ingestre), and grandfather to Henrietta, mother of the 1st Earl of Talbot, who is direct ancestor of the present Earl of Shrewsbury. I have in my

[24] Erdeswicke says : John Vyse bought Standon, not Humphrey his father. Humphrey Vise, gt., grandson of Humphrey, suffered for the King's cause ; he died 1677. "In April, 1645, in an old document, Humphrey Vyse is allowed to come to his house at Staundon, and there to inhabite without molestation of any of the Parliament's fforces." See Erdeswicke, p. 121.

possession an excellent copy of the picture of this John Chetwynd, kindly given me by H. Chetwynd Stapylton, Esqre.

The other monuments in the church are:—One on the south side, to the memory of " Thomas Key, late of Weston, who died Sept. 8, 1784, aged 57 ; also of Mary, his wife, who died Feb. the 21st, 1807, aged 73." This family, which is of long standing at Standon, includes in its number, in A.D. 1687, Thomas Key, signing as churchwarden. Another, on the north side, to Margaret Owen, who died April 28, A.D. 1809, leaving the interest of a sum of £100 for the poor of Standon, which is distributed on St. Thomas's Day.

In the churchyard, William Keen, of Stafford, gentleman, has an altar tomb; he died 11 May, A.D. 1789, aged 54 years. There are tombs to the Adderley family, and many names which by time are becoming indistinct will be found in the 6th chapter.

From the extracts from the churchwardens' accounts, made from A.D. 1679 to 1780, we meet with the following early charitable collections, which were made often for captive Christian prisoners, or fire, or any other causes :—

In 1681, August, Distressed Protestant Churches in Poland, 8s. 9d.

1684, July 6, Runswich Samon Fishing, 5s. 4¼d.

·(I have been unable to obtain any information about this.)

1692, May 28, Captives in Algiers, &c., Barbary, 5s. 9d.

1694, Oct. 14, French Protestants, £1 7s. 2d.

1704, March 26, Orange Protestants, 15s. 0½d.

1708, July 28, Wrottesley, Stafford, 2s. 4d.

1704, July 2, Widows of seamen lost in the storm and tempest.

1702, August, Ely Fire, 5s. 10d.

1720, Oct. 8, Hail Storm, Stafford, 4s. 8d. ·

1724, May 10th, Halifax Inundation, Yorkshire, 2s. 1d.

1737.·—Penkrych, &c., Penkridge Fire, Stafford, 1s. 2d.

1779, Oct. 12th, Propagation of the Gospel in foreign parts, 8s. 6d.

In the year A.D. 1676, Charles II., a religious census taken gives in Standon 164 Conformists, 1 Papist, and 2 Non-conformists.[25] In the year A.D. 1820 we have from William Pitt the following description of Standon and population :—
" Standon is a small parish situated about three miles S.W. of Swinnerton and four miles north of Eccleshall, near a branch of the River Sow. The village of Standon is built on an eminence in a pleasant situation, and surrounded by fertile fields. Standon Church is a small structure of stone, with a tower containing three bells. It is dedicated to All Saints, and is a rectory. The Rev. Thomas Walker is the present incumbent. The population of Standon is 420 persons." In the seventeenth century Standon Church was restored. I give a copy of the agreement of the churchwardens and all other parishioners of Standon for the ordering of the seats and to whom they shall belong, made immediately after the enlarging the church with the new aisle.

" The rowe of seats adjoining to the south side of the church. Ffirst ye Lady Chancel to Mr. Vyse, for Stawne Hall. The next fform to Will. Wetwood, of Weston. Thos. Key. The next to William Stoniland and John Moss, Harding, and Pirkins. Next to Ran. Wetwood, senior, and Thos. Lightwood, Wetwood, ffourd (Ford). Next to John Heifeild and James Read. Next Robt. Gregory. The row of seats in the middle isle (aisle) and southwards : The first to Mr. John Chetwynd[26] and Mr. John Iremonger ; next, Mr. Vyse and Mr. John Broughton, for Walford ; next to Will. Short and Will. Stonyland, Lander, and Harding ; next to the Hall of Weston ; and Will. Badnall next to Tho.

[25] Census of Canterbury, Salt M.S., No. 33, Salt Library. The difference between these two reports of population—1676 and 1820— may be accounted for by the first being a religious census, or else the time soon after the restoration of the Royal Family being not progressive.

[26] This may be either John Chetwynd, father of the first Viscount Chetwynd, or else the second viscount.

Broughton and Will. Badnall ; Bower's House next to
Ffrancis Heames, and John Thorley next to John Glover.
The row of seats in the middle isle (aisle) northwards. The
uppermost seat adjoining to the chancel to the Hall of
Weston ; the next to the Hall of Stawne ; next to the Hall
of Stawne and Walter Asson ; John Edwards to Will. Machin
and Andrew Martin, miller, and Marc Carr ; next to Will.
Wetwood and John Mos. Tho. Key and Pirkins next to
Tho. Martin and John Wetwood. Thos. Naylor and Turner
next to Stawne Mil and Randle Wetwood next to Tho. Roe ;
and William Cooper next to John Heighfield and James Read.
The row of seats to the north wall : The first to the Hall of
Walford ; the next to Mr. John Broughton ; the next to
William Short and John Wetwood ; the next to Andrew
Martin and Walter Asson, and Ffrances Heames ; the next
to John Lloyd and Will. Grinley ; the next to John Thorley.
The row of seats in the wall : The first, where ye old pulpit
was, to Mrs. Wetwood ; the next to John Harding and
Bowers House ; the next, John Peak and John Martin ; the
next, Mrs. Wetwood ; the next, Willm. Grindley ; the next,
William Harding. All ye seats in ye chancel to ye parsonage,
only that joyning to ye desk to the younger brothers of
Standon Hall.

The names mentioned here point to the time I have fixed
for the restoration, for in A.D. 1702 Thomas Broughton is
dead, and John Iremonger appears in accordance with the
date mentioned ; so also do Ralph Wetwood and William
Stonyland.

There is a very good water-colour painting of Standon
Church, which painting was taken before A.D. 1847, the date
of the last restoration ; and as I can find no intimation of
any restoration between the date which gives the different
seats as allotted, I think we may suppose it is a good representation of what existed many years back.

The pulpit is represented in old oak, with a sounding
board ; and at the west end there is the gallery for the choir ;

but the church as it was then is still in the recollection of some of the inhabitants of Standon.

In the restoration of 1847 there was discovered a life-sized fresco of the figure of Death, with a scythe; the colours soon faded. A lead copy was taken at the time. Also there was an old copy of "Foxe's Martyrs" chained in the church.

Some little time back I was interested in seeing in Cheddar Church, in Somersetshire, a man-size figure, painted typifying death, and with the writing, "The sting of death is sin." Soon after this I came across a passage in Sir G. Trevelyan's "Life of Lord Macaulay," which mentions also a chained "Book of Foxe's Martyrs" at Cheddar. No doubt this coincidence would be found by no means uncommon in other churches; but the description of Cheddar Church in "Lord Macaulay's Life," which I give, enhances the circumstance. [27]The writer says: "Nothing caused him (Lord Macaulay) so much pleasure as a visit to any scene that he had known in earlier days . . . . the dining-room in Great George Street, in a corner of which he had written his articles on Lord Holland and Warren Hastings; the church at Cheddar, where as a child he had sat of a Sunday afternoon longing to get at the great black-letter volume of the 'Book of Martyrs,' which was chained to the neighbouring reading desk."

The "Book of Martyrs," which was chained to the pulpit at Standon, has this inscription: "William Lovatt gave this book to the church of Standon, there to be kept for the use of the parishioners to read in before and after prayers on Sundays, holidays, and other convenient times. That they may see the great happiness they enjoy in having the free exercise of religion, and if God gives them grace to rise, it is to his glory they will be happy whilst thay live hear; to all

[27] "Life of Lord Macaulay." By Sir G. Trevelyan, Bart. Vol. II., p. 319.

eternity. That so they might do was the harty prayer of W. L."

The copy is an edition of A.D. 1588.

William Lovatt was churchwarden at Standon in A.D. 1685.

The Rev. W. Jorden, B.D., Rector of Standon, in the year A.D. 1729 to 1788, was tutor and fellow of Pembroke Coll., Oxford, and tutor to the great Dr. Johnson.[28] There is an amusing incident related in Boswell's "Life of Dr. Johnson" about Mr. Jorden and Dr. Johnson.[29] "Mr. Jorden, fellow of Pembroke, was not, it seems, a man of such abilities as we should conceive requisite for the instructor of Samuel Johnson, who gave me the following account of him : ' He was a worthy man, but a heavy man ; and I did not profit much by his instructions. (" Johnson," says Hawkins, " would oftener risk the payment of a small fine than attend his lectures ; nor was he studious to conceal the reason of his absence. Upon occasion of one such imposition, he said to Jorden, ' Sir, you have sconced me twopence for non-attendance at a lecture not worth a penny.'" It has been thought worth while to preserve this anecdote, as an early specimen of the antithetical style of Johnson's conversation.) Indeed, I did not attend him much. The first day after I came to college I waited upon him, and then stayed away four. On the sixth Mr. Jorden asked me why I had not attended. I answered, I had been sliding in Christ Church Meadow, and this I said with as much nonchalance as I am now talking to you. I had no notion that I was wrong or

[28] " Life of Johnson by Boswell," Vol. I, p. 59.

[29] " Life of S. Johnson, LL.D.," by J. Boswell, edited by W. Croker, LL.D. In Vol. I., p. 48, in a note on Mr. Jorden, it is said, " Of the regard which his pupils felt for Mr. Jorden, Dr. Hall has pointed out a remarkable instance in the *Monthly Chronicle*, for November, 1729. About this time the Rev. Mr. Jorden, B.D., fellow of Pembroke Coll., Oxon, was presented by Mr. Vyse, a young gentleman, his pupil, to the Rectory of Standon, in Staffs., vacant by the death of the Rev. Mr. Jarvis." (Jervis.—Editor.)

irreverent to my tutor." Boswell : " That, sir, was great
fortitude of mind." Johnson : " No, sir, stark insensibility."

There is an old oak chest, with three locks and fastenings,
still kept in the church, which held church accounts, and is
an evidence of the equal rights of the rector and two churchwardens to examine such accounts.

The number of bells which are in the church are three,
two of which are ancient, a fuller account of which is to
appear in Mr. C. H. Lynam's book on " Bells in the Diocese
of Lichfield." He, however, says, speaking of the earliest :
" The bell has lettering in an unique style and as beautiful
as any that ever adorned an ancient bell." The inscription
is, " Sancta Maria, ora pro nobis." (Holy Mary, pray for us.)
And this bell is evidently of the Mediæval time. The next in
age has the date on it of A.D. 1674, and has the inscription
on it, " God save His Church." The third bell is modern,
and is cast by Taylor, of Loughborough. Date A.D. 1875.

The bell of A.D. 1674 brings us near or actually at the
restoration of the church mentioned in a previous page.

In addition to those bells, there is a priest's bell at the
rectory (which should be restored to the church), having on
it a label difficult to decipher. It may be Mediæval, or else
later than the Elizabethan age. The name William de
Edgmond, Warwickshire, seems on it.

Mr. Lynam is trying, at the present time, to have it
deciphered, and I trust it will appear in his book, but already
two rubbings, taken at different times, have not as yet made
clear the exact letters.

In A.D. 1847, Standon Church was completely restored,
under the skilful directions of Mr. Gilbert Scott, &c., afterwards Sir Gilbert Scott, Kt.

The work was commenced and promoted in the lifetime of
Mr. J. Stevenson Salt, but he did not see it finished.
However, on his death, the work was completed by his widow,
Mrs. Stevenson Salt, and her five sons and four daughters ;

the church being opened August 1st, 1847,[30] the Bishop of Lichfield (J. Lonsdale) officiating.

The work, under such a skilful architect as Sir G. Scott, would be, no one could doubt, a true restoration, but it is more especially interesting as it has kept distinct mementoes of each period from the Saxon or Norman age, down to a more modern date.

One of the principal features in this restoration is the oak wood-work, the roof in the body of the church being extremely fine ; but when it is said that Mr. Evans, of Ellastone, Derbyshire, undertook all the wood-work and the carving on the screens and seats, under Mr. G. Scott's directions, we may be sure that his talent would not be thrown away.

The monks' stalls in the chancel, with different devices, are, I believe, copied from old work at Nantwich Church, Cheshire.

The Church of Standon and its pretty churchyard are mentioned in "Reminiscences of Lord R. Gower,"[31] the quiet beauty of such a resting-place as Standon churchyard, full of trees, having struck him, surrounded as it is by stone walls, and away from the stir and sound of the busy crowd.

The sixth chapter of this book is devoted to the registers of the parish. In the present day, when so many distant lands are under the government of England, to which lands her sons and daughters have gone out either to conquer or live in, it is not surprising to have repeated applications as to dates of births, deaths, and marriages in families who once resided in our own land, but now have left little but their names behind.

---

[30] The Rev. Joseph Salt, M.A., being Rector. Mr. Richard Shaw and Mr. Thos. Woolf being Churchwardens.

[31] A favourite servant of his mother, Harriett, Duchess of Sutherland, being buried there. "The quiet Staffordshire Churchyard, near Trentham."—Vol. I., p. 217.

Some time back some scheme was suggested for obtaining copies of our church registers. If the ancient copy was kept in the parish, a printed form might be kept at Somerset House, which would aid some to find out the names and abodes of their ancestors, if not to help them to gain possessions which, but for a register, they fail to obtain.

This letter, to the writer of this book, characteristic of its kind, speaks for itself:—"Dear Sir,—Will you kindly look if you are in possession of the marriage of . . . . . . from 1744. Will you kindly let me know if you have seen any names of . . . . Could you get me that baptism of . . . . . born in 1773. I am told that the original registers (were) sent to somewhere in London. We thought he was at the Parish Church of . . . . I have applied to the rector, but cannot get no answer. Would you oblige me with writing to him, but you might get an answer where I can't. If I succeed in getting the money, I shall make you a handsome present.—I am, yours truly, &c., &c., &c. (This was from one of the largest towns in this county).

It is with reluctance I close these pages, and end the account of Standon. I am fully aware of the defects of this work, and know that in all probability others will some day write a further history of Standon, more perfect in its descriptions and more engrossing to readers. This may be sooner or later; it may be when the great fields of commerce and mining of North and South Staffordshire have met in this now quiet country side. Whether this may be so or not, no one can undertake doing so with a greater love for Standon or a greater respect for the inhabitants than I myself, the present writer.

CHAPTER VI.

EXTRACTS FROM THE REGISTER BOOK OF STANDON,
DATING FROM THE YEAR 1558 DOWN TO 1758.

Anno

1558. Anne Lovat was buried the 20th of December.

William Steedman, buried the 15th of March.

William Read, buried the 27th of May.

Richard Short, buried the 3rd of July.

Amey Wettwood, d. of John Wettwood, the younger, was baptised the 14th of May.

Margaret Millington, baptised the 2nd of November.

Thomas Halys and Ffelice Pickstock, married ye 3rd of August.

1559. Margery Martin, daughter of William Martin, was baptised 3rd of December

Jone Cooper, baptised the 25th of January.

William Thorley and Agnes Kenrick, married the 27th of January.

William Stoniland was baptised ye 21st of May, and buried 10th of August.

Anne Read was baptised 8th of October.

1560. Anne Wettwood, daughter of John Wettwood, was baptised 24th of January.

Anno

1560. Jane Lightwood, d. of Geffrey Lightwood, was baptised the 6th of Feb.

Burials.—Humphrey Iremonger, 6th of March.

John Sutton was buried 28th day of March.

James Brodhurst and Ellen Eardley married ye 26th of May.

Christening.—Randulph Thorley was baptised ye 6th of June.

1561. William Short and Jone Sutton, married 28th of November.

Richard Bould and Ellen Event, married 6th of February.

John Lawsey and Ellen Low, married ye 2nd day of September.

Willkin Read was baptised 21st day of December.

Francis Martin, baptised the 17th of January.

Francis Heamis, sonne of Thomas Hemis, bapti. 8rd of April.

John Stoniland was baptised ye ninth of May, and was buried ye 17th of July.

Thomas Lightwood was baptised ye 24th of August.

Elizabeth Badnall, ye 2nd day of October.

Thomas Steedman, bapti. ye 28rd of Oct.

Burial.—Mrs. Ross (or Roos), wife of Ffrancis Ross, Esqre., 29th December. (This must be the monument in the chancel formerly, and now in the vestry —an altar tomb.)

1562. Margaret Lightwood, buried ye 24th of January.

Stephen Glover and Margery Short were married 16th of Nov.

John Glover and Ellin Short, married ye 16th of Nov.

Isabel Read was baptised 19th of March.

Mary Millington, baptised 28th of March.

John Cooper was baptised ye 18th of May.

Thomas Wettwood, baptised ye 11th of June, and buried ye 14th of June.

Anno

1562. Anne Amisson, daughter of William Amisson, bapti.

1563. Christopher Wettwood and Elin Walter were maryed ye 28th of January.

John Salt and Anne Lightwood, married ye 26th of August.

Christenings.—Isabell Martin, daughter of Edmund Martin, bapti. ye 20th December.

Ellin Stoniland, daught. of William Stoniland, bapt. 7th of January.

Richard Read, baptised the 8th of February.

Thomas Wettwood, sonne of John Wettwood, bapt. ye 12th of May.

Thomas Heimes was baptised the 1st of August.

Margaret Short, daughter of Thos. Short, bapt. ye 4th of September.

Margery Ffox was baptised ye 7th of Sept., and buried 23rd Sept.

Margaret Badnall was baptised ye 8th of November.

Burials.—Richard Read was buried 22nd of February.

Anne Vyse, d. of William Vyse (gent.) and Katherine, his wife, buried 14th of February.

1564. Humphrey Steedman, baptised ye 1st of February.

Isabell Martin, baptised ye 1st day of February.

Anne Wetwood, daughter of Christopher Wetwood, baptised ye 18th March.

John Millington, baptised ye 25th of March.

Margery Read, baptised ye 30th of April.

John Bromley, sonne of James Bromley, bap. 24th August.

Randulph Lightwood, baptised ye 30th of April.

Margeret Martin, daughter of Edmund, bapt. ye 14th October.

Burials.—Ralph Cooper, buried at Bristow ye 20th of November.

Margaret Short, buried ye 28th of December.

Anno

1564. Jone Wettwood, wife of Randulph, buried ye 8th of April.

Robert Greatolder, buried ye 11th day of April.

1565. John Buttler and Margery Wintle, married ye 26th April.

{ John Jervis and Sisley Vyse, married ye 6th of November.

Thomas Mills and Anne Vyse, married ye 6th of November. }

Christenings.—Christopher Wettwood, son of John, baptised ye 6th of February.

Thomas Amison, sonne of William Amison, ye 30th of June.

Alis Martin, bap. ye 30th of November.

Burials.—Thomas Iremonger, the 30th of November.

Robert Iremonger, buried ye 23rd of April.

1566. Anne Heymes, bapt. ye 17th of December.

Alis Heath, baptised the 20th of March.

Katherine Badnall, baptized ye 23rd of March.

James Steedman, baptised ye 23rd of March and buried ye 1st of May.

Katherine Steedman, baptised ye 17th of April.

Katherine Martin, baptised ye 30th of April.

James Read, baptised ye 28th of August.

Anne Lightwood, baptised ye 30th of September.

John Wettwood, baptised ye 13th of October.

Gefery Homes, buried ye 18th of May.

Francis Short, buried ye 21st of December.

1567. John Marborow and Anne Steedman, married ye 3rd of February.

Katherine Martin, daughter of Edmund Martin, bap. ye 8th of January.

William Short, baptised ye 28th of March.

Mary Vyse, daughter of Will.Vyse, gent., and Katherine, baptised ye 26th of June.

Anno

1567. William Roe, baptised ye 21st of July.

    Jone Silvester, bap. and buried ye 28th of August.

    Amy Martin, baptised ye 9th of October.

    William Walters, baptized ye 10th of November.

    Burials.—Katherine Wettwood ye 11th of May.

    John Yates, buryed ye 17th of September.

1568. Richard Henston and Ellin Blest married ye 4th of June.

    Tho. Adams and Margaret Steedman married ye 11th of Sept.

    Anne Badnall, baptised ye 8th of January.

    Jane Poole, baptised ye 2nd of April.

    Ursula Heames, born 15th of May and buried ye 13th of August.

    Francis Martin, daughter of John Martin, bapt. ye 5th of November.

    James Astley, bap. ye 14th of November.

    Richard Weaver, baptised ye 15th of November.

    John Vyse was buried ye 8th of February.

    John Steedman, buried ye 1st of March.

    Jane Lawton, buried ye 28th of May.

    Robert Wettwood, sonne of Ralph Wettwood, buried ye 8th of April.

    Timothy Martin, buried ye 21st of June.

1569. Thomas Hodgson and Mary Huntbach married ye 10th of June.

    William Ellkin and Anne Kent married ye 4th of October.

    John Lightwood, baptised ye 12th of December.

    William Millington, baptised ye 24th of February.

    Thomas Rimmer, baptised ye 8th of March.

    Francis and John, sonnes of William Wettwood and Elizabeth Brodhurst, were baptised, and buried the day following: 9th March.

Anno

1569. Lettice Vyse, daughter of William Vyse, Gent., and
Katherine his wife, was baptised ye 7th of May.

Jone Read, daughter of Will. Reade and Isabel his wife,
bapt. ye 18th May.

Will. Mills, son of Thos. Mills and Anne his wife, bap.
27th May.

Thomas Short, sonne of Thomas Short and Jone his
wife, bap. 3rd of July.

Ffrances Roe, daughter of Tho. Roe and Isabel his wife,
bap. 3rd August.

Elizabeth Wetwood, daught. of Randulph and Margery,
bapt. 10th Sept.

Margreat Martin, daughter of John and Anne his wife,
bap. 27th Sep.

Ellinor Heath, daughter of Henry and his wife Anne, ye
23rd of Oct.

Anne Heamis, daught. of Thomas and Margery his wife,
ye 8th of Nov.

William Buntingdale, son of Richard and Jone his wife,
ye 15th Nov.

Ffrances Martin, daught. of John and Anne his wife,
buried 3rd of February.

Humphrey Vyse (gent.), buried ye 5th of June.

John Wettwood, buried the 22nd Dec.

Roger Broughton, buried 31st of January. (Altar tomb
in vestry.)

(The year 1570 is not entered as a year.)

1571. Isabel Mills, daughter of Tho. and Anne his wife, bapt.
30th of November.

Frances Read, daught. of Will. Read and Isabel his
wife, baptised 12th of January.

George Gervis, son of John and Cissley (née Broughton)
his wife, baptised ye 15th of February.

M

Anno

1571. Andrew Amison, son of Will. and Elizabeth his wife,
baptised ye 4th of July.

William Martin, buried ye 14th of May.

Thomas Martin, buried ye 14th of June.

Margreat Badnall, daughter of Will. and Anne his wife,
buried ye 4th of July.

Margreat Royles, wife of Humphrey Royles, buried ye
18th of July.

Richard Broughton, sonne of Mary Broughton, widow,
buried ye 14th of August.

Anne Tunstall, buried 25th of August.

1572. Virgill Stinson, son of Tho. and Elizabeth his wife,
baptised ye 22nd November.

Elizabeth Martin, daughter of Edmund and Katharine
his wife, baptised ye 7th of February.

Isabel Vyse, daughter of Will. and Katharine his wife,
baptised ye 24th of February.

Anne Bucknall, daug. of Hugh and Mary his wife,
baptised ye 20th of March.

Thos. Mills, sonne of Thos. and Anne his wife, baptised
ye 11th of April.

John Rimer, son of Thos. and Ellin his wife, baptised
ye 14th of April.

Anne Iremonger, daughter of Richard Iremonger,
baptised ye 11th of May.

Anne Smith, d. of Richard, baptised ye 6th of August.

Burials.—John Lightwood, buried ye 23rd of December.

Katharine Gervis, daugh. of Richard and Elizabeth his
wife, 6th of August.

Barbara Iremonger, daugh. of Richard Iremonger, ye
14th of August.

1573. William Cleaton, sonne of John Cleaton and Elizabeth
his wife, married Elizabeth Vise, daughter of Will.
Vise and Katharine, ye 20th of July.

Anno

1573. Christenings.—Robert Wettwood, son of Randulph and
Margery, ye 16th of January.

Will Heames, son of Tho. and Margery, bap. ye 12th of
February.

John Lightwood, son of Jeffrey, bapti. and bur. ye 18th
of March.

Will. Caudwall, son of Ralph Caudwall, ye 20th day of
March.

1574. Weddings.—Robert Aston, parson of Standon, and
Mary Broughton, daughter of Mary Broughton,
widdow, marryed ye 18th of February.

Tho. Sherlyald Knight and Ellnor Martin, widdow,
mard. 16th of February.

Christenings.—Rob. Martin, son of John and Anne his
wife, bap. ye 28th of February.

Tho. Read, son of Will and Isabel his wife, ye 17th of
June.

Katharine Wettwood, daughter of Christopher Wettwood,
ye 29th of July.

Margreat Kendall, daughter of Ralph Kendall, ye 9th of
August.

Tho. Poole, sonne of Will. and Margery, bap. ye 20th of
October.

Alis Gervis, daugh. of Richard and Elizabeth, buried ye
13th of March.

1575. Randulph Wettwood, son of Randulph and Margery,
baptised ye 19th of December.

John Vise, son of Will. Vise, gent., bap. and buried ye
1st of February.

Margery Short, daught. of Tho. and Jone his wife,
baptised ye 2nd of February.

John Heamis, son of Tho. and Margery his wife, baptised
ye 18th of July.

Anne Martin, daugh. of John and Anne his wife, baptised
ye 18th of October.

Anno

1575. Thomas Roe, son of Tho. and Isabel his wife, baptised
ye 8rd of November.

Thomasin Caudwall, daugh. of Henry and Margreat,
baptised ye 8rd of November.

Thomas Thorley, sonne of Will, buryed ye 29th of
April.

Amy Wettwood, daugh. of John and Margery, buried
ye 6th of August.

Thomasin Caudwall, daugh. of Henry and Margreat,
buried ye 5th of November.

1576. John Badnall, sonne of William Badnall and his wife,
marryed Amy Denbury, ye 8th of April.

William Martin and Elizabeth Cooper, marryed ye 30th
of April.

John Standly and Jone Ffox, married ye first of May.

Christenings.—Mary Aston, daught. of Robert and
Mary his wife, bap. ye 9th of February.

John Abatt, sonne of John and Margery, ye 23rd of
February.

Robert Heath, son of Henry and Anne his wife, ye 23rd
of March.

Tho. Wettwood, sonne of Christopher and Ellenor, ye
25th of April.

Margery Read, daught. of Will. and Isabel, ye 6th of
May.

Ellen Martin, daught. of Richard and Anne, ye 8th of
June.

Tho. Vise, son of Will. Vise (gent.) and Katharine, ye
16th of June.

Mary Martin, daugh. of Edmund and Katharine, ye
8rd of July.

Edward Shropsheire, son of Will. and Cassander, ye
20th of July.

Samson Smith, ye 8rd of October.

Christopher Cowop, the 17th of October.

Anno

1576. Burials.—Ffrancis Roos, Esqre., buryed ye 18th day of February.

Mary Aston, daugh. of Robert and Mary, ye 4th of March.

John Abatt, sonne of John and Margery, ye 10th of March.

Tho. Shoyle, ye 22nd of March.

1577. Tho. Cash and Margery Cartwright, married ye 16th of May.

Thomas Gerves and Anne Sawle, married ye 21st of July.

William Swinerton and Ffrances Martin, married the 31st of August.

Christenings.—John Wettwood, sone of Randulph and Margery, ye 26th of November.

Andrew Martin, sonne of John and Anne, ye 8rd of January.

Walter Aston, sonne of Rob and Mary, ye 24th of January.

Robert Cauldwall, sonne of Henry and Margery, ye 25th of January.

Will. Abatt, sonne of John and Margery, the 25th of August.

Margreat Williams, daughter of John and Isabell, ye 8rd of Sept.

Mary Short, daught. of Tho. and Jane, ye 8rd of Nov.

Burials.—Margaret Martin, widow, buried ye 81st of March.

Mode Sutton, wife of Robert Sutton, ye 8rd of November.

1578. Wedding.—John Boughey and Alis Bee, marryed ye 29th of September.

Christenings.—Ffrancis Martin, sonne of John and Anne, bapt. ye 6th of January.

Alis Lovat, daugh. of James and Frances, ye 22nd of March.

Anno

1578. Christenings.—John Heath, sonne of Henry and Anne, ye 24th of Aprill.

John Martin, daught. of Robert and Mary, ye 14th of June.

Thomas Turner, sonne of Humphrey and Alis, ye 80th of October.

William Wettwood, sonne of Randulphe and Margery, ye 28rd of Oct.

Shristobell (Christobell) Smithstun, burryed ye 22nd of March.

Thomas Roe, buried the 25th of March.

John Gouldburne, servant to Edmund Martin, buried ye 24th of May.

1579. Weddings.—Will. Thorly, sonne of Will., marryed Ellin Tillsley, daugh. of William and Emye (Amy) wife, ye 5th of August.

Robert Owen and Isabell Roe, widow, marryed ye 29th of Aprill.

Elizabeth Caudwall, daught. of Henry, bapt. and burryed ye 15th of January.

Elizabeth Martin, daughter of John Martin and his wife, bapt. ye 17th Ffebruary, and burryed ye 10th of March next following.

Tho. Broughton, sonne of George (gent.) and Margaret, baptised ye 14th of Aprill.

Burial.—Tho. Vise, sonne of Will (gent.) and Katharine, the 25th of Ffebruary.

1580. Wedding.—William Broughton (gent.), sonne of Mary Broughton (widow), and Anne Younge, daughter of John Young, marryed ye 4th of February.

Christenings.—Mary Caudwall, daught. of Henry and Margaret, bapt. ye 80th of December.

Ffrancis Martin, sonne of John and Anne, ye 9th Ffeb., and buryed ye 10th Ffeb.

Ellin Owen, daughter of Robert and Isabel, ye 11th of Feb., and buryed ye 2nd of June.

Anno

1580. Christenings.—Lettice Martin, daught. of Edmund and
Katharine, ye 6th of May.

Robt. Wettwood, sonne of Christopher and Ellenor, ye
4th of June.

Rob. Short, sonne of Thomas and Jone, the 17th of
June.

Margreat Halloway, daught. of William and Jane, ye
7th of October.

Robt. Aston, sonne of Robt. and Mary, ye 8th of October.

1581. John Lightbourne and Elizabeth Homersley, married
ye 9th of June.

John Dimock and Margery Steedman, married ye 6th of
October.

Christenings.—Anne Heath, daughter of Henry and
Anne, ye 27th of March.

John Broughton, sonne of Willm. and Anne, Gent, ye
18th of Aprill.

Andrew Smith, sonne of John and Margreat, ye 5th of
May.

Edmund Walker, sonne of Hugh and Jone, ye 23rd of
May.

Jone Read, daughter of Anne Reade, ye 1st of June.

Mary Huntbach, daughter of John and Mary, ye 16th
of June.

John Badnall, sonne of William, junior, and Ellenor,
ye 81st of July.

Dorothy Wettwood, daughter of Randulph and Margery,
ye 28th of August.

Richard Aston, sonne of Rob. and Mary, ye 2nd day of
October.

John Barnes, sonne of Thomas and Katharine, ye 4th
of October.

Burials.—Thomas Denson Webster, buryed ye 11th of
December.

William Amison, buryed ye 19th of October.

Anno

1582. Christenings.—John Read, sonne of Willm. and Isabell, bap. ye 80th of November.

Aime Owen, daugh. of Robert and Isabell, ye 17th of May.

Mary Steedman, daugh. of John and Margreat, ye 6th of Sept.

Tho. Martin and William, sonnes of Edmund and Katharine, ye 1st of Nov.

Burials.—Richard Aston, sonne of Robt. and Mary, buryed ye 19th of Dec.

John Vise, gent., ye 25th of December.

Willm. Broughton, gent., sonne of Mary, widow, ye 28rd Jan.

Isabell Vyse, widow, ye 12th of Ffebruary.

Ellin Sutton, ye 27th of February.

Thomas Heimis, sonne of Tho. and Margery, ye 17th of April.

Henry Heath, ye 81st of May.

Jone Greatoulder, widow, ye 21st of June.

Ursula Tillsley, daugh. of Willm. and Emy, ye 21st of Sep.

Ellin Thorley, wife of Willm. junior, ye 6th of Oct.

Margery Cowep, wife of William Cowep, ye 81st of Oct.

Katharine Martin, wife of Edmund, ye 3rd of Nov.

1588. Weddings.—William Thorley, junior, and Ellin, daught. of Richard Tillsley, ye 18th of June.

William Coup and Elizabeth Barnes, ye 26th of Sept.

Christenings.—Ffrancis Cowper, bap. ye 19th of Nov.

Anne Hynly, daugh. of Owford and Anne, ye 29th of Nov.

Richard Wettwood, sonne of Christopher and Ellinor, ye 8th of Dec.

Katherine Aston, daugh. of Robt. and Mary, ye 15th of March.

Anno

1583. Christening.—William Tilsley, sonne of Richard and Isabel, ye 1st of Oct.

Burials.—Mary Broughton, widow, buried ye 2nd of February.

Ellinor Wettwood, wife of Christopher, drownde (drowned) herselfe.

Letice Iremonger, wife of John, gent., ye 11th of November.

1584. John Ffox and Ffrances Amyson, married ye 4th of July.

Walter Hill and Ellin Stonyland, marryed ye 26th of September.

Christenings.—Margreat Steedman, d. of John and Mary Steedman, bap. ye 2nd of Feb.

John Shropshore, sonne of Will. and Cassandar, ye 20th Feb., bap. and buried.

Anne Smith, daugh. of John and Margaret, ye 23rd of Ffebruary.

George Roe, sonne of Gephry and Anne, ye 18th of March, christened.

George Clayton, sonne of William and Elizabeth, ye 26th of April.

William Cooper, sonne of George, ye 8th of May.

Margreat Boughey, daught. of John and Alis, ye 15th of May.

Elizabeth Aston, daughter of Robt. and Mary, ye 22nd of June.

Ffrancis Wetwood, sonne of Randulph and Margery, 1st of October.

Tho. Owen, sonne of Rob. and Isabell, ye 23rd of October.

Amis Cooper, daughter of William and Elizabeth, ye 26th of June.

Burials.—William Cox, sonne of John and Amphillis, buried ye 24th of December.

Anno

1584. Burials.—Richard Iremonger, ye 2nd of Aprill.

Amy Amyson, wife of Thomas, the 7th of May.

George Roe, sonne of Jasper and Anne, ye 27th of May.

Elizabeth Silluester (Sillvester), ye 12th of August.

George Cleaton, sonne of William and Elizabeth, ye 12th of August.

William Thorly (senior), ye 17th of September.

Margreat Broughton, wife of George, gent., ye 28rd of October.

1585. Wedding.—George Cotton, sonne of Edward Cotton, and Margaret Iremonger, daught. of Richard, ye 8th of October.

Edward Shelly, sonne of James, and Anne Ffenton, marryed 27th of October.

Christenings. — William Millington, sonne of John Millington, ye 24th of January.

Elijah Eaton, son of Ralph Newill (Nevill) and Joyce Eaton, ye 19th of Feb., and buryed ye 26th.

John Steedman, sonne of John and Mary, ye 16th of July.

Ralph Cleaton, sonne of Willm., gent., and Elizabeth, ye 29th of July.

John Shropsheire, sonne of Willm. and Cassander, ye 20th of September.

Thomas Ffox, sonne of John and Ffrances, ye 28th of September.

Burials.—Edward Tunstal, buryed ye 22nd of December.

John Broughton, gent., sonne of Mary Broughton, widow, ye 80th of April.

Katherin Homphrey, ye 5th of July.

Robt. Martin, sonne of John and Anne, ye 22nd of July.

Elizabeth Barnes, widow, burryed ye 29th of July.

Humphrey Vise, sonne of William, gent., and Katharine, ye 25th of Aug.

Anno

1585. Burials.—Elizabeth Lightwood, wife of Jeffrey Lightwood, ye 5th of November.

Isabell Read, wife of William Read, burryed ye 7th of
November.

1586. Wedding.—Christopher Hassall and Jone Cooper,
married ye 23rd of Jan.

Christenings.—Margaret Aston, daughter of Rob. and
Mary, bap. ye 21st of Dec.

Mary Hill, daught. of Walter and Ellin, ye 24th of
March.

Burials.—Anne Ellkin, widow, ye 30th of November.

Anne Smith, daughter of John and Margreat, ye 25th
of December.

Margery Heymes, wife of Thomas, ye 6th of Ffebruary.

John Stoniland, ye 14th of July.

John Wettwood, sonne of Christopher, ye 5th of
August.

1587. Wedding.—Lawrence Collier and Anne Hopton married
ye 9th of Nov.

Christenings.—Richard Read, the 1st of Aprill, and
buryed ye 8th of Sept,

Mary Chettwind, daught. of John (gent.) and Mary, ye
6th of Aprill.

Burials.—Willm. Cleaton, sonne of Willm. (gent.) and
Elizabeth, ye 14th of May.

John Martin, ye 28rd of October.

1588. Wedding.— John Kendrick and Margreat Sutton,
marryed ye 29th of Jan.

Christenings.—John Osburne, bap. and bur. ye 9th of
Ffeb.

Richard Bullock, ye 12th of April.

Dorothy Broughton, daught. of John and Dorothy,
gent., ye 12th of May.

Mary Amyson, daught. of Tho. and Cassander, ye 23rd
of July.

Anno

1588. Burials.—Thomas Rimmer, burryed ye 8th of Dec.

John Harrison, the 16th of December.

1589. Weddings.—Willm. Read and Anne Heath, widow, marryed ye 19th Nov.

Jeffrey Lightwood and Anne Martin, widow, ye 8th of February.

Christenings.—Katherine Clayton, daught. of Willm., gent., and Elizabeth, 28th Dec.

Margreat Steedman, daugh. of John and Mary, ye 18th of January.

Ralph Ffox, sonne of John Ffrances, bapt. the 12th of Ffebruary and buryed the 16th of June.

Cassander Hill, daught. of Walter and Ellin, ye 12th of July.

Dorothy Aston, daughter of Rob. and Mary, ye 15th of August.

Margreat Shore, ye 22nd of August.

Burials.—Richard Collye, buryed ye 15th of Dec.

Alice Heath, daugh. of Henry Heath, ye 5th of Ffeb.

Alice Millington, wife of Robt., ye 6th of Ffeb.

Isabell Badnall, daugh. of William (senior) and Anne, ye 3rd of March.

Jone Vyse (spinster), ye 29th March.

Anne Cooper, daught. of Willm. and Elizabeth, ye 3rd of June.

William Vyse, gent., ye 18th of July.

Elizabeth Wettwood, widow, ye 7th of August.

Cassander Shropsheire, wife of Willm., ye 15th of September.

Elizabeth Rider, widow, ye 30th of Sep.

Elizabeth Willson, wife of Ffrancis, ye 31st of Oct.

Robt. Wilson, sonne of Ffrancis, ye 1st of Novem.

1590. Weddings.—Richard Heames and Margery Cooper, maryed ye 14th of Jan.

Willm. Palmer and Amy Kendrick, ye 6th of June.

Anno

1590. Christenings.—Ffrancis Kendrick, sonne of John and Margreat, bapt. and buryed 29th of Jan.

Thomas Buntingdall, sonne of Tho. and Jone, ye 11th of April.

Ellin Tillsley, daug. of Simon and Barbara, ye 7th of Nov.

Burials.—Edward Iremonger, sonne of John and Elizabeth, buryed 10th Dec.

Robert Millington, ye 20th January.

Amy Williams, ye 80th of Ffebruary.

Jane Carrington, ye 8rd of March.

Margery Heames, wife of Richard, ye 2nd of March.

Elizabeth Cradock, ye 19th of March.

Ellin Allin, ye 18th of Aprill.

Elnor Badnall, wife of Willm., jun., ye 4th of August.

William Roe, ye 12th of September.

Thomas Short, ye 24th of October.

1591. Weddings.—Willm. Short, sonne of Jone, widdow, and Margreat Hawkins, ye 80th January.

John Mosse and Anne Wettwood, ye 20th of Aprill.

Christenings.—Thomas Hodson, sonne of Thomas and Mary, baptized ye 1st of January.

George Steedman, sonne of John and Mary. ye 20th of April.

Willm. Martin, sonne of Randulph and Jane, ye 9th of May.

John Cooper, sonne of Willm. and Elizabeth, the 18th of May.

Elizabeth Amyson, daught. of Thomas and Cassander, ye 18th of July.

Humfrey Vise, sonne of Andrew and Elizabeth, borne ye 9th of July and baptised ye 18th of ye same.

Burials.—Anne Chambers, buryed ye 28rd of November.

Christopher Wettwood, ye 5th of Ffebruary.

Anne Willott, ye 9th of March.

Anno

1591. Burials.—Letice Broughton, daugh. of George (gent.),
  ye 6th of May.
  William Badnall, senior, ye 24th of September.
1592. Weddings.—John Hassall and Made (Maude) Kendrick,
  ye 9th of May.
  John Blundell and Amy Martin, ye 29th of July.
  Christenings.—Anne Short, daught. of William and
  Margaret, bap. ye 1st December.
  Alice Moss, daught. of John and Anne, ye 4th of Jan.
  Humphrey Hally, sone of Tho. and Ellin, ye 4th of
  February.
  Richard Tillsley, sone of Richard and Isabell, ye 2nd
  of Feb.
  Alice Smith, d. of John and Margreat, ye 18th Feb.,
  bur. ye 26th Oct.
  Alice Hollins, daught. of Mathew and Ellin, ye 21st
  May.
  Ffrances Vise, daught. of Andrew and Elizabeth, ye
  27th July and buried ye 28th.
  Burials.—Annis Thorley, widdow, buried ye 18th of Feb.
  Kathrine Broughton, wife of Thomas Broughton, gent.,
  ye 18th of March,
  Thomas Amison, ye 15th of March.
  Anne Browne, ye 22nd of August.
  Ellinor Colly, widdow, ye 27th of September.
  Ellinor Smith, d. of John and Margreat, ye 8th of Oct.
  Elizabeth, daughter of John and Margreat, ye 23rd of
  October.
  Lettice Smith, daughter as aforesaid, ye 1st of November.
  Andrew Smith, sonne of ye aforesaid, ye 5th of November.
  John Smith, ye ffather aforesaid, ye 12th of November.
1598. Weddings.—John Thorley and Amy Sutton, marryed
  ye 25th of November.
  John Heyfield and Katherine Steedman, ye 29th of
  January.

Anno

1593. Wedding,—John Unton and Margreatt Martin, d. of
Edmund, ye 12th November.

Christenings.—Ellin Rimer, d. of John and Alice, ye
19th Jan.

Jone and Ffrances Blundall, d. of John and Amy,
baptized ye 13th of April, and Ffrances buryed next
day.

Mary Stringer, d. of Lawrence and Margreat, ye 7th of
July.

Mary Moss, daughter of John and Anne, ye 7th of July.

Tho. Badnall, sonne of Willm. and Ellin, ye 17th of
July.

Ellin Thorly, daught. of John and Amy, ye 17th of
September.

Burials.—Alice Rimer, wife of John, buryed ye 18th of
January.

Randulph Martin, ye 12th of June.

Kathrine Edge, ye 18th of June.

John Bee, ye 26th of October.

1594. Weddings.—Ffrancis Sanbrooke and Alis Heamis, d. of
Tho., 29th Jan.

Andrew Boond and Anne Lightwood, daugh. of Jeffrey,
ye 27th of April.

Thomas Cooper and Margreat Smith, widow, ye 7th of
July.

John Low and Ffrances Cooper, ye 8th of September.

John Tillsley, sonne of Richard, and Margreat Berkin,
ye 31st Aug.

Christenings.—Willm. Heyfield, sonne of John and
Katherine, ye 21st of Dec.

Willm. Tillsley, sone of Simon and Barbara, ye 1st
January.

Robert Sanbrook, sone of Ffrancis and Alice, ye 28th
Feb.

Thomas Heywood, ye 6th of Aprill.

Anno

1594. Christenings.—John and Ffrancis Blundall, sonne and daught. to John and Amy, ye 7th of Aprill; Ffrances buiryed ye 10th and John ye 28th thereof.

Robert Vyse, sone of Andrew (gent.) and Elizabeth, ye 10th April.

Elizabeth Coop, d. of Willm. and Elizabeth, ye 7th of May.

Anne Moss, daught. of John and Anne, 9th July and buryed 10th Oct.

Martha Iremonger, d. of Willm. Joyce, ye 28th Sept.

Elizabeth Wettwood, d. of Willm. (junior) and Alice, ye 30th Oct.

Willm. Broughton, sone of George (gent.) and Bridget, ye 16th Nov.

Burials.—Anthony Broughton, gent., sone of Roger and Mary, bur. 19th of Ffebruary.

Ellin Read, buryed ye 20th of March.

John Iremonger, of Chatcill, gent., ye 28th of Aprill.

1595. Weddings.—John Morry and Anne Hall, widow, maryed ye 7th July.

Peter Roos (gent.) and Mary Huntback, d. of John Huntback (clerck) and Mary his wife, ye 22nd of July.

Christenings.—Clare Broughton, d. of Tho. and Winyfride, ye 2nd December.

Mary Cooke, d. of Robert and Elizabeth, ye 22nd January.

Margreat Short, d. of Willm., ye 28rd January, and buried 3rd Ffeb.

Elizabeth Heamis, d. of Ffrancis and Margreat, ye 6th of April.

— Webe, d. of Anne Web, 8th April.

William Vyse, son of Andrew (gent.) and Elizabeth, ye 5th of May.

Anne Boone, d. of Andrew and Anne, ye 22nd of June.

Robert Steedman, sonne of John and Mary, ye 9th of October.

Anno

1595. Christening.—John Iremonger, sonne of Willm. and Ellin, ye 12th of October.

Burials.—Elizabeth Wisswall, d. of Willm. and Elizabeth, 12th of May.

William Poole, ye 16th of May.

1596. Christenings.—Henry Thorley, sone of John and Amy, bap. ye 31st November,

Robert Martin, sone of Tho. and Elizabeth, ye 23rd January.

Ffrances Brocton, d. of Tho. and Ann, bap. and bur. ye 25th Feb.

James Sutton, sonne of Robert and Jane, ye 29th July.

Isabel Hill, d, of Walter and Ellin, ye 4th of August.

Burials.—Thomas Martin, son of Thomas and Elizabeth, bur. ye 24th of March.

Elizabeth Aston, daught. of Edward (gent.) and Margreat, 1st June.

Jane Rimmer. wife of John Rimmer, ye 2nd of March.

1597. Weddings.—Willm. Boone, of Mere, and Margreat Heyward, wid., ye 2nd Feb.

Tho. Lightwood, sonne of Jeffrey, and Ffrances Roe, d. of Tho. and Isabel, married ye 20th May.

John Wright, of Muckleston, junior, and Anne Blest, ye 29th of June.

William Heath and Margery Walton, married ye 7th of November.

Christenings.—Robert Iremonger, son of Willm. (gent.) and Joyce, ye 24th of November.

Tho. Vyse, sone of Andrew (gent.) and Elizabeth, ye 30th of November.

Anne Thorley, d. of John and Amy, ye 12th of March.

John Hanly, sone of Tho. of Chattkill and Ellen, ye 17th April.

Elizabeth Moss, d. of John of Weston and Anne, ye 9th of July.

Anno

1597 Christening.—Mary Broughton, d. of Tho. (gent.) of
       Bowers and Winifred, 16th August.

    Burials.—Katharine Vise, widdow, 15th of April.

    A poore child from Chattkill, ye 24th December.

    Tho. Badnall, sone of Anne Badnall, of Walford,
       widdow, ye 16th Feb.

    Anne Batham, d. of Simon and Anne, ye 25th Ffeb.

    A poore child from Chattkill, ye 19th of March.

    Ralph Cooper, sonne of Anne Bee, of Standon, wid.,
       ye 28th of March.

    John Cooper, sone of Willm., of Standon, and Eliza-
       beth, ye 9th of May.

    Joyce Iremonger, wife of Willm. (gent.), of Chattkill,
       ye 22nd of August.

    Anne Read, wife of Willm. Read, of Bowers, ye 29th
       of August.

1598. Christenings.—Thomas Anger, sonne of Robt. and
       Ellin, bap., ye 3rd of December.

    Elizabeth Aston, d. of Edward Aston (gent.) and
       servant of ye Right Honble. Earl of Essex, bap. ye
       23rd of December.

    John Heyfield, sone of John and Katharine, of Bowers,
       ye 6th of Jan.

    Edward Vise, son of Andrew (gent.), of Walford, and
       Elizabeth, ye 2nd July.

    Ffrancis Roe, sone of Tho. and Ellin, of Bowers, ye
       7th of November.

    Burial.—Edward Aston (gent.) and serv. to ye Earle of
       of Essex, att Dublinge, 8th of September.

1599. Christenings. — Elizabeth Lightwood, daught. of
       Thomas and Ffrances, bap. ye 18th of November.

    Elizabeth Badnall, d. of Willm. and Ellin, of Walford,
       ye 9th Dec.

    Elizabeth Heath, d. of Willm. and Margery, of Bowers,
       baptized ye 23rd December, and buryed ye 4th of
       January.

Anno

1599. Christenings.—Mary Cooper, d. of Willm. and Eliza-
   beth, ye 3rd of February.
   Willm. Blundall, sone of John and Amy, ye 16th of March.
   Burials.—John Wettwood, brother of William, sone of
   Weston, buryed ye 20th Ffebruary.
   Willm. Read, ye 24th of March.

(N.B.—I give the names after this date without the date in
   the month, and in English of the present day.)

1600. Christenings.—Edward Martin, son of Thomas and
   Elizabeth.
   John Vise, son of Andrew (gent.) and Elizabeth.
   William Hill, son of Walter and Ellen.
   Thomas Heath, son of Willm. and Margery.
   Burials.—Anne Page, servant to William Martin.
   Isabel Hill, daughter of Walter and Ellen.
   William Hill, son of Walter and Ellen.
   Robert Sutton.
1601. Christenings.—Elizabeth Short, daughter of William
   and Margaret.
   Margery Wettwood, daughter of William and Anne.
   Ellen Moss, daughter of John and Anne.
   George Vise, son of Andrew and Elizabeth.
   Peter Hill, son of Walter and Ellen.
   Elizabeth Amyson, daughter of Anne Amyson and
   William, Clocklough.
   Peter Heyfield, son of John and Katharine.
   Elizabeth Sambrook, daughter of Francis and Alice.
   Mary Bonnd, daughter of Andrew and Anne.
   Burials.—John Blundall.
   Elizabeth Wettwood.
   Margaret Hassall.
1602. Christenings.—Ellen Roe, daughter of Thomas and Ellen.
   Peter Heames, son of Francis and Margaret.
   William Badnall, son of William Badnall.

Anno

1602. Christenings.—Edmund Martin, son of Andrew and Mary.
John Lightwood, son of Thomas and Frances.
Weddings.—Thomas Rimer and Katharine Badnall.
John Beardmore and Parnell Reeve.
Burials.—Letice Martin.
Thomas Vise, son of Andrew Vise, gent.
Jeffery Lightwood.
Peter Hemes.

1603. Christenings.—Mary Vise, daughter of Andrew Vise.
Robert Heames, son of Francis and Margaret.
Wedding.– John Holme and Margary Dale.
Burials.—Mary Amyson.
Francis Roe.
Mary Huntback.
Ellen Roe.
William Wettwood.
Robert Webe.
Margaret Danyell.

1604. Christenings.—William Roe, son of Thomas and Ellen.
Elizabeth Iremonger, daughter of William and Dorothy.
Thomas Heath, son of William and Margery.
William Wetwood, son of William and Alice.
Margaret Roades, daughter of Francis and Katharine.
Anne Badnall, daughter of William and Ellin.
Simon Heyfield, son of John and Katharine.
Ellen James, daughter of William and Jane.
Robert Boone, son of Andrew and Anne.
Weddings.—Louis Davis, of the parish of Eglshall, and
Katharine Smalwood, of Whitmoor.
John Greenwood and Anne Aston.
Burials.—Robert Aston, late parson of Standon.
John Martin.
Robert Steedman.
Margaret Roade.
Ellin Vise.

Anno

1605. Christenings.—William Iremonger, son of William and
    Dorothy.

John Greenwood, son of John and Anne.

John Martin, son of Andrew Martin.

Weddings.—Randulph Cotton and Jane Martin.

William Goodwine and Ellen Morry.

Burials.—William Wettwood.

An infant of Frances Kendrick.

1606. Christenings.—Isabel Roe, daughter of Thomas and
    Ellen.

John Heath, son of William.

Edward Lewis.

Humphrey Lightwood, son of Thomas.

Weddings.—William Bond, of Ingstrey (Ingestre), and
    Mary Asply of Dunston, of Penridge.

Thomas Bissell of Aston and Joyce Aston of Standon.

Thomas Browning and Alice Hassall.

Robert Hudson and Jane Steventon.

1607. Christenings.—John Browning, son of Thomas and Alice.

Robert Greenwood, son of John and Anne.

Katharine Boughey, daughter of William Boughey.

Thomas Adams, son of Henry and Elizabeth.

Weddings.—William White and Margaret Potts.

William Machin and Jane Martin.

Randulph Wilkinson and Anne Wood, of Madeley.

Sampson Shelly, of Oulton, and Jane Lander.

Oliver Astley, of Bromley, and Margaret Smith, of
    Audly.

Burials.—Margery Ellkin.

Ellen Thorley.

John Lightwood.

Winifred Broughton.

Ann Thorley.

Thomas Heames.

Alice Blundall.

Anno

1608. Christenings.—Francis Martin, son of William and Jane.

Katharine Bound, daughter of Andrew and Amy.

Randulph Heyfield, son of John.

John Hall.

James Iremonger, son of William.

Thomas Coulclough.

Mary Roades.

Mary Aston, daughter of Walter Aston.

Burials.—Mary Aston.

Edmund Martin.

Weddings.— William Chetwind, son of John, and Margaret Fletcher.

Thomas Gaywood and Katharine Vyse.

1609. Christenings.—Katharine Heames, daughter of Frances Heames.

Elizabeth Mosely, daughter of Francis and Margaret.

Ellen Roe, daughter of Thomas and Ellen.

Kathrine Ffouke, daughter of Griphin and Elizabeth.

Thomas Maxfield, son of Peter and Elizabeth.

Sarah Hanly, daughter of Thomas.

John Gaywood, son of Thomas and Katharine.

Jane Dale, daughter of William and Anne.

Walter Aston, son of Walter and Alice.

Richard Dimmock, son of Margaret.

Weddings.—William Dale and Anne Owen.

William Stanilands and Frances Baker.

Sampson Cotton and Mary Wettwood.

Burials.—Anne Cooper.

An infant of William Iremonger, of Chattcill.

A poor man died in Cotes.

Margaret Caldwall, wife of Henry.

John Gaywood.

1610. Christenings.—Sarah Machin, daughter of William and Jane.

Alice Kendricke, daughter of John and Rachell.

Anno

1610. Christenings.—Francis Hall, son of John and Ellen.
Mary Lovitt, daughter of Robert and Joyce.
Elizabeth Boughey, daughter of William and Anne.
Alice Aston, daughter of Robert and Isabell.
Frances Chettwind, son of Attalanta.
Weddings.—Rowland Allen and Mary Cauldwall.
Thomas Hodson and Katharine Dimmock.
Burials.—Margaret Dale.
Alice Levitt.

1611. Christenings.—William Cotton, son of Sampson and
Mary.
Thomas Gaywood, son of Thomas (gent.) and Katharine.
Jeffrey Lightwood, son of Thomas and Frances.
Richard Butler, son of John and Jane.
Robert Dale, son of William and Anne.
Burials.—Frances Chettwind, son of Attalanta.
William Martin.
Anne Lightwood.

1612. Christenings.—Anne Heath, daughter of William and
Margery.
Mary Greenwood, daughter of John (clerk) and Anne.
Martin Machin, son of William and Jane.
Anne Adams, daughter of Henry and Elizabeth.
John Shropshere, son of Simon and Elizabeth.
Wedding.—Thomas Adamson and Margaret Dale.
Burials.—Anne Boughey.
John Heath.
Anne Heath.
Margaret Poole.
William Moorton.
Cassander Woulssley.
Jane Gaywood.
Martin Machin.
Robert Greenwood
John Fatherson

Anno

1612. Burials.—Robert Owen.
   Mary Moss.
   Margaret Cooper.

1613. Christenings. — Simon Holland, son of Simon of
      Congleton.
   Kathrine Hall, daughter of John and Ellen.
   John Grime, son of Jane.
   Mary Woodburne, daughter of Packet and Jane.
   Edward Moore, son of Edward of Uttoxiter.
   Jane Baylys, of Shelton.
   John Gaywood, son of Thomas and Katharine.
   William Machin, son of William and Jane.
   Anne Aston, daughter of Robert and Isabell.
   Anne Adamson, daughter of Thomas and Margaret.
   Margaret Cotton, daughter of Sampson and Mary.
   Robert Lea, son of Thomas Lea.
   Weddings.—Edward Moore and Katharine Minors.
   Humphrey Vise (gent.) and Elizabeth Aston.
   Burials.—Elizabeth Martin.
   Emma Martin.
   Alman, son of Thomas Alman and Jane.

1614. Christenings.—Elizabeth Martin.
   Mary Heath.
   Richard Harrison, son of Thomas and Anne.
   Sampson Dale.
   Weddings.—William Martin and Frances Adams.
   Francis Dayes and Anne Boulton.
   Burials.—An infant of John Kendrick.
   Robert Lea.
   Isabell Sharp.
   William Greenwood.

1615. Christenings.—William Shropsheire.
   William Adams.
   Ellen Lightwood.
   Andrew Vise.

Anno

1617. Christenings.—Robert Allman.
Thomas Smith.
Mary Roe.
Jane Martin.
Dorcas Jervis.
Katharine Iremonger.
Randulph Bagot, of Meer.
John Kendrick.
Anne Martin.
Weddings.—William Sandles and Jane Heath.
Burials.—Mary Heath.
Francis Lightwood.

1616. Christenings.—Margery Wettwood.
Clare Jackson.
Anne Greenwood.
Anne Lander.
John Eve.
Jane Madex.
Humphrey Aston.
Alice Coton.
Burials.—Francis Lightwood.
William Heyghfield.

1617. Christenings.—Humphrey Iremonger.
Mary Ffloyd.
Katharine Woodburne.
John Machin.
Thomas Dale.
Elizabeth Vise.
Henry Heath.
Edward Adamson.
Randulph Wettwood.
Elizabeth Martin.
Thomas Martin (buried same year).
Francis Clark.
Robert Jones.

Anno

1617. Weddings.—John Serjeant, of Bernard's Inn, gent., and
    Alice Prichet, of Parish of St. Albanes, London.
    Thomas Greatoulder and Margaret Greenwood.
    Thomas Barbor and Bettrice Allwitch.
    Burials.—Jane Coton,
    Walter Barbor (gent).

1618. Christenings.—William Lander.
    William Gascoyne.
    Robert Levit.
    Anne Reeve.
    Mary Snelsen.
    Katharine Vise.
    Burials.—Mary Dimock.
    Robert Levit.
    William Stanylands.

1619. Christenings.—Anne Kendrick, daughter of John and
    Rachell.
    Thomas Jonson.
    Thomas Allman, son of Thomas and Jane.
    Philip Aston, son of Robert and Isabel.
    Thomas Rowland, son of Thomas and Jane.
    Thomas Cotton, son of Sampson and Mary.
    Mary Cash, daughter of Jephrey, of Millmeece.
    Thomas Lander, son of Thomas and Anne.
    Weddings.—William Goodwin, of Meare, and Frances
    Stanyland (widow).
    Richard Bloore, of Audly, and Dorothy Wedwood.
    Burial.—John Moss.

1620. Christenings.—Robert Wettwood, son of John and Alice.
    John Vise, son of Humphrey (gent.) and Elizabeth.
    John Jervis, son of Thomas and Ellen.
    Elizabeth Bennet, daughter of Isabel.
    Elizabeth Greenwood,
    William Martin, son of William and Frances.
    John Badnall, son of Thomas and Clare.

Anno

1620. Christening.—Anne Woodburne, daughter of Packet and Jone.

Weddings.—William Wright of Modersall and Alice Moss.

Thomas Sanders and Margaret Dimock.

Burials.—John Vise, son of Andrew (gent.) and Elizabeth.

Thomas Lander, son of Thomas and Anne.

1621. Christenings.—Margaret Lander, daughter of Thomas and Anne.

Margery Adamson, daughter of Thomas and Margaret.

Anne Wright, daughter of William and Alice.

Elizabeth Levitt, daughter of Robert.

William Kendrick, son of John and Rachell.

Edward Vise, son of Humphrey (gent.) and Elizabeth.

Burial.—John Dale.

1622. Christenings.—Thomas Martin, son of William and Katharine, and buried same year.

Jane Machin, daughter of William and Jane.

William Badnall, son of Thomas and Clare.

Anne Steedman, daughter of Richard and Anne.

Wedding.—William Eardley and Mary Broughton.

Burials.—Edward Broughton.

William Mason,

Thomas Broughton.

William Wettwood.

1623. Christenings.—John Martin, son of William and Frances.

John Richardson, son of Roger and Letice.

Sampson Cotton, son of Sampson and Mary.

Mary Looyd, daughter of Humphrey, of Chatcill, and Anne.

Clare Twiss, daughter of Thomas and Elizabeth.

William Buttler, son of John and Jane.

Elizabeth Eardley, daughter of William and Mary.

Francis Hanly, son of John and Anne, of Mill Meece.

Wedding.—Thomas Twiss and Elizabeth Badnall.

Anno

1628. Burials.—William Martin, son of William and Frances.
Anne Kendrick, daughter of John and Rachell.

1624. Christenings. — John Martin, son of William and
Kathrine.
William Dale, son of William and Anne.
Andrew Wettwood, son of John and Alice.
Thomas Broughton, son of John and Anne, of Whittington.
William Jervis, son of John and Elizabeth, of Chattcill.
Rowland Wells, son of Margaret.
John Steedman, son of John of Meere and Alice.
Thomas Badnall, son of Thomas and Clare.
Weddings.—Ralph Massy and Mary Myles, of Nanytwich
(Nantwich).
Richard Phillips and Anne Taylor, of Stone.
Thomas Lightwood and Dorothy Gregory.
Burials.—Henry Heath.
Anne Levitt.
Anne Morry of Charnes.
Margaret Barnes.

1625. Christenings.—Randulph Bellingham, son of Thomas
and Mary.
William Wright, son of William and Alice.
Richard Badnall, son of Richard and Jane.
William Martin, son of William and Frances.
Richard Caddy, son of John and Ellen, of Stoke-on-Trent.
Ellen Twiss, daughter of Thomas and Elizabeth.
Anne Thorley, daughter of Henry and Margaret.
Frances Greenwood, daughter of John and Anne.
Mary Lander, daughter of Thomas and Anne.

1626. Christenings.—Thomas Eardley, son of William and
Mary.
Thomas Cooke, son of Thomas and Ellen.
Ellen Hanley, son of John and Margaret, of Chatcill.
Thomas Caudway, son of Elizabeth.

Anno

1626. Christenings.—Bridget Hanley, daughter of John and Anne, of Mill Meece.

John Heaford, son of Thomas and Anne Aspley.

James Badnall, son of Thomas and Clare.

Margery Bellingham, daughter of Thomas and Mary.

Burials.—Randulph Levitt.

Philip Hill (gent.).

Frances Linne.

Thomas Martin.

Alice Wettwood.

1627. Christenings.—Thomas Lycett, son of Francis and Elizabeth, and died the same year.

Thomas Vise, son of Humphrey and Elizabeth.

Anne Thorley, daughter of Henry and Margaret.

Kathrine Dale, daughter of William and Anne.

Humphrey Cotton, son of Sampson and Mary.

John Gervis, son of John and Elizabeth.

Anne Twiss, daughter of Thomas and Elizabeth.

Anne Martin, daughter of William and Frances.

John Licett, son of Francis and Elizabeth.

Mary Badnall, daughter of Richard and Joan.

Wedding.—Thomas Pope and Mary Sillvester, of Eagleshall.

Burials.—Randulph Wettwood.

Charles Iremonger.

Margery Wettwood.

Richard Badnall.

1628. Christenings.—Mary Martin, daughter of William and Katharine.

John Lander, son of Thomas and Anne.

John Pickin, son of John and Margaret.

Jane Hanly, daughter of John, of Chatcill, and Margaret.

Wedding.—Thomas Heamis and Frances Machin.

Burial.—Henry Caudwall.

Anno

1629. Christenings.— Elizabeth Wright, daughter of William
and Alice.

Elizabeth Gervis, daughter of John and Elizabeth.

Francis Kendall, son of John and Joan, of Aspley.

Joan Levitt, daughter of Robert and Joyce.

Ralph Eardley, son of William and Mary.

John Thorley, son of Henry and Margaret.

Francis Bellingham, son of Thomas and Mary.

Richard Badnall, son of Thomas and Clare.

Elizabeth Mason, daughter of John.

Wedding.—John Brookes, of Chesserdine (Cheswerdine),
and Ellen Moss.

Burials.—Andrew Broughton.

John Cooper.

Elizabeth Martin.

Francis Heamis.

John Thorley.

Letice Moreton.

Thomas Dale.

Elizabeth Lightwood

1630. Christenings.—Robert Wettwood, son of Robert and
Mary.

Humphrey Gervis, son of John and Elizabeth.

Ellen Kirk, daughter of Katharine, of Aspley.

Bridget Ridings, daughter of Richard and Anne.

Francis Robinson, son of William and Margery, of
Shelton.

William Vise, son of Humphrey (gent.) and Elizabeth.

John Glover, son of William and Bridget, of Slindon.

Kathrine Lander, daughter of Thomas and Anne.

Robert Cooke, son of John and Margery.

Weddings.—Thomas Beardmore and Clare Robinson.

John Lightwood and Mary Tomkinson.

Randulph Pounder and Anne Read.

Thomas Podmore and Mary Brisburge.

Anno

1630. Burials.—Thomas Bevington.

  Elizabeth Win, wife of Richard (gent.), of Pentramorgin.

  John Heamis, of Cotes.

1631. Christenings.—Elizabeth Hall, daughter of John and Elizabeth.

  Francis Heamis, son of Thomas and Frances.

  John Gervis, son of John and Elizabeth.

  Thomas Lightwood, son of John and Mary.

  George Bellingham, son of Thomas and Mary.

  Mary Badnall, daughter of Thomas and Clare.

  Robert Heath, son of Thomas and Mary.

  Weddings.—Robert Edwards and Anne Stasy.

  John Martin and Kathrine Bagnall.

  Edward Bradbury and Isabel Boone.

  Burials.—William Vise.

  William Cooke of Cotes.

  John Huntbach.

  Robert Cooke.

  John Evans.

  Margaret Hayes of Chatcull.

  Elizabeth Cooper.

  William Bettson.

1632. Christenings.—Elizabeth Twiss, daughter of Thomas and Elizabeth.

  Mary Eardley, daughter of William and Mary.

  Francis Reading, son of Richard and Anne.

  Mary Wright, daughter of William and Alice.

  Thomas Thorley, son of Henry and Margaret.

  Mary Vise, daughter of Humphrey (gent.) and Elizabeth.

  Mary Martin, daughter of William and Frances.

  Thomas Lander, son of Thomas and Anne.

  Joan Martin, daughter of John and Katharine.

  Weddings.—Robert Boone and Katharine Heamis.

  Robert Gregory and Frances Potter.

  William Cooper and Dorothy Lightwood.

Anno

1682. Weddings.—Richard Whittaker and Anne Ray.
    William Chesterton and Anne Adcock.
    Burials.—Margery Wettwood.
    Thomas Lightwood.
    Katharine Edwards.
    An infant of George Sadler and Elizabeth.
    Robert Wettwood.
    William Cooper.

1683. Christenings.—Edward Fforshome, son of William and
      Margaret, of Burslham (Burslem).
    Robert Chesterton, son of William and Anne.
    Elizabeth Madox, daughter of John and Margery.
    John Edwards, son of Robert and Anne.
    Thomas Heath, son of Thomas and Anne.
    Elizabeth Tilsley, daughter of John and Katharine, of
      Aspley.
    Mary Lightwood, daughter of John and Mary.
    Elizabeth Thorinwell, daughter of Dorothy.
    Mary Hall, daughter of John and Elizabeth.
    Andrew Kayiney, son of Daniel and Margery.
    Elizabeth Cooper, daughter of William and Dorothy.
    Burial.—Elizabeth Twiss, daughter of Thomas and
      Elizabeth.

1684. Christenings.—Elizabeth Boone, daughter of Robert and
      Katharine.
    Margery Heamis, daughter of Thomas and Frances.
    Margaret Riding, daughter of Richard and Anne.
    Humphrey Badnall, son of Thomas and Clare.
    Elizabeth, daughter of George and Margaret.
    Anne Martin, daughter of John and Katharine.
    Weddings.—John Browne, of Woore, and Katharine
      Gregory.
    Robert Heath and Mary Wettwood.
    Thomas Badeley and Ellen Roe.
    Henry Bloore and Anne Sebrid.

Anno

1634. Burials.—Andrew Vise, Esq.
Elizabeth Vise, daughter of Humphrey, Esq.
Margery Heamis, daughter of Thomas and Frances.
Margaret Aston (widow). ·
Clare Twiss, daughter of Thomas.
Anne Thorley, daughter of Henry and Margaret.
Henry Thorley, of Standon.
Thomas Roe, of Bowers.

1635. Burials.—Francis Martin, of Newcastle (gent.)
Mary Cotton, wife of Sampson Cotton.
Ralph Tomkinson, son of William.
Isabel Owen.
William Moss, of Aspley.
Christenings.—Thomas Wright, son of William and Alice.
William Eardley, son of William and Mary.
Daniel Kayiney, son of Daniel and Margery.
Bridget Vise, daughter of Humphrey and Anne.
Anne Edwardes, daughter of Robert and Anne.
Mary Cooper, daughter of William and Dorothy.
Robert Aston, son of John and Frances.
Wedding.—Thomas Willkins and Mary Roe.

1636. Christenings.—Thomas Heames, son of Thomas and
Frances.
Mary Roe, daughter of William and Elizabeth.
Elizabeth Heath, daughter of Thomas and Mary.
Richard Landor, daughter of Thomas and Anne.
Ursula Tilsley, daughter of John and Katharine.
Anne Boone, daughter of Robert and Katharine.
George Bowers, son of George and Elizabeth.
Jane Cradock, daughter of John and Ellen.
William Line, son of William and Anne.
Weddings.—Robert Berkin and Margaret Daye, of
Chatcull.
Thomas Bagnall and Elizabeth Walker.
James Ffenne and Isabel Lovatt.

o

Anno

1686. Weddings.—Peter Heyfield and Joan Bagnall.
Robert Parnor and Elizabeth Browne.
William Badnall and Alice Bagnot.
Burials.—William Trinder, servant to John Serjeant
(gent.)
Joan Machin, wife of William.
Elizabeth Vise, of Stawne Hall (widow).
Daniel Keyiney, son of Daniel and Margery.
Anne Broughton, of Staune Hall.

1687. Christenings.—Mary, daughter of Richard and Mary
Oulridg.
Peter Heyfield, son of Peter and Joan.
John and Martin, sons of John and Katharine.
John Riding, son of Richard and Ellen.
Sophya Vise, daughter of Humphrey and Anne.
Elizabeth Edward, daughter of Robert and Anne.
Elizabeth Buttler, daughter of Richard and Elizabeth.
Ursula Tomkinson, daughter of Ralph.
Anne Badnall, daughter of Thomas and Clare.
John Aston, son of John and Frances.
Anthony Ward, son of Anthony and Elizabeth.
Burial.—Ellen Cooke, wife of Thomas Cooke.

1688. Christenings.—William Roe, son of William and
Elizabeth.
William Twiss, son of Thomas and Elizabeth.
Robert Vise, son of Humphrey and Anne.
Dorcas Gervis, daughter of John, of Chatcull.
William Rowley, son of William and Thomasin.
Sampson Wright, son of William and Alice.
Elizabeth Palin, daughter of John and Anne.
Weddings.—William Kendrick and Anne Gostley.
Roger Low and Elizabeth Corbitt.
Burials.—Richard Dibdall.
Jane Badnall, wife of Richard Badnall.
Margaret White, wife of William.

Anno

1638. Burials.—Anne Adamson, daughter of Thomas.
Morgan Rogers.
Katharine Martin.

1639. Burials.—Elizabeth Palin, daughter of John.
Elizabeth Ffox, wife of John.
Margaret Heacock.
Dorothy Ashley, wife of John.
Christenings.—Elizabeth Heamis, daughter of Thomas
and Frances.
Mary Heath, daughter of Thomas and Mary.
John Heyfield, son of Peter and Joan.
Robert Levit, son of Thomas and Alice.
Andrew Cooper, son of William and Dorothy.
Sibill Williams, daughter of Eleanor.
Elizabeth Lightwood, daughter of John and Mary.
William Tomson, son of William and Ellen.
Elizabeth Aston, daughter of John and Frances.
Weddings.—John Martin and Anne Smith.
Sampson Dale and Mary Greatoulder.
Edward Adamson and Alice Greatoulder.
Randulph Wettwood and Ellen Greatoulder.

1640. Christenings.—Ellen Roe, daughter of William and
Elizabeth.
John Glover, son of John, of Aspley.
Anne Chesterton, daughter of William and Anne.
Robert Tagg, son of Robert and Margaret.
Robert Dale, son of Sampson and Mary.
John Dale, son of Lewis and Margaret.
William Dale, son of Thomas and Jane.
Ellen Badnall, daughter of Richard and Ellen.
Andrew Vise, son of Andrew and Elizabeth.
Robert Wettwood, son of Randulph and Ellen.
Burials.—Mary Dorington.
An infant of Thomas Badnall and Clare.
Robert Dale, son of Sampson.

Anno

1640. Burials.—Rachell Kendrick, wife of John.

Ellen Badnall, wife of Richard.

An infant of Thomas Levit.

William Badnall.

Margaret Adamson.

Anne Thorley.

Walter Flairly.

Jane Martin.

Weddings.—Thomas Bromley and Frances Pye.

Lewis Dale and Margaret Ashley.

1641. Christenings.—Anne Shropshire, daughter of John and Joan.

John Walker, son of Thomas and Kathrine.

Mary Boone, daughter of Robert and Kathrine.

Joan Hall, daughter of John and Elizabeth.

Edward Martin, son of John and Anne.

John Eardley, son of William and Mary.

Margaret Meate, daughter of Richard and Elizabeth.

Phillip Aston, son of John and Frances.

Elizabeth Levit, daughter of Thomas and Alice.

William Heyfeild, son of Peter and Joan.

Thomas Jervis, son of John.

Burials.—William White.

Margery Madock, wife of John, of Cotes Heath.

Edward Adamson.

An infant of Edward Jervis.

Mary Aston, wife of Robert Aston.

Wedding.—John Johnson and Joan Harding.

1642. Christenings.—Mary Cotton, daughter of William and Anne.

Deborah Roe, daughter of William and Elizabeth.

Dorothy Vyse, daughter of Andrew and Elizabeth.

Elizabeth Chesterton, daughter of William.

Alice Heath, daughter of Thomas and Mary.

Mary Shropsheire, daughter of John Shropsheire.

Anno

1642. Christening.—Thomas Levitt, son of Thomas.
Burials.—Elizabeth Short, wife of Robert.
Robert Dale.
Mary Boone, daughter of Robert and Katharine.
Thomas Adamson.
Anne Hall, wife of John.
Weddings.—Andrew Heath and Alice Adamson.
William Hoome and Margery Adamson.

1643. Christenings.—Jane Badnall, daughter of Richard.
Alice Badnall, daughter of Thomas.
Anne Harrison, daughter of Anne.
Thomas Blower, of Swinerton.
John Tomson, son of William and Ellin.
John Buttler, son of Thomas, of Aspley.
Mary Boone, daughter of Robert and Katharine.
Anne Aston, daughter of John and Frances.
Sampson Dale.
Thomas Key.
Anne Heamis.
William Hoome.
William Wettwood.
Burials.—Mary Martin, daughter of William and
Frances.
William Cooper.
William Hoome.
Weddings.—John Machin and Elizabeth Bradbury.
John Rowley, of Keel, and Margaret Berkins.
Randulph Bagnall and Joyce Gregory.

1644. Christenings.—Mary Martin, daughter of John and
Anne.
Thomas Heyfield, son of Peter and Joan.
Jane Machin, daughter of John and Elizabeth.
Tobias Browne.
Joan Heaford.
William Badnall, son of Richard and Ellen.

Anno

1644. Christenings. — George Vise, son of Andrew and
        Elizabeth.
        Thomas Butler, son of John, of Cotes.
        Burials.—John Heyfield.
        Katharine Heyfield.
        Thomas Vise.
        John Horsley.
        John Kendrick.
        Mary Lightwood.
        Weddings.—Jeremiah Hasles and Mary Plant.
        John Simpkin (married ; no other name).
        Thomas Hasshall and Ellen Lightwood.

1645. Christenings.—Robert Edwards, son of Robert and
        Anne.
        Elizabeth Banks.
        Alice Madocks.
        John Bayly.
        Mary Morris.
        Dorothy Dale.
        Anne Peake.
        Isabel Butler, daughter of Henry and Anne.
        Thomas Aston, son of John and Frances.
        Margaret Boone, daughter of Robert and Katharine.
        Burials.—Margery Birkins.
        Jane Butler.
        Margaret Heamis, wife of Francis.
        Mary Badnall.
        Weddings.—John Barton and Elizabeth Martin.
        John Sutton and Dorothy Cooper.

1646. Christenings.—William Hoome, son of William and
        Margery.
        Thomas Cotton, son of William and Anne.
        Elizabeth Clarke, of Yarnfield.
        John Hassall, son of Thomas and Ellen.
        William Machin, son of John and Elizabeth.

Anno

1646. Christenings.—Elizabeth Barton, daughter of John and Elizabeth.

John Heamis, son of Thomas and Frances.

Mary Rowley, daughter of William, of Cotes Heath.

Elizabeth Vise, daughter of Andrew and Elizabeth.

Elizabeth Martin, daughter of John and Elizabeth.

Burials.—John Hall.

William Short.

Ellen Badnall.

William Wright.

Anne Boone.

Mary Martin.

1647. Christenings.—James Read, son of Edward and Katharine.

Katharine Heyfield, daughter of Peter and Jane.

Jane Peak, daughter of John and Jane (baptised and buried).

Burials.—Joan Maddocks.

Mary Boone, daughter of Robert and Katharine.

1648. Christenings.—Isabell Aston, daughter of John and Frances.

Frances Chesterton, daughter of William and Anne.

Margaret Hashall, daughter of Thomas and Ellen.

Anne Hoome, daughter of William and Margery.

Thomas Badnall, son of James and Anne.

Andrew Boone, son of Robert and Katharine.

Burials.—Margaret Short, wife of William.

Thomas Roe, son of William and Elizabeth.

Robert Levite.

Ellen Roe.

Richard Jones, a "Traveller."

Clare Badnall, wife of Thomas.

Elizabeth Wright, daughter of William and Alice.

Thomas Thorley, son of Henry and Margaret.

Anno

1649. Christenings.—Sarah Peake, daughter of John and Jane.
Thomas Martin, son of John and Elizabeth.
Mary Vise, daughter of Andrew and Elizabeth.
Weddings.—William Bucknall and Elizabeth Jervis.
Robert Wettwood and Ursula Walter.
Burials.—Thomas Thorley.
Isabell Mills.
Ellen Cooke.
Anne Meredith.
William Cotton.
William Greenwood.
Margaret Kendall.
Mary Wright, daughter of William and Alice.
Thomas Martin, son of John and Elizabeth.
John Heatnis, son of Thomas and Frances.
Sarah Peak, daughter of John and Jane.
Packett Woodburne.

1650. Christenings.—Sarah Harding, daughter of John and
Cysley (Cicely).
Andrew Martin, son of John and Anne.
Anne Martin, daughter of John and Elizabeth.
Margaret Arnet, daughter of John, of Cotes.
Anne Badnall, daughter of James and Anne,
Mary Badnall, daughter of William and Elizabeth.
Frances Hashal, daughter of Jho. and Ellen.
Anne Wettwood, daughter of Randulph and Ellen.
Weddings.—Richard Heaford and Ellen Ridings.
Robert Burd and Anne Lander.
John Walker and Elizabeth Whittmoore.
Thomas Langley and Anne Bagnall.
Burials.—Margaret Sutton.
William Machin.
An infant of John Peake.

1651. Christenings.—William Wettwood, son of Robert and
Ursula.

Anno

1651. Christenings.—Sarah Machin, daughter of John and
Elizabeth.

Jane Read, daughter of Edmund and Margaret.

Ellen Badnall, daughter of Thomas and Elizabeth.

Elizabeth Hoome, daughter of William and Margery.

Ellen Peake, daughter of John and Jane.

Burials.—William Dale.

Thomas Badnall.

Ellen Wettwood.

Elizabeth Martin, daughter of John and Elizabeth.

Margaret Clarke, daughter of John.

Ellen Badnall, daughter of Thomas and Elizabeth.

1652. Christenings.—William Dale, son of Sampson and Mary.

John Martin, son of John and Elizabeth.

James Tomson, son of William and Ellen.

Elizabeth Badnall, daughter of William and Elizabeth.

Thomas Badnall, son of Thomas and Elizabeth.

Wedding.—Robert Walter and Anne Cotton (wid).

Burials.—Elizabeth Lin, wife of Thomas.

William Heath.

Rowland Allin.

Elizabeth Machin.

William Lin, son of William and Anne.

Isabell Butler, daughter of Henry and Anne.

Anne Dale.

Elizabeth Badnall.

John Sutton.

1653. Christenings.—John Ffoard, son of John.

Mary Roberts, daughter of Richard and Anne.

Randulph Wettwood, son of Randulph and Jane.

Walter Willsen, son of Walter and Jane.

John Badnall, son of James and Anne.

Mary Yeomans, daughter of Daniell.

William Walter, son of Robert and Anne.

Mary Wettwood, daughter of Robert and Ursula.

Anno

1658. Wedding.—Richard Snelson and Eleanor.
  Burials.—Katharine Martin, wife of William.
  John Butler of Cotes.
  Anne Martin, daughter of William and Frances.
  William Hoome.
  Alice Wettwood, wife of John.
  John Fooard, son of John and Katharine.
1654. Christening.—Thomas Vise, son of Andrew and Elizabeth.
  Weddings.—Abraham Wallis and Anne Snelson.
  Andrew Wettwood and Jane Toft.
  Burial.—William Martin.
1655. Christenings.—Elizabeth Willson, daughter of Walter
    and Joan.
  Jane Yeomans, daughter of Daniel.
  Anne Dale.
  Elizabeth Badnall, daughter of Thomas.
  John Machin, son of John.
  John Read, son of Edward.
  Jane Plant, daughter of Humphrey.
  Burials.—Joyce Levit.
  Alice Wright.
1656. Christenings.—Mary Wettwood, daughter of Randulph.
  Samuel Snelson, son of Richard.
  James Badnall, son of James.
  Jane Peake, daughter of John Peake.
  Anne Ffoard, daughter of John.
  Kathrine Martin, daughter of John.
  Samuel Levit, son of Thomas.
  Mary Eardly, daughter of Thomas.
  Dorothy Edwards, daughter of John.
  Thomas Nevill, son of Edward.
  Alice Wettwood, daughter of Andrew.
  William Eardley, son of Ralph and Mary.
  Burials.—Hester Snelson.
  Thomas Madocks, of Cotes Heath.

Anno

1656. Burials.—Edward Hashall.

Anne Roberts.

John Martin.

Katharine Broughton of Podmore.

Dorothy Edwards.

Alice Wettwood.

Sarah Machin.

1657. Christenings.—Edward Badnall, son of Thomas and Elizabeth.

John Naylor, son of Thomas and Margaret.

John Wettwood, son of Randulph and Jane.

Anne Wright, daughter of John and Anne.

1658. Christenings.—Mary Harding, daughter of John and Mary.

Charles Badnall, son of James and Anne.

Mary Edwardes, daughter of John and Anne.

Richard Eardly, son of Ralph and Mary.

Anne Martin, daughter of William and Anne.

1659. Christenings.—Joyce Fford, daughter of John and Katharine.

Clare Badnall, daughter of James and Anne.

Ambrose Badnall, son of Thomas and Elizabeth.

Thomas Wettwood, son of Randulph and Jane.

John Gregory, son of Robert and Anne.

Mary Naylor, daughter of Thomas and Margaret.

Mary Eardley, daughter of Ralph and Mary.

Benjamin Snelson, son of Richard and Elinor.

Burials.—Dorothy Sutton, widow.

Samuel Nevill, son of Edward and Elizabeth.

1660. Christenings.—John Cooke, son of Thomas and Anne.

Richard Shaw, son of Richard and Mary.

Alice Wright, daughter of John and Anne.

Elizabeth Harding, daughter of John and Mary.

Jane Martin, daughter of John and Elizabeth.

John Martin, son of William and Anne.

Anno

1660. Christenings.—Margaret Lander, daughter of Thomas
  and Alice.
  Thomas Tagge, son of Thomas and Mary.
  Burials.—John Madocks, of Cotes Heath.
  Robert Edwards, son of John and Anne.
1661. Christenings.—Ellen Thorley, daughter of John and
  Bridget.
  Dorothy, the daughter of Ralph and Mary.
  Anne Cooke, daughter of Thomas and Anne.
  Joseph Chesterton, son of Robert and Margaret.
  Thomas Lander, son of William and Margaret.
  Margaret Neylor, daughter of Thomas and Margaret.
  Weddings.—Francis Heamis and Anne Ward.
  Robert Heath and Elizabeth Cooper.
1662. Christenings.—John Harding, son of John and Mary.
  Elizabeth Cook, daughter of Thomas and Anne.
  John Badnall, son of James and Anne.
  Ursula Heath, daughter of Robert and Elizabeth.
  Martha Shaw, daughter of Richard and Mary.
  Frances Martin, daughter of John and Katharine.
  Susanna Heamis, daughter of Francis and Anne.
  Elizabeth Jones, daughter of Peter and Elizabeth.
  Andrew Badnall, son of Thomas and Elizabeth.
  Robert Gregory, son of Robert and Anne.
  Mary Wright, daughter of John and Anne.
  Weddings.—John Vise, son of Andrew and Elizabeth,
    and Jane Wootton, daughter of Thomas and Margaret,
    of Mill Meece.
  John Walker and Elizabeth Harrison.
  Burials.—Ellen Roe, daughter of William and Elizabeth.
  Richard Taylor, of Aulem (Audlem).
1663. Christenings.—Ralph Eardley, son of Ralph and Mary.
  Hester Snelson, daughter of Richard and Eleanor.

---

[1] This is entered so in the book.

Anno

1663. Christenings.— John Eardly, son of William and Elizabeth.

Joshua Mills, son of Robert and Mary.

Mary Baratt, daughter of Thomas and Sarah.

Anne Machin, daughter of John and Mary.

John Edwards, son of John and Anne.

John Thorley, son of John and Bridgett.

William Vise, son of John and Jane.

Elizabeth Shaw, daughter of Richard and Mary.

John Martin, son of John and Elizabeth.

Mary Jones, daughter of Peter and Elizabeth.

Weddings.—John Martin and Elizabeth Heamis.

John Machin and Mary Clarke.

Burials.—Richard Ffoard, son of John and Kathrine.

Ralph Eardly, son of Ralph and Mary.

Jane Robinson.

Joseph Hall.

Mary Baratt, daughter of Thomas and Sarah.

Anne Yardly, wife of William of Weston.

Daniell Yeomans.

Thomas Badnall, son of James and Anne.

1664. Christenings.—Mary Ffoard, daughter of John and Katharine.

William Harding, son of John and Mary.

Rebecca Martin, daughter of John and Elizabeth.

Ellen Cooke, daughter of Thomas and Anne.

William Chesterton, son of Robert and Margaret.

Thomas Lander, son of Thomas and Alice.

William Heath, son of Robert and Elizabeth.

William Lander, son of William and Margaret.

Robert Edwards, son of John and Anne.

Thomas Heamis, son of Francis and Anne.

William Martin, son of John and Katharine.

Humphrey Badnall, son of Thomas and Elizabeth.

Nathaniel Eardley, son of Ralph and Mary.

Anno

1664. Wedding.—William Palmer and Anne Heamis.
    Burials.—Elizabeth Martin, wife of John.
    Martha Shaw, daughter of Richard and Mary.
    Anne Machin, daughter of John and Mary.
    Anne Lander, wife of Thomas.

1665. Christenings.—Andrew Wettwood, son of Randulph
      and Jane.
    Mary Martin, daughter of William and Anne.
    John Martin, son of Edward and Sarah.
    Ursula Badnall, daughter of James and Anne.
    Dorothy Vise, daughter of John and Jane.
    Ralph Gregory, son of Robert and Anne.
    William Martin, son of John and Elizabeth.
    Anne Jones, daughter of Peter and Elizabeth.
    Francis Heamis, son of Francis and Anne.
    Robert Harding, son of John and Mary.
    Mary Chalton, daughter of Thomas and Jane, of
      Chatcull.
    Wedding.—John Stubbs and Ellin Gervis.
    Burials.—Anne Edwards, wife of Robert.
    Peter Heyfield.
    Mary Allen.
    Robert Heath.

1666. Christenings.—Mary Badnall, daughter of John and
      Margaret.
    Anne Shaw, daughter of Richard and Mary.
    Rachell Eardley, daughter of William and Elizabeth.
    Hannah Eardley, daughter of Ralph and Mary.
    Mary Cooke, daughter of Thomas and Anne.
    Sarah Ffoard, daughter of John and Katharine.
    Burial.—William Martin.
    Weddings.—William Preston of Drayton and Elizabeth
      Bibber.
    Philip Wotton and Dorothy Vise.
    Thomas Key and Mary Cotton.

Anno

1667. Christenings.—Wotton Vise, son of John and Jane.
Elizabeth Martin, daughter of John and Katharine.
Henry Edwards, son of John and Anne.
John Heath, son of Robert and Elizabeth.
Anne Lander, daughter of Thomas and Alice.
Margaret Gardenor, daughter of William and Elizabeth.
Margaret Chesterton, daughter of Robert and Margaret.
Thomas Wotton, son of Philip and Dorothy.
Anne Martin, daughter of John and Elizabeth.
Wedding.—Robert Grimly and Mary Cooper.
Burials.—Sarah Ffoard.
Jane and Rebecca Martin, daughter of John.
William Lander, son of William and Margaret.
Robert Short.
Andrew Wettwood.
Anne Cash, wife of William.
Robert Wettwood.
Frances Martin (widow).

1668. Christenings.—Jane Heyfield, daughter of John and
Elinor.
Thomas Cooke, son of Thomas and Anne.
Sarah Harding, daughter of John and Mary.
Andrew Martin, son of Edward and Sarah.
Dorothy Shaw, daughter of Richard and Mary.
Sarah Badnall, daughter of Thomas and Elizabeth.
John Ffoord, son of John and Katharine.
Andrew Wotton, son of Phillip and Dorothy.
Burials.—George Vise, son of Andrew and Elizabeth
John Wettwood, son of Randulph and Jane.
An unbaptised child of John Heath and Mary.
Elizabeth Eardly, daughter of Ralph and Mary.
Anne Holland, wife of William.
William Bagnall.
Dorothy Shaw, daughter of Richard and Mary.
John Martin, son of Edward and Sarah.

Anno

1668. Burials.—John Thorley.

Thomas Wettwood, son of Randulph and Jane.

Joan Heyfeild.

1669. Christenings.—Ellnor, daughter of John Goodman.

Mary Badyly, daughter of Henry and Mary.

Ralph Eardly, son of Ralph and Mary.

Simon Pyatt, son of Richard and Rose.

Elizabeth Eardley, daughter of William and Elizabeth.

Anne Heamis, daughter of Ffrancis.

Thomas Edwards, son of John and Anne.

Elizabeth Gregory, daughter of Robert and Anne

Jane Martin, daughter of John.

Weddings.—John Martin and Thomazin Rowly.

William Meadon and Anne Boone.

Burials.—Thomas Nevill, son of Edward and Elizabeth.

Elizabeth Hall.

Robert Aston.

Elizabeth Gregory,

1670. Christenings. — John Heyfield, son of John and
Ellener.

Ralph Chesterton, son of Robert and Margreat.

Anne Landor, daughter of William and Margreat.

1670. William Martin, son of John and Thomazin.

John, son of Henry Badely and Mary.

Margaret, daughter of John and Margaret Badnall.

Elizabeth Vise, daughter of John and Jane.

Dorothy Shaw, daughter of Richard and Mary.

Burials.—Joseph Harding, son of John and Mary.

Thomas Heath.

Robert Edwards.

Alice Heath, wife of Andrew.

Thomas Cooke, son of Thomas.

1671. N.B.—Only one entry, as follows: Margaret, ye daughter
of Thomas and Margaret.

Anno

1672. Christenings.—Debora Badely, daughter of Henry and Mary.

James Temson, son of George and Mary.

Kathrine Ffoard, daughter of John and Kathrine.

William Shaw, son of Richard and Mary.

Alice Cooke, daughter of Thomas and Anne.

Dorothy Edwards, daughter of John and Anne.

Dorothy Gregory, daughter of Robert and Anne.

Burials.—Edward Nevill, Rector of Standon.

Hester Snelson, daughter of Richard.

William Shaw, son of Richard.

John Barnes.

Humphrey Vise, son of Edward Vise.

Robert Grimley, son of Robert and Mary.

Elizabeth Tomson, from Charnes.

1678. Christenings.—Peter Heyfeild, son of John and Ellnor.

Margreat Heames, daughter of Ffrances and Anne.

Mary Crutchley, daughter of Gamalion and Dorothy.

John Vise, son of Edward and Elizabeth.

Thomas Grimley, son of Robert and Mary.

Mary Cartwrite, daughter of Edward and Isabell.

William Rowley, son of William and Anne.

John Badnall, son of John and Margreat.

Ffrancis Chesterton, son of Robert and Margreate.

Ellen Badely, daughter of Henry and Mary.

William Key, son of Thomas and Mary.

Mary, daughter of Elizabeth Aston.

William Eardly, son of William and Elizabeth.

Peter Jones, son of Peter and Elizabeth.

John Vise, son of John and Jone.

Elizabeth Blackman, daughter of Thomas and Alice.

Margreat Meat, daughter of William and Sarah.

Burials.—Mary, wife of Richard Shaw.

Thomas Lander.

Rose Pyat, wife of Richard.

P

Anno

1673. Burials.—William Lander, son of Thomas.

Thomas Levitt, son of Thomas.

Jane Hoome.

Anne Key, daughter of Thomas.

Weddings.—Daniell Alsager and Mary Vise.

James Read and Jane Bullock.

1674. Christenings.—John Butler, son of Thomas and
Mary.

William Tomson, son of George and Mary.

Mary Martin, daughter of John and Elizabeth.

Jeffrey Tilsley, son of William and Anne.

Thomas Davies, son of Thomas and Elizabeth.

Arthur Glover, son of Thomas and Mary.

Samuel Alsager, son of Daniell and Mary.

Burials.—Mary Martin, daughter of John and Anne.

Debora Badely, daughter of Henry and Mary.

Margreat Heamis, daughter of Ffrancis and Anne.

Mary Horsley.

Ellin Badely, daughter of Henry and Mary.

Thomas Heamis.

Wedding.—Andrew Boone and Alice Heath.

1675. Christenings.—Margreat Heyfield, daughter of John
and Elinor.

William, son of Andrew and Mary Beby.

Benjamin, son of John and Mary Harding.

Humphrey Vise, son of Edward and Elizabeth.

Jone Read, daughter of James and Jane.

John Levitt, son of John.

Andrew Edwards, son of John and Anne.

Sarah Rowly, daughter of William and Anne.

Elizabeth, daughter of Edward and Issabel Charter-
wright.

Humphrey, son of John and Jeane Vyse.

Margaret Heamis, daughter of Ffrancis and Anne.

Robt., son of Robt. Heath.

Anno

1675. Burials.—Alice Levitt.

John Levitt.

Richard Snelson.

Mary Badely, wife of Henry.

Ellin Badely, daughter of Henry.

William Roe.

Thomas Badnall.

Margreat Dearne.

Randulph Wetwood.

Anne Heamis, wife of Ffrancis.

Mary Eardly, wife of Ralph.

Ffrances Aston, wife of John.

John Aston.

Weddings.—Godfrey Fletcher and Elianor Snelson.

Joseph Turner and Mary Wetwood.

1676. Christenings.— Anne, daughter of Thomas Key and Mary his wife.

Anne, daughter of William and Eliza Yardley.

Thomas, son of Thomas and Dorothy Holme.

Mary, daughter of Andrew and Allice Boond.

Elizabeth, daughter of Gamaliel and Dorothy Cruchley

John, son of John and Margaret Low.

Sarah Meat, daughter of William and Sarah.

Deborah Joanes, daughter of Peter and Elizabeth.

Andrew Martin, son of John and Elizabeth.

John Read, son of James and Joane.

Burials.—George Tompson, son of William.

Mr. William Vyse.

Andrew Bond, son of Robert.

1677. Christenings.—Elizabeth, daughter of Edward and Elizabeth Vyse.

William, son of Thomas Glover and Mary.

Thomas, son of John Heifield and Elianor.

Elizabeth, daughter of Thomas and Elizabeth Chalton.

Anno

1677. Christenings.—Anne, daughter of Joseph and Mary Turner.

Elizabeth, daughter of John and Margaret Levitt.

Elizabeth, daughter of Thomas and Dorcas Jarvice.

Thomas, son of William and Elizabeth Lovatt.

Anne, daughter of Thomas and Sarah Wright.

Burials.—Mr. Humphrey Vyse.

Margaret Thorley.

Mrs. Elizabeth Vyse.

Elizabeth Hall.

Jane Taft.

Randulph Wetwood.

John Read.

1678. Christenings.—William Edwards, son of John and Ann.

Elizabeth Adams, daughter of Thomas and Mary.

Katherine Asson, daughter of Thomas and Margaret.

Humphrey, son of Ffrancis and Jane Heamis.

Anne, daughter of Michael and Dorothy Hoome.

Katharine, daughter of William and Elizabeth Gardener.

Thomas, son of Thomas and Mary Key.

William, son of Gamaliel and Dorothy Chrutchley.

Margaret, daughter of John and Jone Vyse.

Mary, daughter of Thomas and Mary Butler.

Burials.—Mary Heath.

Mary Eardley.

Elizabeth Adams.

Edward Read.

Sarah Wright.

1679. Christenings.—Margeret, daughter of William and Sarah Meat.

Andrew, son of Edward and Elizabeth Vyse.

John, son of Robert and Mary Grindley.

William Read, son of James and Jane.

Charles, son of Gerard and Elizabeth Launder.

Edward, son of John and Elizabeth Martin.

Anno

1679. Christenings.—Thomas Chalton, son of Thomas and
Elizabeth.

John, son of Willm. and Anne Rowley.

Burials.—Elizabeth, wife of Edmund Prichard.

Joane Read, daughter of Edward.

Elizabeth Badnall, wife of Thomas.

Edward, son of Thomas Badnall.

Timison, wife of John Martin.

Weddings.—Henry Baddeley and Mary Watson.

William Perkins and Anne Wright.

1680. Christenings.—Thomas, son of Thomas and Jane
Heamis.

Jane, daughter of Joseph and Mary Turner.

Jane, daughter of John Cooper.

Sarah, daughter of John and Elizabeth Martin.

William, son of John Heighfield.

Burials.—Margaret, wife of Thomas Aston.

Weddings.—George Wood and Catharine Barnes.

Thomas Wright and Alice Boone.

John Martin and Mary Tompson.

1681. Christenings.—Thomas, son of Thomas and Alice
Wright.

Dorothy, daughter of Gamaliel and Dorothy Crutchley.

William, son of Edward Vyse, of Bowers.

Thomas, son of John and Margaret Levit.

Benjamin, son of Francis Heamis.

Burials.—John Lightwood.

Mary, daughter of Thomas and Mary Roberts.

Weddings.—William Browne and Margaret Launder.

Samuel Alsager and Ann Beech.

John Barnet and Mary Walshall.

1682. Christenings.—Phillip, son of Phillip and Jone Asson.

Elizabeth, daughter of William and Anne Pirkins.

Jane, daughter of William Barnet.

Thomas, son of John Martin.

Anno

1682. Christenings.—Edward, son of Edward Corbet and
    Mary.
    John, son of Thomas and Alice Wright.
    George, son of William Rowley.
    Burials.—Richard Badenall.
    Elizabeth Goodman.
    John Smith.
    Sarah, sister of James and Edward Hill.
    Weddings.—Randle Standway and Jane Lownds.
1683. Christenings.—Mary, daughter of Samuel and Anne
    Alsager.
    Mary, daughter of Richard and Elizabeth Barnet.
    Anne, daughter of James and Isabel Badnal.
    John, son of John and Mary Holland.
    Samuel, son of William and Sarah Meat.
    Hellen, daughter of John and Hellen Heighfield.
    Anne, daughter of Thomas and Mary Roberts.
    Mary, daughter of Phillip and Jone Asson.
    Joseph, son of Joseph and Mary Turner.
    Elizabeth, daughter of Henry and Mary Baddeley.
    Sarah, daughter of William and Elizabeth Lovat.
    Burial.—Jane Stanway.
1684. Christenings.—Sarah, daughter of John and Elizabeth
    Levet.
    Thomas, son of William and Anne Perkins.
    James, son of James and Jane Reade.
    Jane, daughter of John and Mary Martin.
    Millecent, daughter of Thomas and Mary Roberts.
    Sarah and Mary, daughters of John and Mary Holland.
    Burials.—Margaret Wetwood.
    Elizabeth, wife of John Martin.
    Mrs. Elizabeth, daughter of Humphrey and Elizabeth
    Vyse.
    Weddings.—Phillip Hales and Margaret Wade.
    John Sneylome and Mary Naylor.

Anno

1685. Christenings.—Grissel, daughter of Mr. John and Mrs.
John Vyse.

Thomas, son of John and Mary Sneylome.

John, son of Edward and Mary Corbet.

William, son of John and Mary Holland—being about
7 years old.

William, son of Mr. William and Mrs. Ffelicia Vyse.

Jane, daughter of Thomas and Anne Heamis.

Elizabeth, daughter of Phillip and Jane Asson.

Burials.—Jane Wetwood.

Ursula, wife of Robert Wetwood.

Alice, wife of Richard Butler.

John Holland.

Margaret Eardley, daughter of William of Apsley.

William Lin, *alias* Chesterton.

Elizabeth Eardley, daughter of William of Aspley.

Samuel Alsager, *Rector.*

William Lovatt⎫
Thos. Naylor ⎬ *Churchwardens.*

1686. Christenings.—Joseph, son of William and Mary Meat.

Mary, daughter of John and Jane Shropshire.

Thomas, son of James and Isabel Bagnall.

William, son of Thomas and Mary Adams.

John, son of William and Ann Pirkins.

William, son of Thomas and Mary Adams.

Mary, daughter of Gamaliel and Dorothy Cruthley.

John, son of Michael and Jane Levit.

Katharine, daughter of James and Jane Reade.

Andrew, son of Mr. William and Mrs. Felicia Vyse.

William, son of John and Isabel Cooper.

Mary, daughter of John and Margaret Levit.

Burials.—William, son of William and Elizabeth Lovatt.

Mary, daughter of John and Margaret Bagnall.

William, son of John Martin de Bank.

Anno

1686. Weddings.—John Martin, widower, and Sarah Linne.

George Aston and Dorothy Hall.

Walter Wittington and Ellen Thorley.

1687. Mr. Thomas Hall and Mrs. Dorothy Vyse.

Burial.—Andrew, the son of Joseph and Mary Turner.

Christenings.—Elizabeth, daughter of Weston and Elizabeth Bayley.

John, son of John and Mary Martin.

Anne, the daughter of Henry and Mary Baddeley.

Dorothy, daughter of William and Elizabeth Lovat.

Mary, the daughter of Edward and Mary Corbit.

Elizabeth, daughter of Walter and Ellen Whittington.

Burials.—Thomas Aston, of Weston.

William Thompson, of Bowers.

Catherine, the daughter of James and Jane Read.

Phillip, son of Phillip and Joan Aston.

Mary, wife of Edward Corbit.

Weddings.—John Alman and Ursula Heath.

Daniel Levit and Anne Coutlove.

> Sam. Alsager, *Rector.*
>
> Thomas Key, } *Churchwardens.*
> Robert Heath, }

1688. Christenings.— John, the son of Mr. William and Mrs. Feeld Vyse.

Elizabeth, daughter of Walter and Ellen Whittington.

John, son of Thomas and Ellen Launder.

William, son of William and Anne Pirkin.

Edward, son of James and Jane Reade.

Mary, daughter of Michael and Jane Levit.

Elizabeth, daughter of William and Mary Launder.

Burials.—Old John Martin.

Richard Butler.

1689. Christening.—Mary, daughter of Thomas and Anne Heamis.

Burial.—Old Richard Roberts.

Anno

1689. Christening.—Ellen, daughter of Walter and Ellen
Whittington.

Wedding.—Charles Badnal and Ellen Tagge.

Christenings.—Elizabeth, daughter of Robert and Jane
Gregory.

Anne, daughter of John and Margaret Levit.

Mary, daughter of Thomas and Ellen Launder.

Elizabeth, daughter of John and Jane Cooke.

Ffrancis, son of Samuel and Ursula Nickson.

Thomas, son of William and Anne Rowley.

Elizabeth and Anne, daughters of John and Mary
Smith.

John, son of Phillip and Jane Asson.

1690. Christenings.—Sarah, daughter of Henry and Mary
Baddeley.

John, son of Ffrancis and Jane Heamis.

Ffelicia Vyse, daughter of Mr. William and Ffelicia.

Mary, daughter of Thomas and Mary Roberts.

Elizabeth, daughter of John and Mary Lowes.

Henry, son of James and Elizabeth Badnal.

Mary, daughter of Charles and Ellen Badnal.

Elizabeth, daughter of Michel and Jane Levit.

Matthias, son of Robert and Jane Gregory.

Burials.—Joseph, son of Thomas Avnel.

Mary, wife of Henry Baddeley.

Catharine, wife of Robert Boone.

John, son of Phillip and Jane Asson.

Philip Asson.

Mr. William Vyse.

1691. Burials.—Joseph son of William and Sarah Meat.

Ffelicia, daughter of Mr. William Vyse.

Anne, daughter of Margaret Launder.

Christenings.—Thomas, son of James and Jane Read.

William, son of William and Alice Lithgoe.

Anne, daughter of Samuel and Ursula Nixon.

Anno

1691. Christenings.—Thomas, son of John and Mary Smith.
William, son of William and Mary Launder.
Edmond, son of Phillip and Margaret Dean.
Wedding.—Mr. William Wright and Mrs. Ffelicia Vyse.

1692. Christenings.—Peter, son of Ffrancis and Jane Heamis.
John, son of Thomas and Elizabeth Wallelate.
John, son of Walter and Ellen Whittington.
Richard, son of Thomas and Mary Roberts.
Nicolas, son of William and Anne Pirkins.
William, son of James and Isabel Badnal.
Abram, son of John and Elizabeth Kinner.
Burials.—Margaret Levit.
Susanna Heamis.
William Pirkins, of Weston.
Mr. Edward Vyse.
Robert Wetwood.
Thomas Wright.

1693. Christenings.—Ellen, daughter of Thomas and Ellen
Lander.
Elizabeth, daughter of Peter and Eleanor Pirkins.
Elizabeth, daughter of Thomas and Elizabeth Wallelate.
Mary, daughter of William and Sarah Wetwood.
Anne, daughter of Charles and Ellen Badnal.
Mary, daughter of Robert and Jane Gregory.
Jane, daughter of Michael and Jane Levit.
Burials.—William Yardley, of Weston.
William Eardley, of Walford.
John Nayler.
Wedding.—Austin Tayler and Elizabeth Asson.

1694. Christenings.—Elizabeth, daughter of John and Mary
Smith.
Nathaniel, son of John and Olive Shelley.
John, son of Adam and Elizabeth Madders.
Elizabeth, daughter of William and Margaret Harding.
Elizabeth, daughter of William and Mary Heath.

Anno

1694. Christenings. — Walter, son of Walter and Ellen Whittington.

Thomas, son of Thomas and Elizabeth Wallclate.

William, son of William and Sarah Wetwood.

Burials. — Mr. Andrew Vyse, junior, de Handchurch.

Anne Glover, daughter of Thomas Glover de Rudge.

Margery, the wife of Thomas Arnet de Coates.

Catharine, the wife of George Hood.

Anne, the young child of Thomas Arnet, junior.

Alice, daughter of Thomas Butler.

Mr. Andrew Vyse, senior, de Walford.

1695. (c) Robert, son of Joseph and Mary Beley.

(c) Constantia, daughter of John and Mary Sergeant.

(w) William Morrey and Mary Steel.

(b) Thomas Key, of Aspley, and Weston.

(c) Peter, son of James and Jane Read.

(c) Thomas, son of Thomas and Ellen Lander.

(b) Ralphe, the young child of John Naylor.

(b) Elizabeth, the virtuous wife of William Lovat.

(b) Margaret Riddings.

(c) Ellen, daughter of John and Elizabeth Thorley,

(b) John, son of John and Anne Edwards.

(c) Mary, daughter of Thomas and Elizabeth Wallelate.

(b) Sarah, daughter of Thomas and Elizabeth Lander.

(b) Joyce, daughter of Thomas and Anne Badnall.

(b) John Cooper de Bidge.

(c) John, son of William and Margaret Harding.

(c) Hanna, daughter of John and Mary Smith.

1696. (c) George, son of Thomas and Rebecca Tompson.

(c) Robert, son of Robert and Jane Gregory.

(b) Thomas, son of Thomas and Anne Edwards.

(c) William, son of William and Anne Grindley.

(c) John, son of Peter and Margaret Heighfield.

N.B.—(c) signifies christened, (b) buried, (w) wedded.

Anno

1696. (c) Thomas, son of Charles and Ellen Badenall.

(b) John Wright, of Weston.

(c) Dorothy, daughter of Thomas and Mary Roberts.

(c) Bridget, daughter of Walter and Ellen Wittington.

(w) Peter Heighfield and Katharine Ffoard.

(c) William, son of William and Mary Heath.

(b) Thomas Heamis de Bent.

(w) George Birks and Anne Sweat.

(b) Francis Heamis (senior).

(b) Margaret Lander.

(c) Sarah, daughter of William and Sarah Wetwood.

(c) John, son of John and Elizabeth Thorley.

1697. (w) William Key and Sarah Arnet.

(b) Old John Arnet of Coates.

(b) Mary Tagg.

(b) John Edwards (sen.)

(b) Mary, wife of John Smith.

(b) Anne, the relict of Thomas Heamis.

(b) Robert Linn, alias Chesterton.

(c) Thomas, son of Peter and Katharine Highfield.

(b) Ursula, wife of William Wright of Asson.

(c) Joseph, son of Joseph and Anne Bayley.

(b) Andrew Edwards.

(b) Ellen, daughter of Thomas Lander.

(c) Thomas, son of Peter and Margaret Heighfield.

(b) Jane Martin.

(c) John, son of Joseph and Anne Harding.

1698. (c) John, son of William and Margaret Harding.

(w) John Smith and Rachel Eardley.

(w) John Ffoard and Margaret Snape.

(b) John Harding (junior).

(c) Anne, daughter of Michael and Jane Levit.

(b) Dorothy, daughter of Thomas and Mary Roberts.

N.B.—(c) signifies christened, (b) buried, (w) wedded.

Anno

1698. (b) Thomas Heighfield.

(c) Thomas, son of Thomas and Mary Glover.

(c) Mary, daughter of Walter and Ellen Whittington.

(b) Mr. John Vyse.

(c) Thomas, son of William and Anne Grindley.

(c) John, son of Margaret Badnall.

(b) Mr. Thomas Ffernyhough.

(w) Thomas Lander and Joyce Ffoard.

(c) Mary, daughter of John and Elizabeth Thorley.

(c) Humphrey, son of James Thompson.

(c) Rachel, daughter of John and Rachel Smith.

(c) Mary, daughter of William and Mary Healy.

(c) Jane, daughter of William and Elizabeth Baddeley.

(b) James Badnall, senior, de Brownes Bridge, and his wife Anne. (N.B.—This would be probably in Ootes Parish.)

1699. (c) Thomas, son of John and Margaret Ford.

(b) Isabel, daughter of Widdow Cooper.

(b) Elizabeth, wife of Robert Healy.

(c) John, son of Thomas Glover.

(b) John, son of Thomas Glover.

(c) Mary, daughter of William and Hannah Noel.

(c) Katharine, daughter of John and Rachel Smith.

(c) Peter, son of Peter and Katharine Heighfield.

(b) Thomas, son of Henry Baddeley.

(c) Elizabeth, daughter of Edward and Joane Adderley.

(c) Robert, son of William and Margaret Harding.

(c) Anne, daughter of Thomas and Joyce Lander.

(b) Mary Edwards.

1700. (c) Thomas, son of Michael and Jane Levit.

(b) Catharine, wife of John Ffoard.

(b) William Holland.

(b) Thomas Levit.

N.B.—(c) signifies christened, (b) buried, (w) wedded.

Anno

1700. (c) Margaret, daughter of Thomas and Elizabeth
        Walleslate.
    (w) Ffrancis Levit and Mary Billington.
    (c) Anne, daughter of Francis and Mary Heamis.
    (b) John Badnell.
    (c) John, son of Robert and Jane Gregerry.
    (c) Mary, daughter of Thomas and Mary Glover.
    (c) Margaret, daughter of Peter and Margaret Heighfield.
    (c) Catharine, daughter of John and Rachel Smith.
    (w) Mr. Sam Wilkinson and Mrs. Margaret Vyse.
    (b) Robert Tag.
    (b) Mrs. Dorothy Wootton.
    (b) Mrs. Jane Vyse (wid.).
    (c) Elizabeth, daughter of John and Elizabeth Thorley.
    (c) Mary, daughter of William and Mary Tompson.
    (c) John, son of John and Margaret Ffoard.
    (b) Thomas Glover.
    (b) Jane Meillerear.
    (c) Mary, daughter of John and Joane Collins.
    (b) Joane Asson.

1701. (c) Mary, daughter of John and Olive Shelley.
    (c) Elizabeth, daughter of William and Anne Yardley.
    (c) Thomas, son of William and Mary Heath.
    (c) Thomas, son of Walter and Ellen Whittington.
    (c) Rebecca, daughter of James and Rebecca Tompson.
    (c) Ffrances, daughter of Joseph and Anne Harding.
    (b) William Eardley, de Weston.
    (c) Anne, daughter of Robert and Elizabeth Edwards.
    (w) Richard Henney and Elizabeth Meeson.
    (c) Mary, daughter of Edward and Jane Adderley.

1702. (w) Thomas Green and Mary Boone.
    (b) Mary, daughter of Peter and Katharine Heighfield.
    (c) Ffrancis, son of William and Anne Grindley.

N.B.—(c) signifies christened, (b) buried, (w) wedded.

Anno

1702. (c) Thomas, son of Thomas and Anne Green.

(c) Mary, daughter of Will. and Margaret Harding.

(w) Thomas Key and Elizabeth Perkin.

(w) William Ffoster and Anne Roberts.

(c) Jane, daughter of Robert and Jane Gregory.

(c) John, son of John and Mary Badnel.

(c) John, son of John and Rachel Smith.

(c) Peter, son of Peter and Margaret Heighfield.

(c) Sarah, daughter of William and Sarah Key.

(c) Thomas, son of William and Mary Tompson.

(b) Old Robert Grindley.

1703. (b) Robert Bill.

(c) Sarah, daughter of Robert and Dor. Butler.

(c) Elizabeth, daughter of Robert and Elizabeth Edwards.

(b) Henry Baddeley.

(c) Katherine, daughter of John and Margaret Foard.

(c) Thomas, son of John and Elizabeth Thorley.

(c) William, son of Thomas and Elizabeth Key.

(c) Anne, daughter of Walter and Ellin Whittington.

(c) William, son of Thomas and Margaret Moss.

(b) Anne Gregory.

(c) Mary, daughter of John and Joyce Ffloyd.

(w) Charles Dabs and Margery Boone.

(b) Margaret Naylor.

(c) Anne, daughter of William and Mary Heath.

(c) Mary, daughter of John and Mary Badnall.

1704. (c) Elizabeth, daughter of W. and Mary Thomson.

(b) Old Phillip Asson.

(w) Thomas Leak and Anne Eardley.

(b) Anne Glover.

(c) Mary, daughter of Charles and Margery Dabs.

(c) Elizabeth, daughter of Ffrancis and Mary Heamis.

(b) Elizabeth Eardley.

N.B.—(c) signifies christened, (b) buried, (w) wedded.

Anno

1704. (c) Hanna, daughter of William and Margaret Harding.

(w) Robert Cotton and Eleanor Ridings.

(b) William Tompson.

(c) William, son of Peter and Margaret Heifield.

(c) Mary, daughter of Robert and Elizabeth Edwards.

(c) Thomas, son of Thomas and Elizabeth Key.

(c) Edward, son of Edward and Joane Adderley.

(c) Elizabeth, daughter of Walter and Ellen Whittington.

1705. (b) Old Katharine Martin.

(w) Richard Jenks and Margaret North.

(c) Sarah, daughter of John and Rachel Smith.

(c) Elizabeth, daughter of John and Eliza Bishop.

(c) Thomas, son of Thomas and Eleanor Moss.

(b) Thomas James (child).

(b) William Wetwood.

(c) Mary, daughter of John and Margaret Ffoard.

(c) William and Jone, son and daughter of Arthur and Hanna Glover.

(b) Edward Holling.

(c) Edward, son of John and Elizabeth Thorley.

(b) Dorothy, wife of Gamaliel Crutchley.

(b) Mary, daughter of William and Sarah Key.

(w) Walter Martin and Sarah Martin.

(c) Luke, son of John and Joyce Floyd.

(c) Thomas, son of John and Mary Badnell.

(w) Richard Moyle and Sarah Levit.

(c) Margaret, daughter of William and Mary Heath.

1706. (b) Margaret Lin.

(b) Thomas Wright.

(b) Anne Wallhal.

(c) Thomas, son of Richard and Sarah Moyle.

(b) Bridget Thorley.

(c) William, son of Walter and Sarah Martin.

N.B.—(c) signifies christened, (b) buried, (w) wedded.

Anno

1706. (b) Peter Heighfield.

    (c) Anne, daughter of Joseph and Anne Harding.

    (c) John, son of Robert and Elizabeth Edwards.

    (c) Anne, daughter of William and Mary Tompson.

    (b) Old Thomas Lander de Bent.

    (b) Thomas Priest.

    (c) Anne, daughter of Thomas and Anne Leake.

    (b) Margaret Heighfield.

1707. (c) Samuel, son of W. and Margaret Harding.

    (b) Margaret Dabs.

    (c) Mary, daughter of Thomas and Margaret Moss.

    (b) Mary Gregory.

    (c) Elizabeth, daughter of Arthur and Hanah Glover.

    (b) Anne Heath.

    (c) John, son of Dan and Joane Smith.

    (w) John Burges and Dorothy Lovatt.

    (b) Elizabeth Levit.

    (c) Thomas, son of Edward and Joan Adderley.

    (b) Sarah Morrey.

    (b) Mr. Samuel Alsager, late rector, departed this life, having been constant preaching minister thirty-six years, and was buried December 19th.

    (c) William, son of John and Margaret Fford.

    (c) Peter, son of John and Mary Badnall.

1708. (c) Mary, daughter of John and Mary Read.

    (c) Joyce, daughter of John and Joyce Floyd.

    (b) Thomas Cooke.

    (b) Jane Gregory.

    (c) Ann, daughter of John and Eliza Thorley.

    (b) John Foard.

    (b) Elinor Heighfild.

    (w) John Birch and Sarah Lovatt.

    (c) Jane, daughter of Walter and Elin Witting.

N.B.—(c) signifies christened, (b) buried, (w) wedded.

Q

Anno

1708. (c) Thomas, son of Thomas and Ann Leack.

    (c) Elin, daughter of William and Mary Thompson.

    (c) John, son of William and Mary Heath.

    (b) Ann Wright.

    (c) Thomas, son of William and Mary Glover.

    (b) Sarah Meat.

    (c) Elin, daughter of Thomas and Elin Freeman.

    (b) Jane Heamis.

1709. (c) William, son of John and Sarah Byrch.

    (w) William Hodgson and Catharine Milington.

    (w) Robert Gregory and Mary Shropshire.

    (c) Joseph, son of William and Margaret Harding.

    (b) Thomas Leak.

    (c) Mary, daughter of John and Millisant Wright.

    (c) Samuel, son of Peter and Margaret Highfield.

       Mr. William Vyse baptised, and his mother buried,
         October 27th.

    (c) Eliza, daughter of Thomas and Margeret Moss.

    (c) Mary, daughter of Robert and Mary Gregory.

    (c) William, son of Thomas and Ann Leak.

1710. (c) Thomas, son of John and Ann Key, of Milmeese.

    (c) Mary, daughter of Thomas and Eliza Key.

    (c) William, son of Mary and William Thompson.

    (b) Ellin Wittington (wife) and Walter Wittington.

    (c) Samuel, son of J. and Margaret Foard.

    (c) John, son of John and Joyce Floyd.

    (b) Isabell Badnall.

    (c) Elizabeth, daughter of William and Elizabeth Meat.

    (b) William Heighfied.

    (c) John, son of John and Sarah Byrch.

    (w) Mr. Capting (Captain) Buswell and Mrs. Honora
        Snead.

    (c) Ann daughter of John and Milleson Wright.

       N.B.—(c) signifies christened, (b) buried, (w) wedded.

Anno

1710. (c) John, son of John and Mary Read.

(b) Edward Cartwright.

1711. (c) Sarah, daughter of John and Sarah Heighfield.

(c) Ellen, daughter of Joseph and Anne Harding.

(c) Anne, daughter of William and Margaret Harding.

(b) Thomas Butler, of the parish of Eagleshall
(Eccleshall).

(b) Anne, daughter of William and Margaret Harding.

(c) Elizabeth, daughter of Mary Badnal.

(c) Samson, son of John and Elizabeth Thorley.

(c) Anne, daughter of William and Mary Key, of Aspley
in Eagleshall (Eccleshall).

1712. (w) Thomas Horton and Mary Roberts.

(w) James Birch de Stafford and Anne Hales.

(w) William Adams and Mary Smith.

(c) John, son of Richard and Ellin Shaw.

(c) Samuel, son of Samuel and Anne Glover.

(c) Anne, daughter of William and Margaret Harding.

(c) Jane, daughter of Walter Martin.

(c) John, son of John and Mellissant Wright.

(c) Thomas, son of William Meat.

(b) John Heath.

(b) Eliza, wife of James Badnall.

(b) Richard Horton (a child).

(b) Richard Shaw.

(b) John, son of Robert and Eliza Edwards.

(b) Anne Cooke.

(b) Robert Gregory, gent.

1713. (w) William Crutchley and Ellen Lancaster.

(w) Thomas Wright and Ann Machin.

(w) Edward Guilford and Jane Martin.

(c) Mary, daughter of William and Mary Glover.

(c) Ann, daughter of Robert and Mary Gregory.

N.B.—(c) signifies christened, (b) buried, (w) wedded.

Anno

1718. (c) William, son of John and Mary Badnall.

(c) Eliza, daughter of William and Ann Vyse.

(c) Elizabeth, daughter of William and Mary Adams.

(c) William, son of William and Ann Shaw.

(c) Mary, daughter of John and Eliza Walker.

(b) William Vyse, Esqre.

(b) Thomas Naylor.

(b) Jacob Snape.

(b) Alice Lander.

(b) Robert Edwards de Podmire (Podmore).

(b) Ralph Wild.

(b) Edward Tombes.

1714. (c) William, son of John Stevens de Chalton.

(c) Thomas, son of Thomas and Mary Horton.

(c) William, son of William and Ellen Crutchley.

(b) Thomas, son of William Meat.

(b) John, son of John and Joyce Lloyd.

(b) Ellen, daughter of Joseph and Ann Harding.

(c) Samuel, son of William Clewley de Chalton.

(c) Marmaduke, son of John and Joyce Lloyd.

(c) John, son of Elizabeth Farmer.

(b) Thomas Roberts.

(b) Mary Gilbert.

(b) George Watkin.

(b) James Read.

(c) Sarah, daughter of Robert and Elizabeth Edwards.

(b) Mr. Thomas Lovatt of Cotwallton.

(c) William, son of William and Elizabeth Meat.

1715. (c) Thomas, son of Steven and Ann Forrest.

(b) John Heighfield, junior.

(w) Henry Buckley and Kathrine Heighfield.

(w) John Deville and Eliza Cartwright.

(w) Thomas Maddows and Mary Downward.

N.B.—(c) signifies christened, (b) buried, (w) wedded.

Anno

1715. (c) Thomas, son of William and Mary Adams.

(w) Benjamin Lewis and Margaret Wrottesley.

(c) John, son of William and Ellen Crutchley.

(c) Margaret, daughter of Samuel and Ann Glover.

(c) Thomas, son of John and Millesent Wright.

(w) Robert Ashley and Eliza Smith.

(c) William, son of James and Mary Martin.

1716. (c) Richard, son of Thomas and Mary Horton.

(b) Thomas Smith.

(b) John Smith.

(c) Thomas, son of Charles and Mary Keen,

(c) Ann, daughter of William and Ann Vyse.

(c) William, son of John and Elizabeth Keen de Cotes.

(c) Randle, son of John and Mary Stevens de Charlton.

(c) Walter, son of Walter and Sarah Martin.

(b) William Dean.

(b) John Harding of Walford.

(b) Thomas Kettle.

(b) John Jones.

(b) William, son of John Foard.

(b) Mary Wetwood.

(w) Samuel Heath and Margery Williams.

(w) John Scave and Darcos Stringer.

(w) John Whellenhall and Mary Crutchley.

1717. (c) Elizabeth, daughter of Edward and Ellin Berks.

(c) Richard, son of Adam and Mary Emery of Cotes.

(c) Gemaliel, son of William and Ellin Crutchley.

(c) Mary, daughter of William and Mary Adams.

(c) Mathias, son of Mathias and Mary Gregory.

(c) Mary, daughter of William and Ann Shaw.

(c) Millicent, daughter of William and John Wright.

(c) Sarah, daughter of William and Elizabeth Meat.

(c) John, son of William and Alice Cooper.

N.B.—(c) signifies christened, (b) buried, (w) wedded.

Anno

1717. (b) Widdow Watkin.

    (b) John Levitt of Gostilee.

    (b) Mary Farmer.

    (b) Thomas Adams,

    (b) Widdow Edwards.

    (b) John Riddings.

    (b) Sarah, daughter of Thomas Wilde of Cotes.

    (b) John Eardley from Southwarke.

    (w) Richard Walhall and Ann Sparrow.

    (w) John Mossgrave and Margaret Walker.

1718. (c) John, son of Thomas and Mary Horton.

    (c) John Boulton of Aspley.

    (c) Sarah, daughter of Samuel and Ann Glover.

    (b) Mary Martin.

    (w) John Wiske and Mary Snelome.

    (w) Thomas Bood and Mary Postons.

    (b) Sarah, daughter of William and Eliza Meat.

    (b) Mary Badnall.

    (b) William Chesterton.

    (b) William Wetwood.

    (b) Mary, daughter of John and Millicent Wright.

    (b) Richard Cliff.

    (b) Sarah Martin.

    (b) Ann Shaw.

    (b) Rachel Smith.

    (b) Mrs. Felicia Wright.

    (c) Mary Butler of Aspley.

    (c) Andrew, son of William and Ann Vyse.

    (c) Joseph, son of Joseph and Ann Wootton.

    (c) Joseph Thomas of Chatcull.

    (w) Thomas Warton and Jane Levitt.

    (w) Samuel Dugard and Ester Vyse.

1719. (c) Mary Martin, daughter of James and Mary.

N.B.—(c) signifies christened, (b) buried, (w) wedded.

Anno

1719. (c) Joseph Myott, son of William and Elizabeth.

(c) Walter Turner, son of Robert and Helen.

(c) Stephen Forrest, son of Stephen and Sarah.

(c) Thomas Farmer, son of Elizabeth.

(c) John Knight, son of John and Sarah.

(b) Sarah Arnett of Cotes.

(b) Anne Perkin.

(b) Mary Hues, daughter of John and Elizabeth.

(b) Thomas Key of Weston.

(b) Walter Whittington, junior.

(b) Elizabeth Adams.

(b) William Abell of Aspley.

(b) Michael Levitt.

(w) John Heighfield and Sarah Blakemore.

(w) Thomas Ash and Dorothy Ashley.

1720. July 28rd. William Jervis, A.M., was inducted into the rectory of this church by Mr. Thomas Allen, rector of Stoke-upon-Trent.

(b) Mr. Andrew Vyse, late rector of this church.

(c) Rachel, daughter of William and Mary Adams.

(c) John, son of John and Sarah Heyfield.

(b) Rachel Adams (late baptised).

(c) Mary, daughter of Thomas and Jane Warton.

(c) Mary, daughter of Thomas and Mary Hourghton.

(b) Eleanor Davy.

(c) Richard, son of John and Melicent Wright.

(c) John, son of Joseph and Elizabeth Lovatt of Chatcull.

(b) Mary, wife of Roger Wilbraham, of Madeley Mannour, Esq., daughter of Mr. Samuel Alsager, late rector of this church.

(w) William Freakley and Mary Shelley (banns).

1721. Born.—William, son of William Miller and Winefride, "*Recusants.*"

N.B.—(c) signifies christened, (b) buried, (w) wedded.

Anno

1721. (c) William, son of William and Ann Vyse.

 (c) John, son of Walter Martin and Sarah.

 (c) John, son of Joseph and Anne Wotton.

 (c) Elizabeth, daughter of William and Ellen Crutchley.

 (b) Ellen, daughter of John Thorley.

 (b) Dorothy, wife of Gilbert Lewen.

 (c) Anne, daughter of William and Mary Adams.

 (b) Mr. Phillip Wotton of Sugnell.

 (b) Elizabeth, wife of John Turner.

 (c) Robert, son of Matthias and Mary Gregory.

 (b) Anne, daughter of John Turner.

 (c) Anne, daughter of William and Mary Freakley.

 (b) Elizabeth Knight (an infant).

 (b) Matthias Gregory, son of Matthias,

 (w) Thomas Salt and Deborah Linguard (license).

 (c) Mary, daughter of Peter and Hannah Heyfield.

 (b) Stephen, son of Stephen Forrest.

 (w) John Yates and Mary Whittington.

 (b) Jane, wife of Thomas Warton.

 (b) Alice, wife of Edward Rylands of Norbury.

 (b) John Levett.

 (w) John Lovatt and Katharine Ford.

 (b) Alice Barker.

 (w) Francis Taylor and Sarah Heyfield.

 (b) Thomas Thorley.

 (b) John, son of William Heath.

1722. (b) Edward Wright.

 (b) Thomas Aston.

 (c) Elizabeth, daughter of Moses and Elizabeth Lassels
   of Cotes.

 (b) Anne Alsager, relict of Mr. Samuel Alsager.

 (b) Mary Heighfield.

 (c) John, son of Stephen and Anne Forrest.

 N.B.—(c) signifies christened, (b) buried, (w) wedded.

Anno

1722. (b) Anne Grindley, wife of William Grindley.

(c) John, son of John and Mary Yates.

(c) Roger, son of William and Ellen Crutchley.

(c) Thomas, son of Samuel and Anne Glover.

(c) Robert, son of William and Anne Bedson.

(b) George Wood of Cotes.

(c) Thomas, son of Thomas and Mary Warton.

1723. (c) Abraham, son of Walter and Sarah Martin.

(b) Charles Badnall.

(c) Elizabeth, daughter of William and Mary Adams.

(c) George, son of John and Dorothy Burgess.

(c) Joseph, son of John and Dorothy Burgess.

(b) Gilbert Lewen.

(c) Sarah, daughter of John and Sarah Heyfield.

(c) Thomas, son of Thomas and Ellen Badnall.

(b) Thomas, son of Thomas and Ellen Badnall.

(b) Joseph, son of John and Dorothy Burgess.

(c) John, son of John and Anne Walton.

(c) Anne, daughter of Richard and Catharine Cliffe of Cotes.

(c) William, son of John and Sarah Day of Cotes,

(w) William Heath and Mary Bachelour.

(c) Henry, son of William and Elizabeth Myott.

(b) Elizabeth, daughter of Richard Cliffe of Cotes.

(c) Mary, daughter of William and Mary Freakley.

(c) Mary, daughter of Thomas and Elizabeth Tompson.

(c) Anne, daughter of James and Mary Martin.

(b) Anne, wife of William Littleton of High Offley.

1724. (c) Mary, daughter of John and Melicent Wright.

(c) Edward, son of Thomas and Eleanor Ward of Chatkyll.

(c) Richard, son of Samuel and Anne Glover.

(w) Francis Underwood and Mary Shelley.

N.B.—(c) signifies christened, (b) buried, (w) wedded.

Anno

1724. (b) Mary, wife of Thomas Perkin of Mere.

(b) William Webb, of Handley Green, in Stoke parish.

(b) Mary Adams (widow).

(c) Ellen, daughter of Thomas and Ellen Badnall.

(b) Elizabeth Vyse, widow of Edward Vyse.

(c) Elizabeth, daughter of Robert and Jane Shelley of Chatcull.

(b) Mary Harding (widow)

(c) Joan, daughter of Thomas and Mary Warton.

(c) Jane, daughter of Matthias and Mary Gregory.

(b) John Wright.

(c) Thomas, son of John and Mary Yates.

(c) Moses, son of Moses and Elizabeth Lassels of Cotes.

(c) Mary, daughter of William and Mary Heath.

(c) Jane, daughter of John and Anne Simpkin of Slindon.

1725. (b) Ellen, wife of George Taylor.

(b) Ellen, daughter of Thomas Badnall.

(w) William Key and Mary Plant.

(c) William, son of John and Anne Walton.

(b) Anne, wife of Stephen Forrest.

(c) Elizabeth, daughter of William and Anne Bedson.

(b) Sarah, wife of William Key of Aspley.

(c) John, son of John and Mary Thorley.

(c) Hannah, daughter of Francis and Mary Underwood.

(b) Thomas Cooke of Morefield Green (Cotes).

(c) Margaret, daughter of William and Mary Freakley.

(c) Thomas, son of Thomas and Elizabeth Tompson.

(w) John Gregory and Mary Hodgkin.

(b) Robert Edwards.

(c) Mary, daughter of Samuel and Anne Glover.

(b) John Perkin.

1726. (c) William, son of William and Mary Key.

(c) William and Joan, children of William and Mary Adams.

N.B.—(c) signifies christened, (b) buried, (w) wedded.

Anno

1726. (b) Mary Key of Aspley (widow).

(c) Ralph Chesterton *alias* Lynne.

(c) John, son of Thomas and Elizabeth Lithgow of Swinshead.

(c) Jane, daughter of John and Sarah Bagnall of Mill Meese.

(c) Dorothy, daughter of William and Ann Vyse.

(b) John Smith of Shortwood.

(b) Thomas, son of Fennyhouse and Rachel Green of Lapley.

(b) Edward, son of John and Dorothy Burgess.

(c) John, son of John and Anne Keene of Slindon.

(b) John, son of Richard and Sarah Craddock of Ankerton.

(b) Ellen Deakyn, at Broughton, of this parish.

(b) James Badnall.

(b) Mary Roberts.

(b) Ellen Badnall.

(c) Edward, son of Thomas and Ellen Badnall.

(b) Sarah, wife of Francis Taylor.

(b) John Marten.

(w) William Hewet and Jane Baddiley.

(b) John Heyfield, sen., of Bowers.

(c) Dorothy, daughter of John and Mary Gregory.

(b) John Badnall of Cheswardine, late of Walford.

(c) John, son of Thomas and Mary Warton.

(c) Thomas, son of John and Sarah Day of Cotes.

(c) Robert, son of Robert and Alice Gregory.

1727. (b) Peter Almond.

(b) John Wright of Bowers.

(b) Anne Parton, daughter of Thomas of Ashley.

(c) John, son of Richard and Catharine Cliffe of Cotes.

(b) William Lovatt.

N.B.—(c) signifies christened, (b) buried, (w) wedded.

Anno

1727. (c) William, son of William and Mary Heath, jun.

 (c) John, son of Ralph and Frances Pilsbury of Mill Meece.

 (b) Katharine, wife of Henry Buckley.

 (b) John Read.

 (b) Robert Heath, in 96 year of his age.[1]

 (b) John, son of James and Mary Martin.

 (c) John, son of Francis and Mary Underwood.

 (b) Thomas, son of Thomas and Mary Warton.

 (b) Isabell Cartwright.

 (b) Mary, wife of William Heath, sen.

 (b) William Heath, sen.

 (b) Alice Wright.

 (b) Anne Shropshire of Wetwood.

 (b) Walter Whittington.

 (b) John, son of Francis and Mary Underwood.

 (c) Mary, daughter of John and Sarah Heyfield.

 (b) John, son of John and Mary Thorley.

 (c) Sarah, daughter of Thomas and Elizabeth Tompson.

 (b) Elizabeth Gardiner of Cotes.

 (c) Elizabeth, daughter of Joseph and Margaret Cappock (travellers).

 (b) Joan, daughter of William and Mary Adams.

 (c) Sarah, daughter of Moses and Elizabeth Lassels of Cotes.

 (b) Thomas Lander of Kingstone, late of Bowers.

 (c) Thomas, son of William and Mary Key.

1728. (c) Ellen, daughter of William and Anne Bedson.

 (b) Elizabeth, daughter of William Myott.

 (b) Ellen, wife of Thomas Badnall.

N.B.—(c) signifies christened, (b) buried, (w) wedded.

[1] Robert Heath would have lived in the reigns and during—Charles I., the Commonwealth, Charles II., James II., William and Mary, Anne, and George I.

Anno

1728. (b) Edward, son of Thomas and Ellen Badnall.

(c) Elizabeth, daughter of William and Mary Freakley.

(b) Mary, daughter of John and Sarah Heyfield.

(b) Dorothy, daughter of John and Mary Gregory.

(b) Gamaliel Crutchley.

(b) Thomas Hall, servant to Mr. Shelley, Cotes.

(b) John, son of Edward Cooper of Wetwood.

(w) Peter Read and Mary Abel.

(b) Mr. Daniell Nevill.

(c) Anne, daughter of John and Elizabeth Niklyn.

(b) Thomas Arnett of Cotes.

(b) Sampson, son of John Thorley.

(b) Mary Lister, daughter of Sarah Lister (widow).

(b) Rebecca Wildblood of Wetwood.

(w) Joseph Wilkes and Elizabeth Edwards.

(b) Anne, daughter of William Key of Aspley.

(c) Thomas, son of William and Anne Vyse.

(b) Richard Cliffe of Cotes.

(b) Elizabeth Tombes of Tittensor.

(b) Anne Shelley of Eccleshall parish.

(b) Nathaniel Shelley.

(c) Edward, son of John and Mary Thorley.

(b) Dorothy, daughter of William and Anne Vyse.

(b) Ellen, daughter of William and Anne Bedson.

(b) William, son of William and Mary Adams.

(b) William Myott.

1729. (b) Anne Blakeman (widow).

(c) Mary, daughter of Francis and Mary Underwood.

(w) Thomas Blakeman and Margaret Hand.

(b) William Crutchley of Bowers Bent.

(c) Sarah, daughter of William and Mary Adams.

(b) James Martin.

(b) Elizabeth Chesterton.

N.B.—(c) signifies christened, (b) buried, (w) wedded.

Anno

1729. (b) Andrew Martin.

    (b) Joan, wife of Edward Adderley.

    (c) John, son of Robert and Alice Gregory.

    (c) Sarah, daughter of William and Hannah Hall.

    (b) John Ford.

    (b) Stephen Forrest, at Meare.

    (b) Anne, wife of Mr. Williams Roberts of Walford.

    (b) Mary Key, sister of William Key of Weston.

    (c) Ellen, daughter of Peter and Mary Read.

    (w) William Bayley of Shelton and Mary Blower of Stoke.

    (b) John Thorley.

    (w) William Powner of Trentham and Mary Colley of Beech.

    (b) John Peake.

    (b) Mary, daughter of William and Mary Smith.

    (b) William Gardiner.

    (b) Margaret Ford.

    (b) John Ford.

    (b) Mary Heath.

    (b) William Heath.

    (b) William Key of Aspley.

    (b) Eliza Meat.

    (c) Eliza, daughter of John and Mary Gregory.

    (c) Jane, daughter of William and Ann Bedson.

    (b) Mary, daughter of John and Mary Yates of Eccleshall.

The Revd. William Jervis, rector of Standon and Swinerton, and prebend of Cloughton, *alias* Ufton, in the county of Warwick, and in Commission of the Peace for the county of Stafford, died at Standon, Oct. 26th, and was buried in the Lord's Chancel at Cheswardine, Oct. 29th, 1729, in the 36th year of his age. Was eldest son of Henry Jervis of the Hill, in Cheswardine parish, and Ffrances his wife, who

N.B.—(c) signifies christened, (b) buried, (w) wedded.

Anno

was sister to John Jervis of Darlaston, Esqr. He
was a man of great learning, universall charity,
learned in physick and practised it much to his poor
neighbours and friends' advantage, being commonly
termed the friend of mankind whose study was to do
good. (See chapter V.)

1729. (b) Thomas Peake.

1780. (c) William, son of William and Mary Smith.

(b) Peter Heighfield.

(w) John Beckit and Mary Norris.

William Jorden, B.D., was inducted into ye rectory of
this church by ye Revd. Dean Allen, Dec. 12th, 1729.

(c) Edward Peate, son of Griffith and Mary.

(b) Ann Heamis.

(b) Edward Adderly.

(b) Francis Heamis.

(b) Margaret, daughter of William and Mary Freakley.

(c) George, son of George and Hannah Taylor.

(c) John, son of John and Elizabeth Cartwright.

(c) George, son of William and Ann Vyse.

1781. (b) John Cliffe, of Cotes.

(c) Ann, daughter of John and Martha Plant.

(c) Ann, daughter of Thomas and Elizabeth Thompson.

(c) Mary, daughter of John and Sarah Highfield.

(b) Mary, daughter of John and Ann Eccles, of Newcastle.

(b) Jane Read.

(b) Mary, daughter of George and Ellen Penlington.

(c) William, son of Moses and Eliza Lassels, of Eccleshall.

(b) Mary, daughter of Thomas and Elizabeth Wilde, of
Cotes.

(b) Mary Griffiths, of Ashley.

N.B.—(c) signifies christened, (b) buried, (w) wedded.

Anno

1781. (c) Mary, daughter of Robert and Alice Gregory.

(b) Elizabeth, wife of John Cartwright.

(c) Robert, son of Griffith and Mary Peat.

(c) Mary, daughter of Robert and Mary Harding.

(b) William Adams, of ye Bent.

(b) Eliza Ligo, of Eccleshall.

(w) George Swift, of ye parish of Chebsey and Ann Wooldridge, of ye parish of Seighford.

(c) Mary, daughter of Thomas and Mary Shelley.

(b) Catharine Cliffe, of Cotes Heath.

1782. (b) John Turner, from Standon Hall.

(c) Mary, daughter of George and Ellen Penlington (or Perlington).

(b) Henry Hatchet, of Croxhall.

(c) Josiah, son of Thomas and Rebecca Embrey, of Cotes.

(c) Thomas, son of Francis and Mary Underwood.

(c) Sarah, daughter of John and Mary Gregory,

(c) Ellen, daughter of William and Mary Freakley.

(b) Ellen, wife of Edward Berks.

(w) Thomas Unite (or White), of Drayton, Salop, and Ann Stevenson, of Stoke-on-Trent.

(b) Joseph Harding, of Walford.

(c) Thomas, son of George and Hannah Taylor.

(c) Mary, daughter of John and Mary Thorley.

(b) Thomas, son of George and Hannah Taylor.

(w) John Lindop, of Asprey, Chester, and Elizabeth Baddeley.

(w) John Read and Mary Green, of Stone.

(c) Edward, son of William and Ann Vyse.

(c) John, son of John and Martha Plant, of the Rudge.

(b) Mary, wife of William Key, of Weston.

N.B.—(c) signifies christened, (b) buried, (w) wedded.

Anno

1783. (c) Ann, daughter of Thomas and Mary Wharton.

(b) John Martyn.

(c) William, son of Thomas and Elizabeth Thompson.

(c) Thomas, son of Henry and Ann Hodgkins.

(c) William, son of Peter and Mary Read.

(b) Jane Hickenbottom, of Drayton.

(b) Oliffe, wife of John Shelley.

William Jorden, B.D., did resign the rectory of Standon, Oct. ye 18th, 1783, to William Vyse.

(w) Edward Thorley and Sarah Astbury, of Chebsey.

(c) Thomas, son of John and Mary Read.

(c) Mary, daughter of John and Elizabeth Lindopp.

(c) Paul, son of Robert and Alice Gregory.

(b) William, son of John and Sarah Heighfield.

1784. (c) Sarah, daughter of George and Hannah Taylor.

(c) Catharine, daughter of William and Mary Freakley.

(c) Mary, daughter of William and Ann Tansley.

(w) John Shelley and Mary Martin.

(c) William, son of John and Ann Ecclestone.

(b) Elizabeth Thorley.

(c) John, son of John and Mary Gregory.

1785. (b) Margaret Highfield.

(c) Joseph, son of William and Mary Hawton.

(b) Jane Levitt.

(c) Elizabeth, daughter of John and Mary Read.

(c) Edward, son of Edward and Mary Adderley.

(b) Joyce Lander.

(b) William Grindley.

(c) Margaret, daughter of Joseph and Mary Stockley.

(c) John, son of John and Ellen Forest.

(c) Ellen, daughter of John and Mary Harding.

(b) Joseph Hawton.

(c) John and Thomas, sons of John and Mary Thorley.

N.B.—(c) signifies christened, (b) buried, (w) wedded.

R

Anno

1785. (c) Jane, daughter of Peter and Mary Read.

 (b) Mary Allen, of Coats.

1786. (b) Sarah Wedwood.

 (b) John Knight.

 (c) John, son of John and Elizabeth Lyndop.

 (c) William, son of William and Mary Freakley.

 (b) Mary Cliffe.

 (w) W. Barratt and Ann Allen of Stafford.

 (c) William, son of William and Ann Tansley.

 (b) Henry Hodgkin.

 (c) Richard, son of John and Sarah Highfield.

 (b) Mary Gregory.

 (b) Mary Shaw.

 (w) Richard Salt and Mary Bessick.

 (c) John, son of George and Hannah Taylor.

 (c) Mary, daughter of William and Mary Ford.

 (b) Anne Adams,

 The Rev. Mr. W. Walker, curate of Standon, and Mrs.
  Mary Palmer were married at Standon by the Rev.
  W. Jervis, of Eccleshall.

 (b) Mary Glover (an infant).

 (b) Thomas Keay of Newport.

 (b) John Taylor (an infant).

1737. (b) Richard Highfield.

 (c) Joseph, son of John and Mary Harding.

 (b) Hannah Taylor.

 (b) Jane Gregory.

 (w) Thomas Clay, of Childenall, and Elizabeth Walker,
  of Croxton.

 (c) Peter, son of Samuel and Anne Highfield.

 (c) Mary, daughter of John and Mary Read.

 (b) William Ecclestone.

 (c) Elizabeth, daughter of Thomas and Elizabeth
  Tomson.

  N.B.—(c) signifies christened, (b) buried, (w) wedded.

Anno

1787. (c) John, son of William and Mary Horton.
(b) Eliza Tomson.
(w) John Modershaw and Mary Acres.
(w) Thomas Grimley and Eliza Lightfoot.
(c) Anne, daughter of Joseph and Mary Stockley.
(b) William Smith.
(c) Mary, daughter of Richard and Mary Salt.
(c) Sarah, daughter of Thomas and Mary Turner, of Slindon.

1788. (c) Anne, daughter of John and Mary Gregory.
(b) Mary Adams.
(c) Anne, daughter of Thomas and Susan Adams.
(c) Jane, daughter of John and Elizabeth Lyndop.
(c) John, son of Edward and Mary Adderley.
(c) Anne, daughter of John and Elizabeth Cooton.
(b) William, son of Joseph and Ellen Turnor (infant).
(c) Anne, daughter of William and Anne Tansley.
(c) Robert, son of John and Mary Harding.
(c) Anne, daughter of Robert and Anne Minors.
(b) Peter Highfield.
(c) George, son of John and Eliza Gallimore.
(c) Alice, daughter of Thomas and Mary Wharton.
(c) John, son of Thomas and Mary Turnor.
(c) Mary, daughter of Thomas and Eliza Turnor.
(b) John, son of John and Mary Gregory.

1789. (c) Thomas, son of William and Mary Ford.
(c) Margaret, daughter of William and Mary Freakley.
(c) William, son of William and Mary Haughton.
(c) Anne, daughter of Richard and Mary Salt.
(c) Mary, daughter of Peter and Mary Read.
(c) Margaret, daughter of Samuel and Anne Highfield.
(w) John Nickisson and Eliza Underwood, of Stone.
(w) John Holland and Sarah Stubbs, of Keel.

N.B.—(c) signifies christened, (b) buried, (w) wedded.

Anno

1789. (c) William, son of Richard and Sarah Craddock, of
Aspley.

(c) John, son of Richard and Sarah Craddock.

(c) Mary, daughter of Josh. and Mary Stockley.

(b) Walter Martin.

(b) Thomas Wharton.

1740. (c) Elizabeth, daughter of John and Eleanor Lunt.

(b) Edward Berks.

(c) Mary, daughter of Edward and Mary Adderley.

(c) Mary, daughter of John and Elizabeth Cotton.

(b) Thomas Foard, son of Thomas Foard.

(w) Thomas Wright and Elizabeth Tomkinson.

(c) Ann, daughter of Thomas and Sarah Wood.

(c) Mary, daughter of John and Mary Harding, of
Walford.

(c) Mary, daughter of Thomas and Hannah Adams.

(c) Mary, daughter of Thomas and Mary Turner.

(b) Eliza Grinley, of Maer.

(b) William Perkin.

1741. (c) Hannah, daughter of Thomas and Elizabeth Wright.

(b) Hannah Wright (infant).

(c) John, son of John and Sarah Holland, of Shortwood.

(c) Elizabeth, daughter of John and Mary Thorley.

(c) William, son of John and Elizabeth Lindop.

(w) Robert Bailey, of Newcastle, and Ann Wright.

(c) Elizabeth, daughter of Edward and Mary Adderley.

(w) The Rev. Mr. Taylor, of Chaddesley Corbet, in the
County of Worcester, and Ann Vaughan, of
Summerton.

(w) W. Woolridge, of Eccleshall, and Elizabeth Buscow.

(b) Thomas Palmer, or Parmer, of Eccleshall.

(b) Mira Lunt, daughter of John and Eleanor Lunt.

(c) Eleanor, daughter of Richard and Mary Salt.

N.B. (c) signifies christened, (b) burial, (w) wedded.

Anno

1741. (c) Mary, daughter of Richard and Sarah Cradock, of Aspley.

(c) Joseph, son of William and Mary Haughton, of Mill Meece.

1742. (b) Robert Gregory.

(c) John, son of William and Mary Freakley.

(c) Mary, daughter of James and Rachel Peake.

(c) William, son of John and Sarah Holland, of Shortwood.

(c) Jane, daughter of Joshua and Mary Stockley.

(c) Sarah, daughter of John and Mary Harding, of Walford.

(c) John, son of Samuel and Ann Highfield.

(b) John Shelley, of Bowers.

(c) John, son of John and Elizabeth Cotton.

(c) Mary, daughter of John and Eleanor Lunt.

(c) Sarah, daughter of Aaron and Sarah Dennell.

(b) Mary Houghton, of Stableford.

(c) Elizabeth, daughter of Thomas and Hannah Adams.

(b) Elizabeth, daughter of John and Elizabeth Wild, of Cotes.

(c) Elizabeth, daughter of Thomas and Mary Turner.

(b) Mary, daughter of John and Eleanor Lunt.

(b) Ann, daughter of Thomas and Hannah Adams.

1748. (c) Thomas, son of Thomas and Sarah Wood.

(b) Mary Gregory, of Cuchows Nest.

(b) Elizabeth Glover, of Mill Meece.

(b) Hannah Smith.

(c) Thomas, son of Thomas and Elizabeth Wright, of Weston.

(b) Robert, son of Matthias Gregory.

(b) Ann, daughter of John and Mary Gregory, of Eccleshall.

N.B.—(c) signifies christened, (b) buried, (w) wedded.

Anno

1743. (w) James Gayter and Mary Pool.

    (b) Elizabeth Edwards.

    (b) John, son of John and Elizabeth Wild, of Cotes.

    (c) William, son of John and Alice Taylor.

    (c) William, son of Thomas and Mary Ward.

1744. (c) John, son of John and Sarah Holland.

    (c) Eleanor, daughter of John and Eleanor Lunt.

    (c) Mary, daughter of Edward and Mary Adderley.

    (c) Mary, daughter of Henry and Frances Kyffin.

    (b) Paul, son of Robert and Alice Gregory.

    (c) Hannah, daughter of Richard and Mary Salt.

    (b) John Blakeman, of Stone.

    (c) Joshua, son of Joshua and Mary Stockley.

    (c) William, son of George and Mary Venables.

    (b) Mary, daughter of Henry and Frances Kyffin.

    (b) Sarah Adams.

    (c) Thomas, son of James and Rachel Peake.

1745. (b) Alice Edwards, of High Offley.

    (b) Mary, daughter of John and Mary Gregory, of Eccleshall.

    (w) Richard Wright and Sarah Heighfield.

    (c) Henry, son of Henry and Frances Kyffin.

    (w) William Tamms, of Sandon, and Elizabeth Wright, of Weston.

    (b) Mary, daughter of Margaret Smith.

    (c) James, son of Samuel and Ann Heighfield.

    (c) Ann, daughter of Thomas and Hannah Adams.

    (w) Samuel Taylor, of Chebsey, and Frances Pegg.

    (b) Mary Adderley.

    (b) Elizabeth Lindop.

    (c) Thomas, son of John and Elizabeth Lindop.

    (b) Thomas Turner, of Stawn Hall.

    (c) John, son of Thomas and Sarah Wood.

N.B.—(c) signifies christened, (b) buried, (w) wedded.

Anno

1745. (b) Mary Ward.

    (w) Joseph Wilkinson and Ann Gregory.

    (c) Robert, son of Robert and Ann Minors, of Mill Meece.

    (b) James, son of Samuel and Ann Highfield.

    (w) Thomas Talbot and Hannah Burgin.

    (w) Abraham Martin and Mary Bagnal.

    (b) Ann, daughter of Thomas and Hannah Adams.

1746. (c) John, son of John and Eleanor Lunt.

    (c) Mary, daughter of Gamaliel and Hannah Crutchley.

    (c) Joan, daughter of W. and Mary Freakley.

    (c) Ann, daughter of Edward and Mary Adderley.

    (c) Phœbe, daughter of Thomas and Hannah Talbot.

    (b) Mary Badnal.

    (c) Walter, son of Abraham and Mary Martin.

    (w) Mr. Thomas Plant and Elizabeth Astbury, both of
        Swinnerton, by the Rev. Mr. Robinson, Rector
        of Swinnerton.

    (b) Mary Heamis, of Chebsy.

    (w) William Kent and Ann Peacock, of Eccleshall.

    (c) John, son of Richard and Mary Cliff, of Cotes
        Heath.

    (c) John, son of Joshua and Mary Stockley.

    (c) Samuel, son of Samuel and Ann Heighfield.

    (c) Susannah, daughter of Richard and Mary Salt.

1747. (c) Mary, daughter of Richard and Sarah Wright.

    (c) Elizabeth, daughter of Gamaliel and Hannah
        Crutchley.

    (b) Mary, daughter of Joshua and Mary Stockley.

    (c) John, son of Valentine and Margaret Farmer.

    (c) John, son of George and Mary Venables.

    (b) William Mellor, of Drayton.

    (c) John, son of John and Elizabeth Eardley.

    (c) William, son of Robert and Catharine Edwards.

N.B.—(c) signifies christened, (b) buried, (w) wedded.

Anno

    (b) Ann Harding.

1747. (c) Betty, daughter of Thomas and Elizabeth Wright.

    (c) Thomas, son of Thomas and Hannah Adams.

    (w) Edward Mosgreave and Lydia Wright.

    (w) John Tayler and Eliza Midleton.

    (c) William, son of Richard and Mary Silvester.

    (c) Hannah, daughter of Charles and Hannah Talbot.

1748. (c) Hannah, daughter of Hannah and Gamaliel Crutchley.

    (c) Wm., son of Benjamin and Mary Minshaw.

    (b) Ann Wilkinson.

    (b) William Minshaw.

    (c) Ann, daughter of John and Eleanor Lunt.

    (b) Thomas Wild, of Cotes.

    (c) Mary, daughter of Edward and Mary Adderley.

1749. (c) Christopher, son of Joshua and Mary Stockley.

    (c) John, son of Robert and Elizabeth Bedson.

    (c) Elizabeth, daughter of Thomas and Jane Ward.

    (b) George Hodgson, of Mill Meese.

    (w) Edward Wright and Ann Tomkinson, of Cheswardine.

    (b) Richard Salt.

    (b) James Peake.

    (c) Alice, daughter of William and Alice Martin.

    (c) Mary, daughter of Abraham and Mary Martin.

    (c) John, son of Richard and Sarah Wright.

    (c) Thomas, son of Thomas and Ann Evans.

    (w) John Wain and Mary Dale.

    (c) Mary, daughter of Valentine and Margaret Farmer.

    (b) Sarah Wharton, of Mill Meece.

    (b) Elizabeth, daughter of Thomas and Jane Ward.

    (b) George Taylor.

    (c) Edward, son of Thomas and Elizabeth Wright, of Wetton.

    N.B.—(c) signifies christened, (b) buried, (w) wedded.

Anno

1749. (c) Thomas, son of George and Mary Venables.

    (c) Mary, daughter of John and Mary Wright.

1750. (c) Ann, daughter of Ann and Edward Wright, of Shortwood.

    (c) Ann, daughter of Richard and Mary Silvester, of Stawn Hall.

    (c) Hannah, daughter of Thomas and Hannah Adams.

    (c) Ann, daughter of Samuel and Ann Heighfield.

    (c) William, son of Gamaliel and Hannah Crutchley.

    (b) Margaret Hodgson.

    (c) George, son of Richard and Mary Cliff, of Cotes Heath.

    (w) William Low and Elizabeth Harding, of the Rudge.

    (c) Jane, daughter of Thomas and Hannah Talbot.

    (c) Mary, daughter of Thomas and Rachel Higgison.

    (c) Elizabeth, daughter of John and Elizabeth Cotton.

    (w) William Bedson, jun., and Joan Wharton.

    (c) Thomas, son of Thomas and Jane Ward.

    (w) Edward Taylor, of Eccleshall, and Margaret Smith.

1751. (c) James, son of William and Alice Martin.

    (c) Edward, son of Andrew and Mary Vyse.

    (b) Elizabeth Farmer.

    (c) Mary, daughter of Robert and Catharine Edwards.

    (c) Edward, son of John and Eleanor Lunt.

    (b) William Vyse (an infant).

    (c) Mary, daughter of Joshua and Mary Stockley,

    (b) Thomas Cooke, of Moorfield Green.

    (c) Abraham, son of Abraham and Mary Martin.

    (c) John, son of William and Joan Bedson.

    (c) Thomas, son of Valentine and Margaret Farmer.

    (b) John Grinley.

    (c) Mary, daughter of Robert and Mary Gregory, of the Rock.

N.B.—(c) signifies christened, (b) buried, (w) wedded.

Anno

1751. (b) Ann Kent, of Podmore.

(b) Jane Talbot.

(c) Samson, son of Thomas and Elizabeth Wright, of
Weston.

(c) John, son of Richard and Sarah Wright.

(c) John, son of Gamaliel and Hannah Crutchley, of
Bower's Bent.

(b) Margaret Harding, of Standon.

(b) Thomas Martin, of Bowers.

1752. (b) Peter Ward.

(c) Thomas, son of Andrew and Mary Vyse.

(w) William Edwards and Jane-Bedson.

(c) George, son of George and Mary Venables.

(c) Ann, daughter of Thomas (clerk) and Rachel
Astbury.

(c) William, son of Thomas and Hannah Adams.

(b) Sarah Martin.

(c) Elizabeth, daughter of Thomas and Rachael Higginson.

(c) Lydia, daughter of Edward and Ann Wright, of
Shortwood.

(w) Thomas Lowe, of Ashley, and Jane Williams.

(c) James, son of Richard and Mary Cliff.

(c) Ann, daughter of William and Jane Edwards.

1753. (b) William Harding.

(w) William Kent, of Podmore, and Elizabeth Davenil.

(c) James, son of William and Alice Martin.

(b) James, son of William and Alice Martin.

(c) Mary, daughter of Thomas and Jane Ward.

(w) Joseph Lewtona, of Eccleshall, and Sarah Bailey.

(b) Mary Ashley, of Podmore.

(b) Mary Peake, of Bowers.

(c) Sarah, daughter of Thomas and Rachel Astbury.

N.B.—(c) signifies christened, (b) buried, (w) wedded.

Anno

1753. (b) Edward Thorley.

(c) Richard, son of John and Eleanor Lunt.

(c) William, son of William and Joan Bedson.

(c) William, son of Thomas and Mary Key.

(b) William, son of Thomas and Mary Key.

(b) William Bedson.

(c) Hannah, daughter of Joshua and Mary Stockley.

(b) Hannah Stockley.

(c) Abraham, son of Robert and Mary Gregory.

1754. (c) Julia, daughter of Edward and Ann Wright, of Shortwood.

(w) Roger Crutchley, of Eccleshall, and Mary Davies.

(w) James Kent and Mary Mare, both of Stoke-on-Trent.

(c) Dorothy, daughter of Gamaliel and Hannah Crutchley.

(c) Sarah, daughter of Abraham and Mary Martin.

(b) William Freakley.

(b) John Baddiley, of Walford.

(c) Dorothy, daughter of William and Elizabeth Thomson.

(c) Ann, daughter of Thomas and Ann Evans.

(b) Hannah Abel.

(b) Robert Peake.

(c) Sarah, daughter of Thomas and Rachel Higginson.

(c) Thomas, son of Richard and Sarah Wright.

(b) Hannah Hall.

(c) Andrew, son of Andrew and Mary Vyse.

(c) William, son of Roger and Mary Crutchley.

(c) Joseph, son of Valentine and Margaret Farmer.

1755. (c) Thomas, son of Thomas and Mary Blakeman.

(c) John, son of Thomas and Mary Key.

(c) Elizabeth, daughter of Edward and Ann Wright, of Shortwood.

N.B.—(c) signifies christened, (b) buried, (w) wedded.

Anno

1755. (b) John Key.
 (c) Moses, son of Joshua and Mary Stockley.
 (b) Robert, son of Robert Addison.
 (c) Robert, son of William and Jane Bedson.
 (c) Sarah, d. of Gamaliel and Hannah Crutchley.
 (c) Sarah, daughter of Richard and Mary Cliff (Cotes)
 (c) Joseph, son of Thomas and Hannah Adams.
 (c) Ruth, daughter of Robert and Rachel Addison.
 (c) Martha, daughter of Robert and Mary Gregory.
 (b) Robert Gregory.
 (b) Milicent Thorley.
 (b) Eleanor Crutchley.

1756. (b) Mary Gregory.
 (b) Moses Stockley.
 (b) Sampson Wright.
 (c) Charles, son of Richard and Sarah Shaw.
 (c) John, son of Abraham and Mary Martin.
 (c) Thomas and William, sons of John and Eleanor Lunt.
 (c) Edward, son of Robert and Elizabeth Bedson.
 (b) Mary Badnal.
 (c) Jane, daughter of Edward and Ann Wright, of
  Shortwood.
 (b) John, son of Thomas and Sarah Wood.
 (c) Ann, daughter of John and Mary Wharton, of Mill
  Meece.
 (b) Mary, daughter of Robert and Mary Gregory.
 (b) Elizabeth Till.
 (c) Duke William, son of William and Elizabeth
  Thompson.
 (b) John Key, of Aspley.
 (b) Mary Higginson.

1757. (b) Elizabeth Addison.
 (b) Thomas Wood.

N.B.—(c) signifies christened, (b) buried, (w) wedded.

Anno

1757. (b) Elizabeth Ashley, of Podmore.

(b) Eleanor Banks.

(c) John, son of Robert and Rachel Addison.

(c) Thomas, son of Thomas and Mary Key.

(b) Thomas Lander.

(c) John, son of Thomas (clerk) and Rachel Astbury.

(b) Alice Guest.

(c) William, son of Richard and Sarah Wright.

(b) Elizabeth Cook, of Moorfield Green.

(c) Matthew, son of John and Elizabeth Gregory.

1758. (c) Mary, daughter of William and Joan Bedson.

(c) Thomas, son of Edward and Mary Adderly.

(c) John, son of Roger and Mary Crutchley.

(b) John Yates, of Earnfield (Yarnfield).

(c) Ann, daughter of Valentine and Margaret Farmer.

(c) Elizabeth, daughter of Thomas and Rachel Astbury.

(c) Thomas, son of Richard and Mary Cliff.

(c) John, son of John and Elizabeth Highfield.

(b) James Baggiley.

(c) Rachel, daughter of Thomas and Hannah Adams.

(b) Mary Read.

(c) Sarah, daughter of John and Eleanor Lunt.

(b) Ann, daughter of Valentine and Margaret Farmer.

(b) Margaret Farmer.

(c) William, son of Abraham and Mary Martin.

(c) Sarah, daughter of Thomas and Martha Martin.

(c) Ann, daughter of Robert and Elizabeth Bedson.

(b) Matthew Gregory.

(b) Sarah Lunt.

End of 1758 : Two hundred years of Registers.

N.B.—(c) signifies christened, (b) buried, (w) wedded.

INDEX.